FACING THE SKY

Praise for *Facing the Sky*

More than a poultice for the psyche, *Facing the Sky* shows how composing in words and images mitigates trauma, heals on multiple levels, and makes us better functioning humans, as well as more deeply humane. This book demonstrates that when we nurture the voice we nurture the world and shows us how. It is a book for all of us who must sometime, somewhere, at some critical moment hold another's soul in our hands. Read. Reap.

—Susan Hudson, Boise, Idaho

For teachers and future teachers of writing, *Facing the Sky* is an invaluable resource. By refocusing our attention on the role personal narrative plays in our lives, Fox encourages us to consider seriously what roles the "painfully honest" can, and should, play in our classrooms. Fox's research reminds us of the necessity for our writing classrooms to be sites of emotional inquiry, catharsis, and community-building. This book asks us to consider how critical thinking and written fluency can be fostered when we give language to the images associated with trauma. In the process, Fox proposes a pedagogy concerned with and deriving from the very humanity of our students.

—Benjamin Batzer, University of Iowa

Roy Fox's *Facing the Sky: Composing through Trauma in Word and Image* is an eloquent and timely homage to the power of expressive writing as a way to heal. This alone would be good reason to love this book, especially since Fox isn't content with simply showing how word and image can be transformative; he also examines why this is so, and in the process we come to see the qualities of personal narratives that yield the most meaning for a writer, and in turn, provide teachers of writing with the tools to teach them. *Facing the Sky* makes the courageous claim that we should invite students to write about trauma, and not simply because it might help them to feel better but because it teaches them things about writing that they might not learn as well any other way. Drawing on cases studies, Fox charts the moves that experienced writers make as they use their expertise to go from recording their losses to making meaning from them. These are exactly the kind of intellectual practices that animate any act of inquiry. But here the writers are deeply motivated and especially receptive to seeing the ways language and image can be deployed in discovery. Whether it's Kate trying to come to terms with the sudden death of her husband, or Lucy confronting breast cancer, each writer is inspired by her faith in writing as a way of discovering what she didn't know she knew. But it's a process that involves zigs and zags, and part of the drama of *Facing the Sky* is witnessing each writer switch between public and private writing, and even between genres, as she attempts to find the stories that yield understanding. *Facing the Sky* is an especially timely and welcome contribution to the conversation about the importance of narrative in writing instruction. It's a book that challenges the Common Core's diminishment of narrative writing as little more than a "technique." On the contrary, Fox shows that it is a powerful method of analysis and reasoning that also bears the priceless gift of self-knowledge.

—Bruce Ballenger, author of *The Curious Researcher* and *The Curious Writer*

LAUER SERIES IN RHETORIC AND COMPOSITION
Editors: Catherine Hobbs, Patricia Sullivan, Thomas Rickert, & Jennifer Bay

The Lauer Series in Rhetoric and Composition honors the contributions Janice Lauer has made to the emergence of Rhetoric and Composition as a disciplinary study. It publishes scholarship that carries on Professor Lauer's varied work in the history of written rhetoric, disciplinarity in composition studies, contemporary pedagogical theory, and written literacy theory and research.

BOOKS IN THE SERIES

Facing the Sky: Composing through Trauma in Word and Image (Fox, 2016)
Expel the Pretender: Rhetoric Renounced and the Politics of Style (Wiederhold, 2015)
First-Year Composition: From Theory to Practice (Coxwell-Teague & Lunsford, 2014)
Contingency, Immanence, and the Subject of Rhetoric (Richardson, 2013)
Rewriting Success in Rhetoric & Composition Careers (Goodburn, LeCourt, Leverenz, 2012)
Writing a Progressive Past: Women Teaching and Writing in the Progressive Era (Mastrangelo, 2012)
Greek Rhetoric Before Aristotle, 2e, Rev. and Exp. Ed. (Enos, 2012)
Rhetoric's Earthly Realm: Heidegger, Sophistry, and the Gorgian Kairos (Miller) *Winner of the Olson Award for Best Book in Rhetorical Theory 2011
Techne, from Neoclassicism to Postmodernism: Understanding Writing as a Useful, Teachable Art (Pender, 2011)
Walking and Talking Feminist Rhetorics: Landmark Essays and Controversies (Buchanan & Ryan, 2010)
Transforming English Studies: New Voices in an Emerging Genre (Ostergaard, Ludwig, & Nugent, 2009)
Ancient Non-Greek Rhetorics (Lipson and Binkley, 2009)
Roman Rhetoric: Revolution and the Greek Influence, Rev. and Exp Ed. (Enos, 2008)
Stories of Mentoring: Theory and Praxis (Eble and Gaillet, 2008)
Writers Without Borders: Writing and Teaching in Troubled Times (Bloom, 2008)
1977: A Cultural Moment in Composition (Henze, Selzer, and Sharer, 2008)
*The Promise and Perils of Writing Program Administration (*Enos & Borrowman, 2008)
Untenured Faculty as Writing Program Administrators: Institutional Practices and Politics, (Dew and Horning, 2007)
Networked Process: Dissolving Boundaries of Process and Post-Process (Foster, 2007)
Composing a Community: A History of Writing Across the Curriculum (McLeod and Soven, 2006)
Historical Studies of Writing Program Administration: Individuals, Communities, and the Formation of a Discipline (L'Eplattenier and Mastrangelo, 2004). Winner of the WPA Best Book Award for 2004–2005.
Rhetorics, Poetics, and Cultures: Refiguring College English Studies Exp. Ed. (Berlin, 2003)

FACING THE SKY

Composing through Trauma in
Word and Image

Roy F. Fox

Foreword by Peter Elbow

Parlor Press
Anderson, South Carolina
www.parlorpress.com

Parlor Press LLC, Anderson, South Carolina, USA

© 2016 by Parlor Press
All rights reserved.

Printed in the United States of America
S A N: 2 5 4 - 8 8 7 9

Library of Congress Cataloging-in-Publication Data

Names: Fox, Roy F., author.
Title: Facing the sky : composing through trauma in word and image / Roy F.
　Fox ; foreword by Peter Elbow.
Description: Anderson, South Carolina : Parlor Press, [2016] | Includes
　bibliographical references and index.
Identifiers: LCCN 2015044950 (print) | LCCN 2015045388 (ebook) | ISBN
　9781602354494 (pbk. : alk. paper) | ISBN 9781602354500 (hardcover : alk.
　paper) | ISBN 9781602354517 (pdf) | ISBN 9781602354524 (epub) | ISBN
　9781602354531 (ibook) | ISBN 9781602354548 (Kindle)
Subjects: LCSH: Creative writing--Therapeutic use.
Classification: LCC RC489.W75 F69 2016 (print) | LCC RC489.W75 (ebook) | DDC
　615.8/516--dc23
LC record available at http://lccn.loc.gov/2015044950

1 2 3 4 5

Lauer Series in Rhetoric and Composition
Editors: Catherine Hobbs, Patricia Sullivan, Thomas Rickert, & Jennifer Bay

Cover design by David Blakesley. Cover image by Roy F. Fox.
Printed on acid-free paper.

Parlor Press, LLC is an independent publisher of scholarly and trade titles in print and multimedia formats. This book is available in paper, cloth and eBook formats from Parlor Press on the World Wide Web at http://www.parlorpress.com or through online and brick-and-mortar bookstores. For submission information or to find out about Parlor Press publications, write to Parlor Press, 3015 Brackenberry Drive, Anderson, South Carolina, 29621, or email editor@parlorpress.com.

Contents

Foreword
Peter Elbow   ix

Acknowledgments   *xi*
Introduction: An Unfinished Furrow   *3*

1 Composing through Trauma   *13*
2 Beyond "Just Academic Stuff": The Course, The Teacher, The Study   *43*
3 Lucy   *77*
4 Seven Writers Composing in Word and Image   *124*
5 Kate   *163*
6 Common Threads   *207*
7 Recommendations   *226*

Notes   *251*
Works Cited   *253*
Appendix A: The Course Syllabus   *263*
Appendix B: Research Questions   *282*
Appendix C: Assessing Thinking in Writing   *288*
About the Author   *291*
Index   *293*

For
Lucy Elicker Stanovick
Hero

Foreword

I'm happy to recommend this book to a wide variety of readers. I find it important and useful—and I admire its strong humane prose style.

Writing for healing used to be a controversial idea. I remember a time, not so long after my 1973 *Writing Without Teachers* began gradually to be noticed, when a number of people in English and Composition accused me of wanting to "practice therapy without a license." I would immediately deny the charge. "Oh no, I'm just trying to improve people's writing." Of course I was being disingenuous; of course I harbored the belief I knew many other teachers of writing shared, namely that private writing and exploratory expressive writing, even very personal writing, would help people write better, and indeed, *be* better.

In fact out of my own need, I "invented" freewriting for myself—before I'd heard about it from Ken Macrorie. In the late 1950s I'd felt subjectively tortured by an uppity Oxford tutor who made fun of my writing. (It didn't help to learn that this was just how people act when they think they are at the best university in the world.) I was desperate and instinctively took to my typewriter to pour out my feelings nonstop about my pain and inability to write—all of this of course in writing. It gave me genuine relief. For centuries, really, many journal keepers have used writing in the same way.

I'm happy to say that now there is ample evidence to show that writing for healing—*Writing through Trauma* in Fox's formulation—need no longer be controversial. Ironically, people in the academic fields of English and composition have often been slowest to accept this fact. One of Fox's most useful chapters summarizes extensive research showing the benefits that come from writing out of pain—some of these benefits being physically and empirically measurable.

This book is a rich compendium of case studies. It's full of extended examples of writing from a wide variety of people of various ages. Fox provides extensive commentary where he describes, ruminates, and puzzles about what the writer is doing, how the language is functioning, and how all this relates to healing. (By the way, one of his chapters explores drawing and other visual imagery that people can use to deal with their suffering.) His statement about his original goals is probably right (though I can't vouch for knowing all the scholarship out there):

I could not locate anything like what I had in mind—hardly any studies that zoned in on people's actual writing, thinking, and imagery. I also became convinced that the future will bring much more attention to addressing all types of trauma, some of which we have yet to "discover."

Fox is both anthropologist and theorist. Reading his book gives us remarkable perspective—and in the end distance—on how writers have used symbolic systems to deal with pain. Yet all the while he is opening windows that cannot but lead *us* to experience some of the pain that his subjects write about.

Fox's writing itself is powerful for its plain simplicity in treating what is often extreme. His writing reminds me of the pungent example from Truman's journal where he wrestles bluntly with the concrete reality of having compromised his ideals and committed shady and even criminal acts—naming them—for the sake of goals he considered good. Fox admires Truman's plain prose and I admire Fox's. But it is pain, after all, that all these words are about, so that must be what led Fox to a rare rhetorical loftiness in his comment about the words of one of his subjects: "Such writing is very much like prayer, whether or not we believe in a God. This, we have to believe, is the highest, holiest use of language imaginable."

How This Book Applies to Writing

Many readers of this book will be interested not just in the practice of writing from pain, but also in the practice of writing itself and the nature of the writing process. Indeed I hope that one of his main audiences will be teachers of writing.

So there is good evidence that writing from suffering brings some measure of healing; but does it help heal writing? What about my original lamely given excuse, namely that freewriting and personal writing can improve writing? This question continues to be a matter of controversy among teachers and scholars of writing. On this point, Fox makes a claim I find convincing: "While improvement in writing itself is not an explicit point or chapter in this book, I believe it reverberates in every line in the pages ahead." In addition, he's had a career as teacher and scholar of writing and offers countless good insights about many aspects of writing.

Peter Elbow
Seattle, Washington

Acknowledgments

I am grateful to the University of Missouri for a sabbatical leave allowing me to collect data for this book. I am indebted to students, colleagues, and editors who responded to drafts, offering superb feedback. I thank my students, past and present, for their enthusiasm and willingness to dive into unknown, risky territory. I am indebted to David Blakesley for his independence and vision. Catherine Hobbs provided careful, insightful guidance in the final stages of preparing this manuscript. My wife, Bev, again served as the sanest sounding-board and editor I could ever hope to have. Finally, I stand humbled before the people who agreed to become a part of this book, for trusting me, for believing that their experiences could help others.

Facing the Sky

That is at bottom the only courage that is demanded of us: to have courage for the most strange, the most singular and the most inexplicable that we may encounter. That mankind has in this sense been cowardly has done life endless harm; the experiences that are called "visions," the whole so-called, "spirit world," death, all those things that are so closely akin to us, have by daily parrying been so crowded out of life that the senses with which we could have grasped them are atrophied. To say nothing of God.
—Rainer Maria Rilke, *Letters to a Young Poet*

Wisdom is like the sky, belonging to no man, and true learning is the astronomy of the spirit.
—Rabbi Abraham J. Heschel

Introduction: An Unfinished Furrow

The gravel in the parking lot of the old church across the road shone zinc white in the sun. This church held ice cream socials to raise money, sold cardboard fans with gaudy pictures of Jesus on them, and, for a dollar, bottles of imitation vanilla. I knew people used it in cooking but could not understand why it was a big deal. I once saw my eighty-five-year-old great aunt dab a fingertip of it behind each ear as a kind of perfume, but it still didn't add up. As a ten-year-old in Paradise, Missouri, in the sweltering August of 1959, I moved inside a glass jar and a huge, resounding stillness. Nothing moved.

The only competition with my great aunt's squat, relic-like presence was my grandparents' brown plastic View Master and its white disks that rotated photos of Niagara Falls. A more exotic treat was a five-cent Hershey bar or an orange Nehi soda from Hafferty's Farm Implement store. There was nothing to read, either, if you discounted the tiny gray print of *The Smithville Democrat Herald*, which reported the locals' activities, such as, "Mrs. Claudie Archer's nephew and his family, from Platte City, visited on Sunday." The only other reading material was the archaic gibberish in the Bible.

Across from the church and down the road, the vacant house overgrown with brown weeds, tangled trumpet vine, and sticky burrs stood perfectly silent as usual, but I would not poke around in it on this day, even though the marbles, shells, and pebbles of glass randomly lodged into its outer plastered walls remained just as mysterious as ever. What kind of people in the middle of rural Missouri would make a house like that? On this day, though, the ghosts that I was sure hovered there would have to dissolve inside themselves and wait for another day. It didn't occur to me to go there, because, on this day, everything was different.

I knew that the yard, house, chicken coop, wire fences, and cellar were not *really* different. It was just that they no longer mattered. Like they weren't even there. Or they had somehow shifted from being three-dimensional into being faded, cardboard props. My grandfather, Pop, had just disappeared from the earth, and inside of me, everything was churned up, voided. I was confused and cut loose from an anchor I didn't realize was there. My grandfather, Daniel Harrison Fox, was soft-spoken, tall, lean, and gentle as a lamb's ear. Never critical, often quietly bemused. Why him?

Instead, I wandered in my grandparents' yard, away from the shuffling, small groups of elderly farm neighbors who milled about the porch and steps quietly paying their respects, carrying covered dishes of green bean casserole, potato salad, and pies, especially the sticky-sweet pecan pies. There seemed to be dozens of each. I didn't know what to do or where to go, and I found myself in the back of their small home, where they had moved after leaving their farm. The garden was half-plowed. In the middle of an unfinished row, a rusted hand-plow rested. Next, I spotted a small homemade bench made of weathered boards in a simple T-shape, stuck into the ground. Not steady, but good enough to sit and catch your breath.

After the hushed, humble neighbors shuffled off, it was time for Sunday afternoon-dinner, which we often had with my grandparents, though this time, my grandfather would not be shaking extra salt on his ham or, afterward, drying the dishes handed him by my grandmother—the only times I ever saw them talk together. My great aunt, Betty Rupe, the widow of a country doctor, lived with them. She was small, squat, chatty as a parakeet, and did not believe that the earth rotated on its axis because, if it did, "we'd all fall off." Aunt Betty left her false teeth on the table beside her glass during dinner. I couldn't bear looking at them, lest they came clacking down the tablecloth and clamped onto my fingers. Dinner usually consisted of green beans, smoked and salty ham from Dave Lizer's locker, fried chicken, baked oysters, rolls, mashed potatoes, and fruit salad with tiny marshmallows.

My parents, grandmother, aunt, and everyone were placing plates and bowls on the table as I watched in silence. How could they? Didn't they know he had just died? The well inside me came surging upward. I broke into tears and ran outside. I sat on the slope near the garage and quieted down, then laid back on the grass and stared at the clouds blowing across the sky, giving way to blue expanses, unfolding into oblivion. I wasn't there long before returning to the dining room. I don't remember what any of the adults said to me. Likely nothing. It just wasn't something you talked about.

We all have our first experience with death. I had no warning about what would happen or what the funeral would be like, how the burial would work. In those days, these things were not talked about. As I sensed at the time, the adults in that dining room were also grieving, carrying around their own weighty sadness and confusion on their insides. It just wasn't something you talked about.

Three decades later, I am with my friend, Tom, in a sunny backyard in Idaho. I had recently buried our cat, Buford. I looked up as my daughter, Emma, five years old, was leading Tom to the outer edge of the yard, under the huge fir trees. She started chirping out of the blue: "Wanna know what happens when you die?" she asked.

"What?" Tom said, not missing a beat. "Well, first they wrap you in a towel, then they put you in a box, then they put you in the ground," she answered.

A few days earlier, we'd buried Buford, our gentle, elegant, orange and white cat, and I'd hoped she'd forgotten about it. At least she was talking about her first experience with death, however tersely practical her summary. I'd just read aloud to Emma E. B. White's *Charlotte's Web* (her first *real book*, as I wrote on the flyleaf) about the spider, Charlotte, that spins webs for her friend, Wilbur, the pig, to read. Wilbur, the runt of the litter, had been rescued from death by Fern Arable, the owner's daughter. Wilbur again faced his fears of death when the geese told him that his new owner, Mr. Zuckerman, was planning to fatten him up for the Christmas dinner.

Charlotte promised to save her new friend. When she spun the phrases, "some pig," "terrific," and others into her web, Wilbur began acting like some pig, doing tricks and stunts to amaze the people around him. This beautifully-crafted, simple story has much to say about people and nature and the cycle of life and death. But it's also about the powers of expression, of words and what they can do, especially during those times when our lives become redefined for us. At that time in Paradise, Missouri, it never occurred to anyone to talk things out, much less to write it up. Somehow, the word and the image did not exist for such purposes. But when we're jerked into a new reality, facing the unfathomable, composing through words and pictures can help us sort things out, understand, and go on.

***

In this book, I use *writing* interchangeably with *composing*, and both terms apply to any medium or symbol system. As well, *composing through trauma* has two meanings here. First, to create or write or compose something in words and images related to the trauma. If you compose in word and image, you'll often arrive at the second meaning—to compose yourself—emotionally, physically, and spiritually. This all means *coping*, yes, but it goes beyond that.

At a recent international conference called "Making Sense of Pain," there was much talk about "coping strategies," from medical doctors, medical anthropologists, counselors, and others. Just as often, the question kept surfacing from different people: "But what do we *do* with pain?" I finally spoke up, first explaining that while I understood the usefulness of the phrase, "coping strategies," I found it limiting, and second, more importantly, what we should *do* with pain—physical, emotional, spiritual—is simple: *transform the pain into something else*—create a mission, perhaps a mission that is connected with the pain, one that can help others: a written composition, a film, an essay, a scholarship, a garden, a poem, a barn, or a video. The first step in transforming pain is to get it out into the light, through purposeful action. Only then does it become more visible and, therefore, less scary, subject to reflection, manipulation, revision, and re-conceptualization into a more ordered and calmer internal landscape.

I've believed in composing *through* trauma for a long time—creating words, piling up brush for burning, painting a portrait or a house, constructing *anything*—in order to bypass the pain, to lessen its gnawing at my consciousness. I've somehow found these construction sites all along the roads I've taken through my personal and professional life. As a kid—since I could sit at a table, according to my mother—I spent all my time drawing and painting. The best thing my mother ever did for me was to keep me supplied with *blank* white paper. I guess that I was told that I, too, was "some pig" and maybe even "terrific," so maybe I believed it. I was an art major for a few years before going into English, but I've continued composing to this day. I've spent my life shamelessly cajoling my students to compose, too, whether it be basic writing or advanced composition, or technical and professional writing, or poetry, or creative nonfiction, or doctoral dissertations and research articles.

No matter when or where or who, I'd often encounter people who somehow changed when they wrote about what was most important and confusing and troubling to them. The traumatic experiences that had festered within them had never been freed because they thought it was "not academic," or because, if and when they did venture such writing, they were shut down by their teachers. I've seen this scenario time and again: in "mainstream" college writing courses; in remedial writing classes; in teachers and students in a state-run youth offenders program; in undergraduate and graduate students studying to be schoolteachers and college professors. People need to make sense of what's most important to them. Their issues seep under doors and ooze out of closed lids and cracks. Many teachers receive such trauma-focused writing from their students, regardless of what is assigned.

More often, composing through trauma occurs, sadly, only by accident, when circumstances happen to align. When we carry a serious trauma within us and fail to *do* anything with it, then it is often *published* in *some* way. If it's not written or somehow processed through language or art or some other form, it can be acted out with far more severe consequences—acted out through violence or social isolation or substance abuse.

Cleanly defining *composing through trauma* always seems to fall short, but here's my version. The essential concept runs under different aliases: "writing as healing," "expressive language," "writing for wellness," "transitional writing," "therapeutic writing," and more. Regardless of the label, any useful definition has to be broad; if not, it defeats the whole enterprise. In short, I define composing through trauma as *any* kind of communication or product that focuses on *any* kind of traumatic experience—any experience that harms, worries, saddens, scares, or makes the writer anxious; any experience that creates feelings of violation, dissociation, isolation, alienation, confusion, depression, or inferiority.

Some topics that are often written about include, but are not limited to, the following: death of a loved one; suicide; rape; alcohol or drug addiction; divorce and other forms of separation; gender orientation; disease and illness; relationships with parents, children, and siblings; Post-Traumatic Stress Disorder (PTSD); cultural and racial bias; and all forms of physical and psychological abuse. Keep in mind that these "traumas" necessarily exist on a continuum—from the less serious to the most severe. This notion of "How severe is your trauma?" calls to mind the posters in doctors' offices that show a series of ten circular faces, progressing from Mr. Frowny to Mr. Smiley. However, I'm not sure that pain can be a number. As well, one woman's minor irritant may be another man's demon. We have to take people at their word, as to the degree of severity of any given trauma, at any given time.

Lucy, whom you'll meet in the pages ahead, defines composing through trauma this way:

"And when you say writing as healing—what am I healing? It's not like I am going to heal or be on the mend—so I guess what I am healing is my . . . spirit, my identity—how to integrate this new aspect of my life that has caused a rupture in who I was, how I saw myself." Lucy understands that she must fuse her "new" present into her past. As Anderson and MacCurdy (2000) state, "the chief healing effect of writing is . . . to recover and to exert a measure of control over that which we can never control—the past" (7). Also, the term *healing* is problematic for Lucy, as it is for many of us, which is why it should be treated with some nuance, as Anderson and MacCurdy recommend:

> Healing is neither a return to some former state of perfection nor the discovery or restoration of some mythic autonomous self. Healing, as we understand it, is precisely the opposite. It is change from a singular self, frozen in time by a moment of unspeakable experience, to a more fluid, more narratively able, more socially integrated self. (2000, 7)

In the following brief excerpt, David, who described himself as a "latchkey kid" after his parents' divorce, illustrates this definition:

> Alone in those hours, I created a world of my own self-expression. I sang loudly in operatic voices, my reedy swellings filling the great acoustic voids of the empty house. I talked to my dog, to our paintings, to myself. I read aloud, dramatically, and in monotone: I would say the same sentence one time for every word in the sentence, each time emphasizing a different word to see what difference it would make in meaning. I sat before the television, repeating dialogue of the talk show hosts, the newscasters, the PBS painting instructors—trying to say their own words before they said them, trying to predict what they might say, what they might think. I watched Mr. Rogers without the sound, supplying my own explanation soundtrack for tours of dairy farms and goldfish aquariums. (Course Document 1993)

As an adolescent, David fought his intense loneliness through exercising his voice, through engaging in language with television and painted imagery. He seemed to *neuter* his loneliness by hearing a real human voice, even if it was his own—in a sense, explaining his isolation to himself as he resisted it. Also, as an adult, David accomplished much the same thing by writing about these experiences. Then and later, he reduced or even avoided being "a singular self, frozen in time" by this negative situation. His breaking free of "time-binding" is an important victory when composing through trauma, as Anderson and MacCurdy (2000) clarify:

> Traumatic events, because they do not occur within the parameters of "normal" reality, do not fit into the structure and flow of time. Instead, they are imprisoned within the psyche as discrete moments, frozen, isolated from normal memories. Because they are not connected to the normal, linear flow of time-bound memory, these moments emerge into consciousness at any point, bringing the force of the traumatic event with them. (6)

Voice and language and writing help David become more fluid and narratively able, which allows him to more precisely articulate the issue—and doing so usually indicates that one inhabits a more socially integrated self. Lucy, too, seems driven to narrate her "unspeakable experience," to integrate it with her "previous" sense of self:

> Not only did I privately recite narratives or storylines of hope, read narratives of hope and envision narratives of hope, I had to publically tell my own new narrative. I had to tell my story over and over, out loud, as a way to gain some control over it. Like wrangling a monster to the ground. My disease was so big and overwhelming, I had to find a way to incorporate this new narrative into the existing life I had been living—the 42 year old Lucy, mother of two, professor *without* terminal cancer. I had to hear my voice, the one I knew, the one that has been narrating my life all along tell this new part. Whether at a department meeting or in class, I told them. Whether it was relevant to the class or not, and as self-indulgent as it might have been, I needed to speak it. (Stanovick 2012)

Overall, though, most definitions remain limited unless they are grounded in specific experience, as David's and Lucy's are. Along with such unanchored definitions, writing-through-trauma research, since the early 1990's, has focused on how writing affects specific and observable changes in our health, such as blood pressure or heart rate. This is a rich, extremely valuable body of work—summarized later—that's been long over-due. Of course, the bulk of this research is quantitative in nature.

However, we know almost nothing about how, specifically, the written products and processes function in improving health. Researchers in writing, rhetoric, and pedagogy have not focused on how writing about trauma works, in terms of its specific language or its thinking and composing processes. What motivates them to write in the first place? How do they conceive of their audiences? How do they organize their pieces? What evidence appears in their writing—and in their reflections on this writing—that reveals specific critical thinking strategies? What language devices do they employ in their writing?

For these reasons and many more, I embarked on what became a ten-year study to describe, as closely as I could, *how and why* experienced, effective writers compose to "heal" themselves—the focus of the following chapters. Most of the people described in this book are language experts who have devoted their lives to the study and teaching of reading and writing. These professionals were tenured faculty members in university English and education departments, conducted research, published widely, presented frequently at professional meetings, and received awards for their work. Others were experienced teachers pursuing graduate degrees. A few are middle-school, junior high, and high school students.

In Chapter 1, "Composing through Trauma," I describe the foundational principles or "pillars" of such composing. Only by immersion in "the thing itself" can we better understand such complex feelings, so I'll try to anchor these principles in the experiences, products, and processes of all kinds of people, who, in many different ways, seek to compose their way through trauma.

Regardless of the age, background, or expertise level of these writers, trauma has a way of leveling the field on which they find themselves. While improvement in writing itself is not an *explicit* point or chapter in this book, I believe it reverberates in every line in the pages ahead. One argument behind this book is that writing not only wrestles with trauma, but in so doing, it develops many writing skills. Readers will find identification of numerous thinking strategies in nearly every discourse examined—especially those types of thinking that have long been heralded as necessary for academic prose and success in the workplace. In fact, I think that readers will find that improvement of discourse *cannot help but occur* when we write about trauma. After all, such writing occurs when we are literally driven to understand immediate issues weighting us down, when hesitancy, self-censorship, and cultural artifice have fallen away, when such "shackles" become, somehow, no longer very relevant. Writers, themselves, recognize when their words and voices ring true, when their knots of fear and confusion get laid out in clearer, straighter lines.

Chapter 2, "Beyond 'Just Academic Stuff . . . '" provides the main contexts for this work, describing the course, the teacher, and the resultant study. Writing, reading, visualizing, reflecting, revising, and talking about our trauma not only make us better writers, but they create an environment that leads to deeper, wider understanding of those unspeakable moments that too often lay frozen within us. However, this composing through trauma is by no means a magic bullet. Composing about trauma is not a cure-all or remotely similar to any kind of vague, mystical panacea. Instead, it's hard work that demands commitment, time, extensive writing, thinking, and many other activities and processes.

Most of the people you'll meet in the chapters ahead have experienced much worse traumas than I did when I couldn't grasp the death of my grandfather. At that time, my only way to manage my grief was to bolt out of the dining room, run out to the yard, lay back in the grass, and watch the clouds drift above. Suddenly, brazenly, the world made no sense. When the people in this book turn to composing their way through trauma, they look face-up into that same sky that goes on forever, as they work toward understanding.

Traumas that we are compelled to write about are powerful human ones, which require a uniquely human response—writing to and for ourselves and trusted others—small, human voices that rail against the universe. Such writing is very much like prayer, whether or not we believe in a God. This, we have to believe, is the highest, holiest use of language imaginable.

1 Composing through Trauma

> *Sweet are the uses of adversity,*
> *Which like the toad, ugly and venomous,*
> *Wears yet a precious jewel in his head;*
> *And this our life exempt from public haunt,*
> *Finds tongues in trees, books in the running brooks,*
> *Sermons in stones, and good in everything.*
>
> William Shakespeare, *As You Like It* (2.1.14–19)

Claire, a bright young student in my graduate course focused on writing about trauma, insisted that she "didn't have anything to heal from." At semester's end, she did not turn in the long narrative and analysis of a traumatic event. I had constantly assured her that "traumas" reside on a continuum, from the most severe to the least serious, and she could choose topics heavy or light. She finished most of the assignments, but when it came time for the final project, in which writers combined and synthesized their various writings into a single piece, she did not turn anything in. I had to assign her a grade of "Incomplete."

What most concerned me was that her calm, rational observations about why she could not complete this project caused me to question the premise of my course. Would there be future students who simply have nothing to say about *any* kind of trauma or issue, regardless of its degree of severity? Claire had struck me as an honest, forthright person, so maybe others felt the same way but said nothing? I'd long known that writing about trauma is not for everyone, nor should it be. But this didn't stop me from worrying that this course—which the other twenty-two students seemed to find valuable—could not happen again. A few months after the class ended, Claire sent me this email.

Hello Dr. Fox,

I know my name is probably the last thing you wanted to see in your inbox. I want to talk to you about my paper. It's finished, and I was wondering if I could still turn it in. To be honest, my real concern is about the content of the paper. Dr. Fox, I let it out. I let it all out. What you are going to read is the bare bones . . . plain Claire with nothing extra. I debated for a long time if I were going to write about what my logic was telling me or what my soul was propelling me to write about. I know this sounds corny and clichéd, but it's the truth. I initially told myself that I was going to write about the relationship between my brother and my mom and the fistfight they had when I was eight. It just wasn't coming out, because I had another subject pressing on my mind. It has been a subject that I wanted to talk about for years, but have been scared of the repercussions. Dr. Fox, I talk about repeatedly being molested . . . by my brother. Just last year, I would not have even thought about writing that down, but the floodgates have been opened and I can't shut them. This has been both easy and difficult for me to write. It was easy because there was so much that I wanted to say. (Personal Communication 2003)

Claire's case solidified three important lessons for me. First, it ingrained in me that writing about trauma is *not* for everyone. Second, it's not for everyone *at certain times*. We can suggest and nudge people to write about trauma, but we cannot force them. (I didn't try to persuade Claire to do anything she did not want to do, and grades were off the table, but the fact remains that she was enrolled in a college graduate course.) Finally, this situation underscored the fact that writing about trauma *does* work, much of the time, and for good reason: The positive effects that writing has on wellness have been documented through qualitative and quantitative research studies, conducted over time, with different populations and rigorous methods.

In "Writing as Physical and Emotional Healing: Findings from Clinical Research," Jessica Singer and George Singer (2008) provide a comprehensive review of clinical research on the positive effects of writing on a variety of maladies. The authors review how writers, by using expressive language and self-disclosure, can mediate the adverse effects of physical traumas, including the Epstein-Barr Virus, blood pressure, cancer, chronic pelvic pain, HIV, and physical recovery from surgery. Stephen Lepore and Joshua Smyth (2002) and other researchers have concluded that expressive writing is linked to a general improvement of our immune systems. More specifically, James Pennebaker (1990, 8) summarizes the physiological benefits of expressive writing, which include

> better lung function among asthma patients and lower pain and disease severity among arthritis sufferers (Smyth et al. 1999), higher white blood cell counts among AIDS patients (Petrie, Booth, and Pennebaker 1998), and less sleep disruption among patients with metastatic breast cancer. (De Moor et al. 2002)

Singer and Singer (2008) also evaluate research results of writing's positive effects on psychological issues, such as depression, the loss of jobs, Post-Traumatic Stress Disorder (PTSD), and intimate-partner violence (IPV). Lepore and Smyth (2002) and other researchers have concluded that expressive writing is linked to a general improvement of our immune system. Here, too, Pennebaker (2004) offers a more specific account of expressive writing's psychological effects, as one of experiencing

> immediate feelings of sadness but long-term effects of happiness; lower levels of depressive symptoms and general anxiety; improved performance in school; enhanced ability to deal with one's social life; reduced feelings of anger; increased employability or success in job interviews; and increased feelings of connection with others, [or] social integration (8–11).

Expressive writing therapies are used in major medical organizations, such as Duke University, North Carolina; the City of Hope Cancer Center and The John Wayne Cancer Institute, California; and Piedmont Hospital, Georgia. Writing is used in the treatment of physically and psychologically abused women, AIDS/HIV patients, soldiers experiencing Post-Traumatic Stress Disorder (PTSD), and suicidal people (Anderson and MacCurdy 2000).

In current and clinical contexts, there's little doubt that composing through trauma positively affects our physical and emotional health. While these "new scientific facts" provide assurances to many people, we shouldn't be surprised at how writing has forever helped us. For eons, writing has breathed life into human culture. Writing systems using graphic symbols to represent the sounds of a language seem to have evolved independently in Mesoamerica (650 BCE), China (1250 BCE), and Mesopotamia (3200 BCE) (Schmandt-Besserat 2006). Writing is the basis of government, law, religion, economy, science, art, and technology. In huge and grand fashion, writing has been key to the development and survival of the human race.

We've always regarded the values of writing as self-evident. After all, through the mists of time, we had only to look around at the rich, written products surrounding us—from the magnificent library in ancient Alexandria, to the timeless beauty of Shakespeare's *King Lear*, to the strength of a Milton sonnet, to the brilliance of Mark Twain, to the insights of Joan Didion. We know the inestimable value of writing because it has forever sustained us, guided us, and moved us forward.

Our Storied Past

Composing through trauma works because it's been effectively practiced throughout human history, including by some impressive minds. Thomas Jefferson, for example, penned a long dialogue, "My Head and My Heart," in which his two internal forces debated with each other over his deep affection (if not love) for Maria Cosway, a young married woman he had met in Paris when he served as the US Minister to France in 1786 (Brodie 1974). The dialogue comprised the bulk of Jefferson's long letter, beginning with his sadness at seeing Cosway leave France for her home in England.

> I was at home. Seated by my fireside, solitary & sad, the following dialogue took place between my Head & my Heart:
> Head. Well, friend, you seem to be in a pretty trim.
> Heart. I am indeed the most wretched of all earthly beings. Overwhelmed with grief, every fibre of my frame distended beyond its natural powers to bear, I would willingly meet whatever catastrophe should leave me no more to feel or to fear.
> Head. These are the eternal consequences of your warmth & precipitation. This is one of the scrapes into which you are ever leading us. You confess your follies indeed; but still you hug & cherish them; & no reformation can be hoped, where there is no repentance.
> Heart. Oh, my friend! This is no moment to upbraid my foibles. I am rent into fragments by the force of my grief! If you have any balm, pour it into my wounds; if none, do not har-

row them by new torments. Spare me in this awful moment! (493–94)

While the most common form of writing through trauma is direct, expressive language (discussed later in this chapter), *all* forms of writing can be therapeutic: from poetry to drama, from letters to obituaries, from lists to PowerPoint presentations. An imagined dialogue is a more creative form that emphasizes interaction and thinking, as one voice responds to another, allowing ideas to evolve and become more comprehensible. Jefferson's imaginary dialogue served as a kind of "bridge"—from his internal conflict to reality, from his feelings of fragmentation, to a greater sense of wholeness. I believe this dialogue provided Jefferson a bit of "distance" from his struggle, hence allowing him greater control.

Several decades later, another US President engaged in poetic language, which was, in all likelihood, a way for him to express and distance himself from personal trauma. Here are the final three stanzas from his nine-stanza poem, "The Suicide's Soliloquy," identified by historian Richard L. Miller (Shenk J. 2004):

> Yes! I'm prepared, through endless night,
> To take that fiery berth!
> Think not with tales of hell to fright
> Me, who am damn'd on earth!
> Sweet steel! Come forth from your sheath,
> And glist'ning, speak your powers;
> Rip up the organs of my breath,
> And draw my blood in showers!
> I strike! It quivers in that heart
> Which drives me to this end;
> I draw and kiss the bloody dart,
> My last—my only friend!

This poem was first published in the August 25, 1838, *Sangamon Journal,* by a twenty-nine year-old Abraham Lincoln. Scholars agree that Lincoln suffered bouts of serious depression, twice talking about suicide to his friends. Compared to today's standards, the poem is over-wrought, but that was the style back then. Nonetheless, its imagery and metaphor are starkly effective.

Imagery and metaphor have long been staples of writing for purposes of healing. They work because our minds themselves are metaphoric. We use such a poetic language as another "window" for describing problems and finding solutions. Poetic language, especially metaphor, can *transfer* meaning from one experience or concept to that of another. Casting our thoughts in imagery, metaphor, or imagined dialogue, as Jefferson did, can loosen or remove the issue that is tied to us.

One way that poetic language accomplishes this is by its interactive quality: Its ambiguity often suggests more than one possible meaning, so it forces us to think, to consider more than one alternative. When we see options (as readers and as writers), then we are invited to think independently. The specificity of poetic language largely bypasses linear, logical thinking. This concreteness also helps us bypass resistance, if we have experienced the same message in generic terms. Therefore, (and to conjecture for a moment) Lincoln may have directly told himself that suicide was wrong; his friends may have explicitly told him it was wrong, or may have even commanded him not to think about it or do it. Let's assume that merely telling him does not work, nor would telling him again be effective. This is the point where the indirectness of poetic language may be most effective; Lincoln implies, but doesn't say, he would commit suicide.

Nearly a hundred years after Lincoln, another US President, Harry S. Truman, engaged in extensive writing that he called "longhand spasms" (McCullough 1993). When facing complex issues and vexing problems, Truman would often check in, alone, to Kansas City's Hotel Muelbach, where he would write his way out of the problem. Following is an example of such writing from early in Truman's career, when he served as a Jackson County Judge (now referred to as a "County Commissioner").

> This sweet associate of mine, my friend, who was supposed to back me, had already made a deal with a former crooked contractor, a friend of the Boss's . . . I had to compromise in order to get the voted road system voted out . . . I had to let a former saloonkeeper and murderer, a friend of the Boss's, steal about $10,000 from the general revenues of the county to satisfy my ideal associate and keep the crooks from getting a million or more out of the bond issue. Was I right or did I commit a felony? I don't know. . . . I've got the $6,500,000 worth of roads on the Ground and at a figure that makes the crooks tear their hair. The hospital is up at less cost than any similar institution in spite of my drunken brother-in-law, whom I had to employ on the job to keep peace in the family. I've had to run the hospital

job myself and pay him for it. . . . Am I an administrator or not? Or am I just a crook to compromise in order to get the job done? You judge it, I can't. (McCullough 1993, 499)

While Truman's language here is far less poetic than Jefferson's or Lincoln's, I admire it more than theirs. First, Truman was a plainspoken man, with more than a trace of a now-disappearing rural Missouri accent. These facts led many people to dismiss Truman as a "hick," similar to the way Lyndon Johnson was often perceived, due to his Texas drawl. This is far from true for both men. Truman was more literate and cultured than most of his peers; he just never took pains to show this side of himself. He constantly read history and loved Shakespeare. He was an intense student of classical music, who wanted to be a concert pianist. When traveling, Truman took his own record player and LPs, or long-play albums, of classical music with him. The second reason that I admire Truman's habit of writing through trauma is that he chose to write in common, everyday language—expressive language. It's not pretty or stuffy or preachy. It's direct and honest. It doesn't hold back.

Expressive language is the "matrix" from which all other forms of language are born—from academic and scientific reports to business contracts and poems (e.g., Britton 1975, 11–18). The main reason is this: Before you can write in language that is manipulated and cast in specific ways for a specific audience (e.g., a lab report aimed at molecular biologists), you have to be able to explain it first to yourself or to a close, trusted friend (explaining specialized vocabulary when needed). If you can't clearly explain it to yourself, then you'll have a helluva hard time explaining it to a specialized reader. In short, expressive language is the kind in which we think. Its uncensored, trusting, and informal qualities are what make it malleable, flexible. This, in turn, allows us to generate *more* and *different* thinking.

Expressive language and writing about trauma share many characteristics, which you'll find in this excerpt from Truman's writing. For example, he begins with concrete, observable details, sticking close to his reality ("6,500,000 worth of roads"). While he emphasizes the personal, he keeps the larger context in his view (accomplishing projects for the public good). Truman also connects feelings to specific events, as a kind of *evidence*, and he connects one incident to another. He asks questions of himself and twice expresses frustration at not answering them directly, though here he suggests his *answer* merely by posing the question.

He later answers an implied question by explaining why he had to hire his inept brother-in-law. Truman is also flexible with time, including observations of the past and present; he also implies his concern for the future, in his satisfaction with the new roads and hospital. Truman describes some tension by including positive and negative observations and events. He also uses ironic, direct, and colorful names for people ("sweet associate"; "crooks"; and "saloonkeeper and murderer"); he uses fragments or incomplete sentences, contractions, lists, and the first-person pronoun "I" and second–person pronoun "you" for addressing the reader. All of these are common characteristics of expressive language and writing about trauma.

As far as I know, Truman never explained how or why he engaged in such writing. His label of "Longhand Spasms" suggests a certain dismissal of such writing. On the other hand, he must have believed in its value because he practiced it throughout his life. Historian David McCullough's (1993, 499–500) description of one instance leaves little doubt about Truman's purpose:

> Truman had had all he could take. Alone at his desk upstairs at the White House, on a small, cheap ruled tablet of the kind schoolchildren use, he began to write. It was the draft of a speech, a speech that he had no intention of giving, but that he needed to get off his chest.

I don't know if anyone ever praised Truman for his literate and insightful habit of writing through trauma, but I do. I'll just chalk it up as another quality for which this modest man never received credit. The major difference between today and the times of Jefferson, Lincoln, and even Truman is that writing is no longer the province of the elite or educated few. Composing about trauma is now simply more available to everyone, including Claire, whom you met at the opening of this chapter.

Our Storied Present

Throughout that semester, Claire had insisted that she had no real traumas to explore in writing, until a couple of months after the course ended, when she sent me a thirty-six-page paper describing and analyzing her repeated sexual abuse inflicted by her older brother, whom she revered:

I adored Kent growing up. I wanted to be just like him. I didn't want him to join a gang or get arrested. I simply admired his independence and toughness. I felt safe when he was around. (Course Document 2003)

The following excerpt recounts the first episode when Claire was about seven years old. She and her sisters were "playing house" with Kent. With Claire's younger sisters sent out of the living room by their make-believe father, they laid under a blanket stretched between the living room couch and a coffee table to form their bedroom. Claire describes how they talked to each other as pretend parents:

"So honey," I began to say, "How was your day at work?"

"Fine," he said with his back facing me, "I had a long day and I'm tired."

"Okay honey, go to sleep," I replied in a motherly way.

I turned on my side and pretended to go to sleep when I heard Kent moving around. I could tell at that point he was looking at me, and it felt like he was closer to me than before. I was always cautious when Kent was silent and near me. He was always trying to pull some kind of prank. I quickly turned toward him, to see what he was doing. He was laying on his side, raised on his left elbow, facing me.

"You didn't give me a good night kiss," he said playfully.

"Ugh," I replied automatically, "That's nasty."

"Well, that's what mamas and daddies do and you said you wanted to play house." I stared at him suspiciously, but he had a point.

"Not a real kiss, just a little one. We're just playing," he said matter-of-factly.

"Okay," I said cheerfully, "just a little one." I kissed him on the cheek. It didn't hurt and it didn't feel too weird. I had kissed Kent on the cheek before and plus I had kissed DeShawn Perry last year in 1st grade under the jungle gym. At that moment, Darla started complaining about Trish messing with her in the other room. Without thinking, I jumped up and reprimanded Trish. I walked slowly back to my pretend bedroom. I was hoping that Kent was asleep. He wasn't. He was lying on his back with his head resting on the pillow and watching me as I crawled in. At that moment, I realized how small the room was. I didn't say anything to Kent and laid down with my back facing him. He broke the silence.

"We didn't finish," he said quietly. He was practically whispering, "Mamas and daddies do other things." I knew he was talking about sex. Mama had the birds and the bees talk with me seven months ago. I looked at him and then the light blue ceiling. It was semi-transparent so I could faintly see the white tile of our real house. I guess my silence signaled him to go ahead. He climbed on top of me. He started moving his body up and down, just like the people on TV before mama turns the channel. My clothes were on and so were his, but for the first time I realized he had a penis. I knew that boys had different genitalia from me, but I had never thought of that in terms of my brother. It seemed like forever he rocked on top of me. The weight of his body caused my chest to hurt and I wanted him to get off. I didn't say anything. He rolled off of me and put my hand on his penis and held it steady. I held my breath; I was scared to breathe and more scared to move. He began to fondle me as I lay stiff. I kept looking at the ceiling.

Kent could tell I was nervous. He looked at me and said, "Remember we're just playing." I nodded but I knew we stopped playing. He didn't sound like a daddy, I didn't sound like a mama, but instead we reverted back to brother and sister.

I always hate myself when I think back on that day. I could have ended it all right there, but I didn't. What makes me more ashamed is the reason why I didn't stop it. While I was lying there, I knew what we were doing was wrong. I knew that I should have run out from under that blanket and called Mommy and Daddy, but I didn't. I let Kent do that to me. For many years, I told people and myself that I was frozen with fear. This was the truth, but it wasn't all of the truth. I was scared of what Kent would say or do to me if I left, but I was scared also because part of me enjoyed it. I remember now that I had a window of opportunity to get out of that situation. Darla and Trish started fighting again, and I went to pretend spank them, then I quickly returned to Kent, to finish our business. (Course Document 2003)

As Claire stated earlier, this was painful for her to write; it's even painful to read. While there are far more differences than similarities among Jefferson, Lincoln, Truman, and Claire, they are similar in their risk-taking and courage in writing about these topics. It is not surprising that Jefferson, Lincoln, and Truman have long been cited in the top tier of America's leaders. I suspect that Claire will be regarded as a top educator. Their writing quoted in this chapter shows fluency with language and vigorous thinking—two extremely important and entwined processes that I'll take up next. Following this, I'll briefly explore three additional pillars of writing about trauma: form and structure, other symbols, and other people.

FLUENCY AND THINKING

About her writing of repeated molestations, Claire stated, "As I began writing, more and more incidents began to pop in my head." This is the magic: Words trigger thoughts, and thoughts elicit words, and so, the cycle continues. The most basic reason, then, for Jefferson's, Lincoln's, Truman's, and Claire's using writing as a means of comprehending, organizing, and therefore, better controlling their traumas, is a simple one—they could write and write easily. They were used to it; they were comfortable with it; they trusted it.

They were confident that, through writing, they could impose some semblance of order on chaos. Composing through trauma works because writers can generate visible language, which in turn prompts thinking, which in turn leads to more and different writing, and the cycle of fluency continues. We often think of "fluency" as referring to how much language—spoken or written—we can produce. But, this is only half of the equation as generating language also means generating thought. The two cannot be separated, even though we have managed to do so, for a very long time. Consider the following writing, completed by a fifteen year-old boy.

> I have a question for you dad is it wrong to love someone who you hate so much to want to die and hope to be released, and to be saved what would you say if I said I don't think it would bother me to watch you die at my feet does that make me insane? Or am I just lost and confused about who I am supposed to be am I the monster the world outside of me and my beast portrays me to be do I kill to survive or take the cowards way and hide when the world looks at me what do they see a coward a hero or just a lost and abused soul so dead so dark my heart

no longer beats with life as I sit there wishing that I could die I am so fucking weak inside of me I feel gone do I have this right to want to watch you bleed and fucking scream for turning me into a beast? I have a question for you before you leave when I was so messed up on my drugs that I was almost dead inside did it hurt you or did you just laugh at the thought I was hurting deep inside. (Anonymous, from state government youth services instructor, 2006)

Most readers will find much to criticize here. Sadly, the first criticism will likely be, "This kid can't write! What lousy grammar!" While I love grammar as much as Professor Poindexter or Mrs. Grundy, it's always the easiest response to glom on to, stopping us from seeing any *larger* qualities. When we neither know nor care about something, we look toward an authority—the rulebook. Another common response to this writing will likely be, "This spoiled, self-centered kid is not taking any responsibility for himself, blaming his father for everything!" This may be wholly or partly correct. I have no idea. The third common response is likely to be, "This is not *real* writing; it's a rant, a mind-dump—just another piece of *Dear Diary* trash."

Of these three common responses, the last one is closest to the truth. But, it's misguided because there is nothing wrong with "rants," "mind-dumps," or even "Dear Diary Trash"—if you believe that fluency and self-disclosure promote thinking and health, as abundant research tells us (e.g., Pennebaker 2004; Singer and Singer 2008).

"Mind dumps" may not be pretty, but they start the generative sorting-out process, which leads to a less fragmented self. While we may not like what this young man says or how he says it, at least he's fluent enough to *begin* the process of the writing-thinking cycle. Would his writing improve if he supplied and evaluated evidence? Definitely. Would his writing benefit if he revised, qualified, and elaborated his ideas? Absolutely. But if we don't have language fluency first, then we'll never get close to thinking and revising and reflecting—and a less fractured sense of self. How, then, are language and other symbol systems connected to thinking?

While I never separate these two crucial processes, they are commonly put into different boxes, often on different shelves. Among many others, Judy Willis, though, links writing with higher-process thinking:

Consider all of the important ways that writing supports the development of higher-process thinking: conceptual thinking; transfer of knowledge; judgment; critical analysis; induction; deduction; prior-knowledge evaluation (not just activation) for prediction; delay of immediate gratification for long-term goals; recognition of relationships for symbolic conceptualization; evaluation of emotions, including recognizing and analyzing response choices; and the ability to recognize and activate information stored in memory circuits throughout the brain's cerebral cortex that are relevant to evaluating and responding to new information or for producing new creative insights—whether academic, artistic, physical, emotional, or social. (Willis 2011, 1)

The language most often used for critical thinking, as well as "healing"—what Willis describes as "**evaluation of emotions, including recognizing and analyzing response choices**"—*is*, you guessed it, expressive language, the very "Dear Diary Trash" we love to hate. In addition to those expressive elements that Truman demonstrated in the earlier passage, expressive language is also marked by condensing or packing a lot of meaning into a few words, which only the writer can completely unpack.

Another primary characteristic is asking yourself questions and trying to answer them, even providing several possible answers. Along with speculating and hypothesizing, other elements include expressions of doubt and qualification, litany or listing, and metaphor. In short, thinking on paper or screen. Expressive language is much like Lev Vygotsky's (1986) concept of "inner speech," one of the major ways in which we think (Britton et al. 1975). In the following excerpt from Claire's paper, she wonders about her sensations when being raped. We can see the cogs and wheels in motion. We can hear her thinking on paper.

> I'm trying to figure out why I got pleasure from that. It could be that I enjoyed the time with Kent. He hated me, Darla, and Trish so much when we were little. But, I adored him. I wanted to be just like him. I thought he was cool and that he knew everything. Maybe that's why I did it. I don't know.
>
> I'm lying. I'm lying. I'm lying. I do know why I did it, but I'm scared of how people will judge me if I say it, write it, or even think it. Putting on this "I need his attention" act is just to cover

up and suppress the truth. I'm embarrassed about how I really feel. But if you must know . . . I did it because I enjoyed that tingling feeling. You know? That tingling feeling? The kind they warn children about on "The More You Know" commercials? Well, those commercials implied that the tingling feeling was bad and that it would hurt you. It didn't hurt me. . . .

I feel as if something is wrong with me. How could I allow a family member to turn on me? The thought of it sickens me to my stomach. I keep trying to tell myself that I'm not weird and that if anyone or anything touched a woman's privates, she would get excited, right? My body was responding normally, right? For whatever reason, this explanation doesn't settle with me. How could a little girl like being molested? I know what you're thinking, "You were only seven. You didn't know any better." Well, that's what I kept telling myself for years, but it's not working anymore. I'm old enough to assess the situation. Do women like being raped? If they do, is it still rape? I finally realized that I was old enough to know it was wrong, and I was old enough to make a conscious decision to return to him. So, what do you think? Do I still deserve your sympathy . . . empathy . . . or whatever it is?

. . . .

When other people share their experiences, I keep my mouth shut. Generally, they feel that something was stolen from them. I can only empathize. I don't feel that Kent took something from me. If anything, I gave it to him. I was a willing participant. Does this qualify me as a victim? (Course Documents 2003)

Such expressive language may not supply easy answers or resolutions to dilemmas (though it happens), as we want Claire to learn about the social and cultural forces that have conditioned women to submit quietly to men. Nonetheless, expressive language *does* lift burdens off of our shoulders, rendering problems visible, giving them shape and form, so that we can better see them and define them and analyze them in different ways. This unburdening, in turn, helps us distance ourselves, rhetorically and emotionally, from the trauma in question. In an opposite way, expressive language also functions as a more direct conduit to our feelings, emotions, and thinking. Demystifying problems makes them less scary. It is an act of unifying or "suturing" our splintered selves, so that we can become more whole (Anderson, Holt, and McGady 2000, 58–82).

When we somehow distrust our readers, we not only censor ourselves, but we also produce fewer words, in total, as well as fewer words per minute (e.g., Elbow 1998). This *lack of fluency* often means that we cut short the time and language we need to arrive at our intended meaning. That is, visible language generates more language and more thinking, in turn extending the thinking-writing cycle. We need to generate enough ideas in our writing to discover exactly what it is we want to say, what we most need to write. If we lack fluency, then we're likely unable to generate enough detail to more fully comprehend it and to analyze it, or to revise it in productive and healing ways.

The reverse is also true: When we indeed trust our readers, we gain confidence in ourselves as writers, have reduced fears of evaluation, and hence increase our production rate. The writers in this study always trusted their readers (if they were even thinking of their readers), and therefore were highly fluent, providing extensive diaries, email messages, and website postings.

Being committed to the topic we're writing about also affects our fluency and thinking. We have to be invested in our subjects, cognitively and emotionally. This occurs when we have complete freedom in our choice of topic, purpose, and audience, as did the writers explored in this book. Under these circumstances, we can become deeply absorbed in our activities, to the point of becoming unaware of the passage of time and of our immediate surroundings. Mihaly Csikszentmihalyi (1990) calls these "flow experiences," which become intrinsically rewarding for us—the best kind of motivation, which, in turn, promotes writing fluency and thinking.

Even the processes we engage in as writers influence our production rate and thinking. Research on composing processes reveals that writers constantly engage in mentally shuttling back and forth between larger "global" plans, such as audience appropriateness and organization—and smaller "local" concerns, such as word choice and syntax (Perl 1994; Flower and Hayes 1989).

When we compose for purposes of healing, we likewise grapple with words and ideas, tugging and pulling between many types of *oppositions*, including: (1) the whole idea, tone, or attitude we wish to convey versus the individual parts; (2) the past time period in which the traumatic experience occurred versus the current time period; (3) the need to focus on negative experiences versus the impulse *not* to sound completely negative; and (4) the experiences we wish to *show* in our writing (i.e., sensory images and details objectively conveyed) versus the meaning we want to *tell* or summarize, via using generalizations and adjectives. In such writing, we also engage in analysis (breaking wholes into parts) and synthesis (forming wholes from parts). These simultaneous mental actions create tension or "critical thinking," as well as creative thinking (John-Steiner 1997; DeSalvo 1999).

Thinking, then, resides deep in the heart of composing through trauma. In the people you'll meet in the chapters ahead, you'll see them courageously engage in a host of specific thinking strategies, such as making decisions about identity, motivation, audience awareness, genre, rhetoric, and imagery. You'll also see how these writers wrangle with how they are alike and how they differ from other people, as they try to *fit* themselves into their radically altered realities brought on by their trauma. You'll see these writers grapple with all types of "oppositions" or tensions, as they try to gain some resolution on more level ground.

In doing all of these things, they tap into their inner stream of consciousness—witnessing it, focusing it, and suspending it. It's important to clarify that this type of thinking is indeed "higher-order" thinking—maybe the *highest* of all types of thinking, because logical deduction and induction become merged with reason, emotion, and spirituality. In the combustible heat of writing through serious and immediate trauma, all of these big guns fire at the same time. Have no doubt: Expressive language, fluency, and thinking are the first pillars of composing through trauma. Of course, anything as complex and unwieldy as this needs other support beams, a few of which I'll take up now.

SHAPE AND STRUCTURE

Composing through trauma works because it's flexible enough to thrive without structure, as well as to be shaped (later) into any genre. Shape and structure greatly help everyone: They contain meaning in recognizable vessels, helping readers to understand the whole message. Shape and structure also provide some familiarity, safety, and confidence for writers. Even though a piece may not be intended for anyone else to read, a defined shape can increase the writer's feelings of wholeness wrought from fragmentation or chaos.

However, you can seldom *begin* with a form or a shape in mind when writing about trauma. Fluency must come first, or else you have nothing to mold into a shape or assemble into a structure. It really is as simple as that. If you begin with a structure or a form in mind, then everything you do is tailored to *fit* within your pre-fab mold. This approach will stunt or smother your ideas and thinking before they have a chance to grow and bloom. In many ways, then, the point of composing through trauma is to *avoid* structure and form, as long as possible, because structures tend to force us into tidy little boxes of closure—"the right answer" or "the point." While forms can help readers understand our meaning, they do not necessarily help us *discover* our own meaning, unless, of course, we are satisfied with our discovered meaning and somehow want to mold it into a more definite shape.

It is also true that we often perceive a lack of organization (and thinking, purpose, and even sanity) unless a writing has a clear *thesis* at the beginning, followed by a few paragraphs of evidence and a conclusion paragraph. Discourse can be organized in many different ways, and just because a message does not conform to this particular, deductive sequence doesn't mean it was composed by a willy-nilly writer. It only means the reader was trained to see one pattern in a world of infinite design possibilities. Consider the following piece by Jake.

> I will tell you about the fear, and what I did about it.
>
> In my dream, there is an owl flying around the restaurant, circling above our heads, or maybe just mine. I can't tell if I'm alone or not. When I say to the owl, "Get out," a voice dripping with sarcasm and hate repeats my words from off screen. Suddenly I know, in that instant and positive way that knowledge arrives in dreams, that it's the devil and he's in the bathroom. Then there is a couple, standing, arms linked, younger than I am. Their faces are familiar. "How do I know you?" I ask them. The girl answers me, and though she is directly in front of me, her words are miles, even dimensions, away. It sounds like she says, "We told you this would happen," and the boy gives her a warning look, like I'm not supposed to know. "Know what?" I ask. Another instant flash of dream knowledge arrives—I have, in fact, seen them before, and they are both dead. This startles me into consciousness.
>
> I hear myself breathing, gasping, gulping. I try to open my eyes but I can't. I try to turn over, but I feel heavy, or that I am

held down. I try to move an arm, a foot, a finger, an eyelid, anything. It's all shut down. I'm still struggling for air. I become somewhat detached from my panic and think, "What the hell is happening?" Then I'm back to panicking again. Alarms are going off in my head. *Panic.* I should be able to move. *PANIC!* I don't know how long it lasts—twenty seconds? Three minutes? Half an hour? I summon up all the strength I imagine that I've got and prepare to rock myself into movement. Have you ever had a door shut on you, and when you try to open it, realize that someone is holding it closed? So you get a running start to blast the door open, but the person holding it has let go, anticipating what you are about to do, and you almost kill yourself trying to get out? I nearly fall out of the bed trying to turn over, but I am mobile.

A mixture of fear and confusion swirls in my chest as I turn on my lamp and grope for my glasses. Where is it? My nightstand is a clutter of magazines and notebooks, scrap paper and empty glasses. Fumbling, sweeping, my hands are bricks. One thought repeats itself, "I know it's here, I know it's here," trying to keep obvious questions from forming. I know it's here, but it is buried beneath more and more temporal matter. There. I locate that familiar reptilian red skin on the bottom shelf, gathering dust. I seize it, the Holy Bible. It falls open wherever it will, and I tear into it like a sinner on fire. Looking for some kind of soothing communication from the Almighty, I flutter the fragile, onion skin pages until I come across Isaiah 54:6, which reads, "'For a brief moment, I abandoned you, but with deep compassion I will bring you back. In a surge of anger I hid my face from you for a moment, but with everlasting kindness I will have compassion on you,' says the LORD your redeemer." A modicum of comfort drips into my shaking skin, an IV divine. Maybe there is meaning behind this. Is this event some kind of wake-up call from God? Has my recent behavior disturbed Him? Do I need to get myself right?

When this happened I was 17, and I assumed that I had had a physical visitation from some being, benign or malign, I wasn't sure which. This was the beginning of a sometimes terrifying, sometimes amusing, always educational journey in which I learned much about "cloth-like dolls," night terrors, the grays, fugue states & waking dreams, God, the Devil, and me. (Course Document 2003)

Most of us would say that this piece has no discernible shape or structure. We're not sure what the point is. Is it about Jake's fear of dreams? His regret and/or return to formal religion or belief in God? His fear of a "visit" from aliens? ("Grays" are described on the Internet as aliens responsible for abductions of humans and cattle slaughters. Of course, the Grays are also described as a short-lived rock band and a professional, independent baseball team.) The point here is that this piece has no point. It doesn't need to, because it's exploratory. If Jake had begun with a clear point or thesis, then we would know that he had already made up his mind; that he had already discovered his "truth," and he only wanted to communicate it to us. But, if you don't understand your trauma, if you can't make any sense out of it, then you have to "write your way there." Exploration, then, is the first rule of writing through trauma.

Nonetheless, there *is* form in Jake's piece. First, it's a narrative; it tells a story. Stories are an ancient, durable form of entertainment; they transcend all barriers of race, class, gender, environment, and age. Narratives occur within a time frame, often chronologically. They usually serve a purpose, come from a specific point of view, and contain selected information, while leaving other information out. Narrative is fundamental to composing through trauma because it relies on specific events represented in imagery created with words, as well as actual images, such as photos, paintings, or videos (explored in the following section). Guy Allen (2000) summarizes why narratives are key to composing through trauma:

> Stories, Buford writes, "protect us from chaos, and maybe that's what we, unblinkered at the end of the twentieth century, find ourselves craving." Buford goes on: "Implicit in the extraordinary revival of storytelling is the possibility that we need stories—that they are a fundamental unit of knowledge, the foundation of memory, essential to the way we make sense of our lives. . . . We have returned to narratives—in many fields of knowledge—because it is impossible to live without them" (279).

Rebecca Dierking puts it this way:

> Siegel (2007, 308), looking at narrative from a neurological standpoint, found that narrative is not just a story, not just a

distilled memory, but "a deep, bodily and emotional process of sorting through the muck in which we've been stuck" (2012, 50).

As crucial as narratives are for sorting through trauma, they can also help us to spin our wheels in the same old sludge. The savior, chronology, is also the culprit here. We think and live according to the iron clockworks of sequence. Chronological order forms deep lines in our psyches, and breaking this pattern can be hard. Chronology can meld us to the same ways of thinking about a trauma. Because traumatic memories are so strong and so rooted in time sequence, creating a narrative in a *non*-chronological order can help extract us from this rut. For this reason, much of the writing in my course does not depend on time. I suggest that students use flashback and flash-forward—and never begin at the beginning. Of course, within these blocks of discourse, narrative still prevails, but the primary chain is broken and new perspectives of making meaning often arise.

Another form or structure Jake uses is less visible to most readers, but is very common to writing about trauma. Different researchers (e.g., Wilma Bucci 2002 and Louise DeSalvo 1999) have identified this rough pattern in writing about trauma: (1) sensory detail; (2) linking these details to the event, which provoked these details; (3) blending these details and events into a narrative; and (4) analyzing and/or reflecting on the details and events. Writers do not set out to follow this form; it's just that this rough shape is commonly found in such writing, after the fact.

Jake's piece begins with a few intriguing sensory details: an owl circles above his head; an unknown voice sarcastically mimics him; he speaks with a young couple whom he recalls is dead. From there, he moves to the event itself—his struggle to wake up and orient himself, find his glasses, fumble through the pages of a Bible, and read a passage. He briefly analyzes why he is writing; it gives him a "modicum of comfort." He continues to reflect briefly in the final paragraph. Like any writing process or product, there's often a lot of recycling of elements. For instance, sensory detail often occurs throughout the piece, as it does in Jake's writing. In all, form and structure reside in Jake's piece, but it flies under the radar, so that it cannot stunt or hijack his ideas, distracting him from his search to identify and understand his trauma. At many stages of composing through trauma, we don't need any kind of form or structure or recipe to follow—just a willingness to get it out, to create.

Forms and structures can be helpful but are not needed as we work to demystify a trauma. However, once we *have* generated an abundance of material that we have thoroughly developed, probed, questioned, offered possible answers to, analyzed relevant secondary sources and integrated them into our own thinking, casted them into different genres, and all other ways of perceiving them from multiple perspectives, then a structure can further help us gain distance and perspective on our issues.

Chih-Ning Chang is an intelligent, hard-working language expert who chose a demanding form to express her trauma, *after* she had thoroughly processed it in many different ways. Following is her poem, which she later converts to a video:

> I am defeated
> And I refuse to believe that
> I can make a difference
> I know it is hard but
> "Dreams come true"
> Is a joke and
> "Nobody can change the fate"
> So I told people
> I don't trust myself
> My life is broken because
> The monster
> Is more powerful than
> My strength
> The monster stole my identity and hope
> I would be lying to you if I said
> I will have a great future ahead
> Before everything I must know
> Failures are inevitable
> Why is it?
> Shame and insecurity are so ingrained in me
> I don't think
> My life will be filled with joy and the sense of great achievement
> My self
> Is controlled by
> The fear
> There is no way to turn things around
> It is foolish to presume
> I will succeed
> If only I could reverse the perception, my life would be different.
>
> (Course Document 2008)

Chih-Ning, whose second language is English, wrote this poem in response to the "Monster and Angel" prompt, in which writers wrote a poem or a letter to their monster or trauma and then literally deconstructed the monster and re-assembled it into an angel. Chih-Ning chose to do this as a palindrome, which makes sense read from top to bottom, as well as from bottom to top. In her video, the poem appears in white font on a black background as she reads it aloud to soft, tinkling piano music. The monster version reads from top to bottom, scrolling downward, to emphasize the trauma. The poem's final line signals the opposite meaning: that the positive quality of the angel, is about to begin. Next, the same poem appears on a pink background, illustrated with a flower, as Chih-Ning reads it from bottom to top, the upward movement serving the positive message.

The palindrome is a demanding master. Chih-Ning was able to recast her trauma into this stringent form for a few different reasons. First, because she had completed and revised several projects focused on her trauma, she felt grounded and confident enough for this new challenge. She knew her message inside and out and was prepared to compose it in a different way, for a wider audience. Second, like other international students who had been educated in school systems that rarely or never allowed students to experiment or "play," Chih-Ning vigorously seized the chance to do so as a graduate student. She had just encountered the palindrome form on a YouTube video and had to try it out for herself.

In this context, the "tight" structure of the palindrome was perfect. It extended or further distanced Chih-Ning from her original trauma, which consisted of arriving in America from her native Taiwan without a means of financial support and experiencing severe culture shock throughout her first year in her new home. Like many forms, her palindrome demanded a lot of control—over the structure of the content, and, I believe, over the original trauma itself. In this case, her verbal and visual palindrome became a kind of artifact that she could now place on a shelf and reflect upon from a greater distance than ever before—a kind of end-point in her composing and healing processes about this episode in her life.

Much more can be said about the roles of shape and structure in composing through trauma. Here I've only sketched the two extremes—loose form and tight form. But lots of useful techniques reside somewhere in the middle. I'll only note one of them now: subheadings. In the throes of "getting it out," most writers don't consider the simple use of subheads, and well they should not. But they are a wonderful first step toward coherence when writers think about them on their first rereading of what they wrote. They only have to look for "chunks" and add a subhead where they see them. Adding subheads benefits the writer as much as the reader. In a few words or phrases, the writer can see and grasp the whole complicated discourse she has just poured out. This can help unify or synthesize the writer's message to himself, thus motivating him to go one-step further and then maybe another step, until, like Chih-Ning (and Jefferson and Lincoln), they approximate the greatest distance from their original trauma.

OTHER SYMBOLS

Composing through trauma also works because it can be communicated to ourselves and others through any medium, not just words, creating a broad spectrum of meanings to a wide range of readers. In addition to written language, Chih-Ning used other symbol systems in her composing through media—video, music, and actual images. I've long encouraged the use of visuals in tandem with writing about trauma. Like Chih-Ning, writers also sometimes choose to integrate videos, music, song lyrics, and even advertisements into their pieces. In Chapter 4, you'll meet several people who effectively integrate visuals that they create themselves or find on the Internet, often manipulating these images in some way, to address their own purposes.

For many years, I've fiercely believed in *any* form of imagery. I continue to believe that any imagery represents the most basic building block of thinking and communicating—the DNA of language, media, and mind (Fox 1994; Fleckenstein, 2003). Traumatic memories are mainly stored as images (e.g., Sheikh, 2003), so when we write, we connect them to the events, people, and places which generated them, ushering them into the light of day, the first step in demystifying the trauma. When you think of imagery within these contexts, its influence is equal to or greater than that of the word.

Semiotics is the study of meanings in signs and symbols, especially in language and images. Although it's poorly understood by most of us, it's the wellspring of using words and images to write about trauma. Semiotics extends from the ancient Greeks, to John Poinsot's *A Treatise on Signs* in 1632, to Umberto Eco (1978). From Leonardo Da Vinci, to William James, to the Gestalt psychologists, we have learned much about images and visual thinking. Cognitive psychologists also focus on the significant role played by mental imagery in thinking: Stephen Kosslyn, William Thompson, and Giorgio Ganis (2006); Ulric Neisser (1976); and Gavriel Salomon (1994) share Allan Paivio's (2001) conclusion that perception and imagery are at least as fundamental as language when it comes to how we think. In short, words trigger other words, as well as images—and images elicit other images, as well as words. Suzanne Stokes's (2001) meta-analysis concludes that, "using visuals in teaching results in a greater degree of learning." Vera John-Steiner's (1997) case studies of the thinking and creative processes of professional scientists, artists, musicians, writers, and others, documents the rich interplay of visual and verbal thinking in these accomplished professionals. Visual thinking also helps people who are learning English as their second language (Kim 2010, Fox and Kim 2011). Platforms such as Second Life have been vigorously adopted by education, business, libraries, museums, and other professional organizations. (See, for example, the "Virtual Worlds Group" of EDUCAUSE at www.educause.edu).

Other research has explored how imagery *directly* affects physical and psychological issues. Anees Sheikh and others review imagery's effects on blood pressure, blood flow, sexual response, body chemistry, ocular changes, electro dermal activity, electromyography (EMGs), and the immune system (Sheikh, Kunzendorf, and Sheikh 2003, 342). Other topics include imagery and cancer, smoking cessation and weight management, cerebral laterality, music, and pain management. It's long past time to recognize these basic research findings that clearly point to imagery as central to thinking. As Rudolf Arnheim summarizes, "We think by means of the things to which language refers—referents that in themselves are not verbal but perceptual" (Arnheim 1986, 207).

Even more relevant here, trauma, language, imagery, and memory may be connected: These have to do with the notion that trauma produces a mental picture that is stored but not accessible to the cerebral cortex. In 2000, Marian MacCurdy examined how traumas are sensory, and that the body reacts to them whether or not the conscious mind can apprehend this information.

> Traumatic memories become locked in a part of the brain that is preverbal and are often accessed unexpectedly. These images pop up sometimes unbidden when we smell hear, see, or touch something that takes us back to the time the traumatic event oc-

curred. It is these images that must be accessed if a story about the trauma is to be told. (Singer & Singer 2008)

Images communicate more directly and quickly, helping writers to crystallize their meanings. When writers use both images and language and then share their writing with a small group of supportive people, then fireworks are more likely to ignite.

OTHER PEOPLE

Writing about trauma is one of the most private and singular activities imaginable. Such writers begin (and often remain) isolated. Eventually, though, most writers greatly benefit from involving other people. Because working through trauma by composing involves other people in so many ways, at some time, they *have* to become part of the equation. Because composing about trauma is undeniably personal and risky, we're often not comfortable with "self-disclosure." Nonetheless, the most human of all kinds of communication demands other humans. A small, prepared response group anchors our writing about trauma, demonstrating for us that we are not alone, that whatever worries or misgivings or confusions beset us *can* be understood by others—others who can help in abundantly different ways. This is the core principle of small response groups: the individual internalizes the behaviors of group members, thereby widening her repertoire of how to write, how to think, how to behave.

Getting started is simple: gather a handful of like-minded spirits who can meet on a regular basis to share their pieces—their ideas, plans, drafts, revisions, images, and even responses to common readings. Each group figures out what's needed to communicate effectively. It takes time for people to build rapport and trust each other, so they should begin with non-threatening tasks, such as sharing why they're interested in composing and trauma, what led them here, or discussing influential and relevant readings.

There are no rules for the register or level of formality in which anyone can speak; the only rule is that writers somehow *communicate* with their group members by responding as a human being, not as a grammar cop. About the worst feedback they can give to someone who's just written about her terminal disease is, "In line two of paragraph one, you need a comma after that subordinate clause." Far down the line, the writer may choose to revise for a wider audience and a specific purpose, such as publication. If and when that time comes, then that comma comment may be appropriate. But even before looking at grammar and mechanics, other useful responses include some basic principles of general semantics: Are some words too general and vague? Does the writer present ideas only in black and white terms, leaving out any middle ground? Does the writer make blanket judgments instead of qualifying what she says? What is the ratio of words with positive meanings and connotations to those that are negative? Most of the time, though, we have to respond with empathy, as one human to another. Nothing less.

In small groups, everyone has to be prepared to accept anything. What is offered to our peers depends upon us, upon how much we want to disclose at any given time. It's natural to disclose more detail as our level of trust grows. Initially, some group members may fear that such writing will re-open old wounds, as they interrogate and excavate an unspeakable moment. This discomfort is not unusual. However, I've learned from others and my own experience that such discomfort is short-lived. In the long run, most people find that it was worth it.

Another concern that can surface early on (or fester, if unspoken) is our awareness that popular culture is drenched in confessional dramas, from the television program, "Cheaters," in which wayward spouses confront each other, to YouTube confessions, to the politician or evangelist "coming clean" for past transgressions. This backdrop of popular culture can trivialize the serious efforts of sincere people trying to help themselves by composing about trauma. This is a hard obstacle to deal with, but it's worth putting on the table for groups to explore and discard. We need to keep in mind that there are clear differences between public confessions for ratings, profit, and instant fame, on the one hand, and for personal, contextualized disclosure for personal growth, on the other hand.

Not just popular culture can influence our composing about trauma. Larger cultural forces, of course, can play a role, too. These are issues that can definitely help writers see that "they are not alone," that such forces exert a kind of gravitational pull on all of us. I firmly believe that learning about such forces—biological, environmental, and cultural—should be integrated into our composing about trauma, but not until the trauma's specific events, places, people, and feelings have been well developed and processed. At this point, it's time to "enlarge the context" by researching relevant facts and issues, and then integrating them into our narratives.

One writer, for example, wrote about her adoption when she was an infant. After she'd thoroughly explored this issue, I suggested that she investigate the entire adoption issue for the population in the state and region where she was adopted, as well as the same timeframe as her own placement: What were the requirements for adoption, on both sides? What were the most common reasons, circa the late 1950's, for babies to be put up for adoption? What was the social and economic context during this period of her new family? This look into outside sources positioned the writer in a place and time, clarifying and broadening her issues. Mainly, this enlarged context weakened or diluted her anxieties.

Another writer focused on the shame and ostracism suffered by his family when his younger brother was arrested for using marijuana. They lived in a small, conservative town in the Midwest. This situation needed to be enlarged, so that the writer could understand that, in many other areas of the country, and with different groups of people, a pot-bust would not be considered a huge deal, for many reasons.

Claire, who, as a child, was repeatedly molested by her brother, gained a wider context and more understanding when her writing explored the possibility that her parents suspected what was going on, but did nothing to stop it. After all, she reasoned, they were a very successful and religious family, well respected within their urban community; their mother avoided conflicts and did not want to upset their family's life; and Kent, her brother, had reason to feel that his father loved Claire and her two younger sisters more than him, as he did not receive a new bicycle when they did, even though he had long wanted one.

Claire also explored her trauma's larger context when she described a midnight conversation with her sisters, Darla and Trish, which happened four years after Kent first raped her. The whole family had returned late from a Pentecostal church service in a neighboring state. Since it was summer, the girls were allowed to stay up even later, as their parents went to bed. They agreed to watch a television program featuring a *real* judge and courtroom—"reality TV." In this program, a ten-year-old girl was suing her sixteen-year-old brother for rape. Claire sits in the dark, fearful of showing her tears of embarrassment.

> I lay on my belly on the side of the brown and white flowered velvet armchair, hoping that it was too dark for Trish and Darla to see my depressed countenance. Neither of them knew what had happened between Kent and me. I had been keeping it a secret. I knew that Darla wouldn't understand, and I thought

> that if I told Trish, out of concern, she would tell Mamma and Daddy. I couldn't risk it. I couldn't risk adding to the pile of dirty laundry our family had developed. Darla was sitting in the loveseat diagonally to my left, by herself, and Trish was seated on the couch in the back of the room. The dim light cast shadows on their faces. I watched them from the shadows of the armchair as they watched the program. It almost seemed as if they were in deep thought of their own. . . . I was actually trying to hold my breath to prevent the need to cry from setting in. A few tears came out, but I was too hidden for Darla and Trish to see.

The TV judge gently coaxes the young girl to admit that her brother had raped her, as Claire continues her narrative:

> The atmosphere in the living room changed. Darla began coughing. I could tell she was faking. She couldn't handle the intensity of the silence either. Trish was in the back of the room leaning on her left elbow and rubbing her temples. She always did this when she was nervous or about to cry. . . . The show went off and all of us were still attempting to mask our embarrassment. Finally, Trish broke the silence.
>
> "Did Kent do anything to y'all?" she asked softly with a slight smile on her face.
>
> She wasn't smiling because she was amused, but because that was the only way she could hide her humiliation. We all smile when we get in trouble, from Daddy on down. She didn't have to clarify. We all knew what she was talking about.
>
> "Yeah," I whispered. I knew Mamma and Daddy were asleep, but I still had to whisper. I was scared to hear myself admit to it aloud. I imagined sirens and bells going off soon as the words left my lips.
>
> "Did he for real?" she asked, relieved to know that she wasn't the only one.
>
> "Uh-huh."
>
> "How many times?" she asked softly, now smiling with excitement.
>
> I don't know if my boldness to talk about this came from being so relieved that someone had been through the same thing, or that they were willing to talk about it first. Either way,

> it was easy to talk about it. "Four times," I said, feeling embarrassed again when the words came out of my mouth. "How many times did it happen to you?" I asked Trish, as if I was trying to retaliate.
> "I don't know. A lot of times." The room became silent again. I looked at Trish and she took a deep breath trying to hold it all back. "What about you, Darla?" she asked quietly. I forgot Darla was in the room. I was too wrapped in fear, excitement, and connecting with Trish that I failed to think about how this one, minute conversation would impact Darla. "Did Kent ever do anything to you?"
> "Yeah," she replied, shrugging her right shoulder as if she was guessing.
> "How many times?" Trish asked.
> "Once," she replied. She put her head down and began to cry. I didn't move to comfort her. I didn't know how. It was too big for a hug and a pat on the back. Trish and I sat there and watched Darla cry. She was only nine.

Claire then explains how this molestation specifically influenced the lives of her younger sisters. While this conversation brought the three sisters closer together, I also have to believe that self-disclosure helped each of them begin to mend. As Claire stated in another message to me, casting the entire trauma into this powerful narrative helped her move forward in life. Claire also noted that she was seeing a counselor now and doing well. (At this writing, Kent was serving a prison term.)

In composing through trauma, making all types of connections is crucial for mending the rupture. Connecting from a micro-context to a larger one is often over-looked if writers get lost in the tangled details related to one specific trauma. Every exploration of trauma should look inward very deeply, as well as outward. Sharing trauma narratives with trusted individuals or in small groups is vital to making them work, to "bringing them home" to readers and writers. I would never think of *not* consulting a trusted friend and *not* using small response groups in my classes. At semester's end, students unanimously cite the bonding and trust with group members as being nearly as helpful as their composing in word and image. Richard Miller (1994), Mary Louise Pratt (2002), and others call this a "contact zone," which demands commitment and participation from everyone. As Pratt states, "no one is excluded, and no one is safe" (129).

Whether made up of students or homemakers, accountants or steelworkers, the give-and-take of response groups is crucial for understanding and learning. As Janet Lucas summarizes, "without contact—without disclosure—there is no contact zone, no point where cultures can meet, clash, converge, and understand" (Lucas 2007, 370). The operational word here must be "understand." Composing through trauma and engaging in disclosure, to ourselves, and, whenever possible, to trusted others, remains the brightest jewel in the head of the venomous toad.

2 Beyond "Just Academic Stuff": The Course, The Teacher, The Study

> *Everything we name enters the circle of language, and therefore the circle of meaning. The world is a sphere of meanings, a language.*
>
> —Octavio Paz

Introduction

Most of this book focuses on "naming"—describing how writers interact with trauma and symbols (verbal and visual) as they work to integrate past disruptions into their current lives. The writing processes and products explored in the forthcoming chapters have often been ignored, abandoned to sit at the curbside, outside the circle of meaning. Therefore, in order to contextualize these phenomena, this chapter focuses on three larger and more familiar circles of meaning: the course, the teacher, and the research study.

The first section describes my graduate course, "Teaching Therapeutic Language, Literature, and Media," beginning with how it was born and evolved. Even though this course was aimed at gradute students in our English Education program, I believe that much of it can be adapted for other levels and situations. Indeed, some of the teachers in this course soon asked their own junior high and high school students to engage in the same activities they were doing on campus. This course has a dual purpose: to vigorously engage teachers in composng about trauma as well as to demonstrate how they may go about it with their own students. Implicit in these purposes is convincing teachers that composing about trauma is a serious academic pursuit that is not only worthy of inclusion in an already-crowded curriculum, but desperately needed.

The second section, "The Teacher," explains my roles in this course, which I hope will help others to follow my own rough-hewn paths in their own ways. Finally, "The Study" explains how the case-study research reported in this book was designed, how the data was collected, and how it was analyzed. I hope that you'll come to accept these three common names as more than "just academic stuff . . . as really *doing* something."

THE COURSE

Somehow, my lifetime of teaching and researching how people interact with language and media led me to this book and the people and issues that generated it. For this luck, I feel fortunate. My experiences teaching high school English in a high-poverty rural area taught me that students are not learning machines sitting at desks waiting with baited breath to please what teachers give them. Rather, they are people with all the problems of adults, intensified because they did not yet have the life experiences that adults draw upon. (Some of my students had grown up within a few miles of the Mississippi River but had never seen it.) My students would sometimes turn in personal writing about their current traumas even when I had not asked for it. I realized that their problems with their jobs or families or friends "got in the way" of their learning about J. Alfred Prufrock and John Donne, as worthy as these fellows are.

What I began learning back then, I kept re-learning in different ways throughout my career. As a graduate teaching assistant, I learned that my freshmen's most coherent and natural writing flowed best when they wrote about what they knew, including their current traumas. They, too, managed to "work in" their life difficulties, regardless of what the assignment requested. These students were nervous and afraid of having their writing evaluated, to the point that they wrote very little, in halting, hiccupping ways, often crossing out words they were unsure of. These experiences led to my dissertation, which was focused on how to reduce such students' writing apprehension. In my first university teaching job, my "developmental" writers, enrolled in a non-credit but required course which met off-campus in a small house owned by the university, had the same fears and needs. I observed the same issues at work in subsequent professional contexts, from directing a university writing program, to teaching technical communication to students as well as workplace professionals, to teaching teachers how to teach writing, reading, language, literature, and media. All of these experiences demonstrated—in living color—how and why literacy affects our thinking and feeling—how we relate to the world, adjusting or not. This fact keeps writing teachers going.

In 1999 I taught my first graduate course focused on writing about trauma. At that time, such a course was a definite risk. Few people, especially academics, considered trauma worthy of study, let alone a legitimate topic for a university graduate course in a College of Education. It was definitely successful. I was most pleased with the dedication and fearlessness of my students and their writing.

The following year, working in the Republic of South Africa, I gained a first-hand view of the huge societal needs for using writing as a way to cope with severe trauma. At this time, Cape Town was racked by domestic as well as international terrorism. Every day, the teachers, students, and others I worked with lived in palpable fear. In hushed tones, they warned me of violence at every turn. Paranoia enveloped this environment like a thick fog. People of all kinds warned me about staying safe, making sure I knew to do things like allow sufficient distance from the car ahead of me so that I had room to speed away in case I was car-jacked; not to go here, avoid going there, and never do that. Their concern was authentic and touching. The violence and crime was certainly real. However, every time I received a warning, I would invariably ask the person if such things had actually happened to them, and they often said no. My second question was always, "How long have you lived in South Africa?" and it was usually "forever" or many years. I reached the point where I had to turn off their voices of warning that had begun echoing too much inside my head. I decided to do and go where I wanted. At that time, in that place, it became evident to me that this shroud of paranoia seemed to be well-fed by language—a potpourri of sensational news headlines, television reports, rumors, and talk among people, all occurring in a "closed system" where not many competing voices existed. Language and symbols seemed to hold people hostage. The teachers I worked with did not write about their fears, and I regret that there was no structure in place during my stay, nor was there enough time to begin such work.

That year, my colleague from the University of the Western Cape agreed with me for the need to address trauma in writing, and we began plans to work with HIV-positive patients and their writing. This was formalized two years later, with my group of USA graduate students—

none of whom were HIV-infected—and his group of South African writers, who were. Too many complications of distance prevented these two groups from working directly with each other, but my colleague and I learned a lot about how to focus and implement our efforts. We next planned to create a humanities curriculum that would be infused with HIV/AIDS education: what it is, how to cope with it, how to communicate about it—all woven into the study of art, literature, and mass media. Unfortunately, my colleague was killed in a car accident and the project ended. Finding a like-minded colleague a world away was not easy.

I then decided to teach my next writing about trauma course with a major change: I would include media, especially visuals, with writing. I was convinced that imagery and language could work in tandem to "heal" a variety of traumas—that working with both symbol systems simultaneously would create more "combustion" for us to re-see, re-frame, and extend our perceptions of trauma. Despite my fears, the course was again a solid success. Students held nothing back, as they plunged deeply into verbal and visual renderings of their own traumas. For examples, see Chapter 4, "Seven Writers Composing in Word & Image."

Finally, in creating and revising this course over several years and researching this book, I was also encouraged by responses from many conference talks I gave around the world. My sessions attracted relatively small but sincere audiences. I still recall a woman at UCLA coming up to me after my session who said, "This is not just academic stuff—You're really *doing* something!"

THE SYLLABUS

What I want to *do* in this course is immerse students in the topic of trauma, so that they may understand it, and, maybe someday, engage in it with their own students. Therefore, I want students to write it, think about it, read it, talk about it, visualize it, analyze it, and synthesize it. The complete course syllabus for *Teaching Therapeutic Language, Literature, & Media* appears in Appendix A. While this course is aimed at masters and doctoral students in English Education, much of it can be adapted for other levels and situations. If you have the luxury of working with teaching assistants, they can be very useful for everyone involved. For the course referred to here, two graduate teaching assistants volunteered to work in the class, even though they could not be paid. They simply wanted to participate. Rebecca Dierking collected data for her own dissertation throughout this course, and Deb Holland wanted to figure out if she also wanted to focus her dissertation on writing and trauma. They were especially helpful because the three of us could talk about how the class was going as it progressed and brainstorm possible changes, all in ways that usually did not specify individual students.

The required books and articles listed in the syllabus are intended not just to convey important and relevant information, but also, to convince students that writing about trauma is a serious topic, researched by scholars in many disciplines. Also, the book, *Finding a Voice: The Practice of Changing Lives through Literature* (Trounstine and Waxler 1999), documents the powerful roles that literature plays in working with adolescents, whose traumas include committing crimes and subsequent arrests. Instead of sending youthful offenders to prison, they are "sentenced" to reading well-selected books of fiction, then meeting in a library and discussing the literature with a librarian, a parole officer, and sometimes a judge. These programs in Massachusetts, Kansas, and a few other states have reduced the recidivism rate of those participating. My students read this book near the end of the course; it opens their eyes to another effective application of using language to defuse current traumas, as well as to limit future ones.

Following is the course description, which I hoped would challenge students, as well as communicate the spirit of experimentation.

> What do we mean when we speak of "composing as a way of writing about trauma" and the "therapeutic uses of language and other symbols"? New fields of inquiry are emerging, but with inconsistent names (e.g., "Resilience"; "Emotional Literacy"; "Spiritual Studies"). How should we use words, images, music, and other symbols in such ways—whether it be temporary academic or personal problems, psychological trauma, or disease? How is "writing to heal" similar to "writing to learn" and "writing to communicate"? What roles do other literacy activities and symbol systems—especially reading and viewing—play in using therapeutic language?
>
> How can writing processes and strategies that are described primarily from a cognitive perspective—one that values linearity, sequence, cause-effect, logic, and propositional thinking—and those that are rooted in "other ways of knowing"—ways which value emotion, images, silence, intuition, spirituality, chaos, and the unconscious—be integrated or reconciled to as-

sist people who engage in writing about trauma? How do the therapeutic uses of symbol systems align with professional standards for English and Language Arts professionals? This graduate seminar will explore these thorny (but endlessly fascinating) issues.

This course, then, will provide you an opportunity to engage in the following activities:

Use evidence-based and standards-based teaching to *also* enhance students' wellness.

Use a variety of writing prompts and literature to elicit and develop oral and written language to explore major life events.

Revise writing as a means of increasing one's control over major life events.

Employ specific elements of general semantics to explore major life events in rational, grounded ways.

Of course, we could not resolve so many complex questions, but the activities occurred throughout the semester. Finally, every time I've taught this course, I've included a professional "counseling psychologist on call." It helps if this person can visit and speak with the class. Fortunately, I've never had to call upon this counselor for specific advice.

Following are the course's three major requirements. First, students had to complete weekly "projects" that included text and visuals. These were responded to in small peer groups, as well as by the instructor, and then revised as many times as the student wished. Near the end of the course, these projects were to be re-conceptualized into a "Collage Essay" (See Elbow, 1997). Specific information for all requirements appears in the syllabus in Appendix A. The second requirement was a "Mini Case Study" in which students were to apply their knowledge to a specific student, interview the student, and analyze her writing. The case study was intended to help "move" students away from focusing on themselves and their colleagues, and move "toward" their own students. This requires a lot of "quick distancing" for some students and may not be appropriate for your own situation. Third, students had to participate in Socratic Seminars focused on the assigned readings.

In short, this course employed three major types of pedagogy described by Lauer (2004): 1) the "natural ability pedagogy," in which students write about what is most interesting to them and provides feedback, all within a supportive environment; 2) the "imitation pedagogy," in which students also read extensively for examples of what they are composing themselves; in this course, such imitation was never directly requested; instead, it was left up to writers how (and even if) they wanted to somehow emulate another student's example or a professional piece; and 3) the "practice pedagogy," in which students write frequently and receive a variety of types of feedback, written and spoken (121).

While the major requirements each contain a percentage of the total course points, I tell students that I will not place any kind of grade or number or other symbol on their papers—but they will indeed receive much feedback, through my comments on their papers and my talking with them. I tell them that I do this because I can get away with it! Less cheekily, I explain that if they have come this far in their careers, they should have at least one experience in a class that does not use grades of any kind. I emphasize that grades would create an impenetrable barrier to what we're trying to accomplish—that if they write and explore personal issues, they will not feel free to do so if a grade dangles over every word they write. I emphasize that this course is an "experiment" for all of us, and one does not judge results *as* they are occurring. I stress attendance, participation, and completion of all work. More importantly, I emphasize the necessity of responsibility—for themselves, for their colleagues, for me, and for their profession, which includes their dedication to finding "better ways."

The Weekly Projects

On purpose, I exclude these projects in the syllabus. Instead, they are "reeled out" as we get to them, pretty much in the order presented here, two or three at a time. The reason is that I want to maintain a sequence that moves from the very open and exploratory, to the more focused and creative. I don't want students to be overly influenced by an assignment too far down the road, thereby influencing what they write in the early projects. Receiving the prompts in batches allows the assignment to germinate in their minds for a longer period. You will find examples of how various students have responded to these projects in Chapter 4, "Seven Writers Composing in Word & Image." However, Chapter 3, "Lucy" and Chapter 5, "Kate," focus only on their self-sponsored journal writings and public writings. These two chapters were collected over a much longer span of time, during which I collected data on twelve "writing experts" who had *not* taken this course or anything similar to it.

For these verbal/visual projects, I suggest a text length of one or two written pages, single-spaced or 1.5 spaces, emphasizing that they can choose whether to go shorter or longer. Most or all papers should be shared in small groups. Students should be free to "try out" various issues, but I expect them to settle on one of them for most of the papers. Most projects require PowerPoint images and manipulation of them, and they may choose to integrate music, voice-over narration, and sound effects. Near the course's end, for the last project, I ask students to choose from those assignments remaining.

In the following sections, each project's instructions appear exactly as students received them. I follow a few of the projects with italicized explanations.

Project 1: The Mirror

At home (or in class; bring a hand mirror), for 15 minutes you should stare at yourself in the mirror. Do not look away from the mirror, except to make notes on what you are seeing, thinking, and feeling. When the music stops, you should stop. (When all of the writing is completed, I give them this final instruction.) Next, write up your notes into a good paragraph or page. Next, count the total number of positive or benign comments or words; do the same for the negative comments or words. Finally, write a reflection on the whole experience.

I am indebted to Dr. Sut Jhally of the Media Education Foundation for this activity. Dr. Jhally asks students to simply look at themselves in a mirror for an extended time and to take notes on what they see. I do this during class to ensure that we gaze at ourselves for at least 15 minutes or longer. (It's harder than you might think.) Jhally's purpose is for students to demonstrate to themselves and others that they mainly see all the "bad" things in their own faces, all the imperfections, such as the too-big nose, the blemish above the eye, the odd shape of the head or ears. This leads to a discussion of advertising and how consumers are conditioned, over time, to regard themselves as never matching up to the models and perfect people within the constant streams of media which surround us. My purpose in beginning with the mirror activity is similar, but goes beyond this. Sharing our notes, we learn that most of us find fault with ourselves, that we are made to feel inferior for many reasons, not just through advertising. This places us, at the course's beginning, on a somewhat level playing field.

As a possible follow-up activity to this project, after reading and discussing the "Introduction" in Anderson and McCurdy's Writing and Healing *(1999), especially the discussion of the "existence of self," and after responding to the Mirror papers in small groups—ask writers to write about what they believe about the existence of a "core" self.*

PROJECT 2: SYNESTHESIA (COMPLETED IN CLASS)

On a long sheet of butcher paper unrolled on the floor, find a place with plenty of room between you and others. Use markers and crayons to draw whatever images come to mind, especially those related to your issue. To begin, you'll listen to music for a few minutes with the lights turned off. Next, with the lights back on, begin to sketch anything that may be related to one of the traumas you're considering writing about for this class. This sketch can include words or phrases, if you like, but try to keep it pictorial, however rough it may be. You'll take your sketch and doodles home, so that you can write a reflection piece on this activity. Turn your drawing in along with your writing. Please refer to the whole drawing and specific parts.

The first music played should last for about 20 minutes and should sound "sad" or "bleak," such as portions of Verdi's The Requiem. *The next music should switch to something upbeat and lively, such as a Benny Coleman saxophone piece or the Beatles'* Here Comes the Sun.

PROJECT 3: FIXING THE PHOTO

See the example presented in class. Select a photo that is in some way related to your issue. The photo should include people and/or places that represent a relationship(s) that is somehow relevant to your specific traumatic event. Scan this photo into your computer and use Photoshop or other program to *manipulate it and change it* in a variety of ways (think adding, subtracting, substituting, altering color, background, etc.). You can even draw on the electronic photo. Place the original photo and your altered photo into a PPT, along with your analysis and explanation of both photos—why you chose the original and why you made the changes you did, especially, how and why the altered photo may better represent your perception of these people and this event. Include a brief reflection on both photos and the whole experience.

I've used this durable assignment for many years because it generates great writing. It began long before it was easy to deal with photographs and text electronically. It was first called, "The Snapshot Paper," and asked students to find a significant and meaningful family photo and place it within their written paper—a literal copy, cut and pasted. The only restriction was that the photo not contain too many people (if so, writers often wrote a little about each person, and a cataloging was not good!). I next asked them to study the photo's details carefully and select one such element to serve as a kind of visual metaphor for the larger issue the writer developed in her text. For example, an arm draped over another person, a slight distance of one person from another, a car in the background, or a raised eyebrow might be the visual counterpart of a discussion of what was occurring during the time the photo was taken, before it was taken, or after it was taken. A description of this visual element often occurred near the beginning of the paper, but writers were free to integrate it anywhere and often returned to it at paper's end. This Snapshot Paper morphed into the "Fixing the Photo" assignment.

PROJECT 4: IMAGINING MAMA, PART I

Read the assigned chapter from Maya Angelou's *I Know Why the Caged Bird Sings*, recounting her childhood visit to Dentist Lincoln. First, write an objective, detailed narrative of *your* issue, no more than two pages. Exclude all thoughts, feelings, or any other subjective "colorings" of the event. That is, write of yourself in 3rd person, as if you are an objective reporter. Second, select 6–8 key images (created or found) to visually communicate your no-frills narrative. On each PowerPoint slide with an image, place 1–3 key sentences from your narrative, to further help tell your story.

PROJECT 5: IMAGINING MAMA, PART II

Change the ending of your no-frills written narrative (or the whole piece, but retaining much of the original message) and PPT narrative, so that the story ends in a neutral or positive manner, just as Angelou imagined a different response from Mama to Dentist Lincoln.

PROJECT 6: YOUR OBJECTIVITY PLUS THEIR OBJECTIVITY

Return to your objective narrative from the Angelou assignment ("Angelou Imagining Mama, Part I"). Select three key quotes from this paper and place them in the left-hand column of a split-page or screen (the page or screen should have a vertical line down the middle). Next, research the topics of each of these key quotes, and choose a few direct quotes to place into the right-hand column. If at all possible, these quotes must be data-driven information or "hard evidence" from experts that place your own quote into a larger or different context—or even refutes or disproves your quote. That is, you'll end up affirming or refuting your own quote in some way. If you are unable to do so, you may instead list all possible factors entering into this situation and assign a percentage of influence to each.

Project 7: Entrance into Another World

Follow the written directions given in class, "Entrance into Another World Paper Guidelines." You will also hear or read an example in class. In short, you will "enter," in detail, a portion of a world different from yours. You will write about it in the present tense, as if you are there. You may choose to carry this world to absurd extremes. Because you are limited to two pages, you must be highly selective by focusing on a limited part of this other world. The world you select should be somehow related to your issue, directly or indirectly. You should also create a PPT (captions or other language optional) that visually depicts this other world. Use created or found images from popular media culture, etc. Note: You <u>may</u> find it easier to begin with the visual part.

Project 8: The Monster and the Angel

Following basic directions given in class, list all of your "monsters"—major issues that severely depress and frustrate you—or, you can use the list created on the first night of class. Next, select one of these and write a letter to this "monster" OR write a poem for this monster. Next, create or find an image of the monster you wrote to, and place it into a PPT slide. Then, take the image of the monster apart, tear it up, piece by piece, and reassemble it to depict your new "angel"—or some other creature that is far more benign than your original critter. Physically and actually take apart the pieces and re-arrange them into something more friendly and positive. Finally, write a piece that explains, analyzes, and reflects on this experience.

I am indebted to Deborah Holland and Bari Bumgarner, who introduced me to the first part of this project, writing a letter to one of your demons or monsters. To this I added three more parts. One asks writers to create a visual of their monster, preferably one that they create and not merely lift from the Internet. Second, I then ask writers to physically tear up the monster and re-assemble it into their "angel." Third, they write another letter, this time to their angel. I wanted students to physically deconstruct their visual representation of their monster (or trauma), and then to physically reconstruct it into its positive or benign counterpart. They engage in the same process with language. You'll find examples of how writers executed this project in Chapter 4. I believe that language represents reality, but for many people, a photograph or visual is a "closer" approximation of the real.

PROJECT 9: ALL ISSUES GREAT & SMALL

First, create or find the absolute *single image* of your issue. Feel free to enhance it if you like, to make it as evil or scary as you think it should be. Next, place it into a PPT slide so that it fills the entire space. Then, create or find five images that somehow represent the *best* elements in your life, past and/or present; place all five of these positive elements onto a single slide. Third, again on a single slide, place all six images, good and bad, but be sure that the negative image is far larger than the five positive ones. Fourth, place all six images onto a single slide (the five positive and the one negative image), making them all the *same* size (and necessarily smaller). You may choose to place a photo or other representation of yourself in the center of the slide, with the six smaller images "orbiting" around it. Fifth, again on a single slide, make each of the six slides a different size: the most positive image should be largest; the second most positive should be the next-to-largest, and on down. Position your negative image in any way that you wish. Sixth and finally, several days later, write your analysis-reflection on the whole experience, highlighting why you chose these images and what you were thinking and feeling as you created each slide. Include your overall reflection on this "order," and try to title or name your entire set of slides.

PROJECT 10: GETTING INSIDE THE QUOTE

Select a direct quote from another source that strongly appeals to you, one that somehow "matches," parallels, or somehow "speaks to" your issue(s). Choose a quote from any of our readings or from those shared in class, or from any other source, as long as it focuses on language and "writing about trauma" or spirituality in some way. Return to your earlier writings and explain how and why this quote applies to or parallels you and your issue. You may choose to "parse" or break the quote down into smaller chunks or organize this paper however you wish. You may do this assignment as a standard paper or as a PPT paper or some other way.

Project 11: Conversation across Time

Create a conversation, dialogue, or Q&A session between the current you—and the "you" of 25–30 years from now. Label the speakers however you wish (e.g., "Me Now" and "Me Older"), as long as they are cleanly differentiated. Limit this dialogue to no more than 2 pages. Place all or selected portions onto PPT slides that show a visual rendering of each of you on each slide containing bits of conversation. The slides need not be the same ones repeated (though that's fine). Finally, write a 1-page analysis-reflection on this experience.

Project 12: Therapeutic Meets Professional

Explain which projects or parts of projects would lend themselves to serving as a springboard for a professional publication. Which could be integrated into such an article?

These projects are challenging for students, indicated by their visible thinking, questioning, and talking with fellow students (another great benefit of small peer response groups). In many projects, I try to integrate either an actual visual rendering or ask students to engage in mental imagery or imagination—all of which I like students to manipulate—to juxtapose, alter, shrink, and enlarge. The role of meta-language is also important, so I ask for written reflections about their processes and products to accompany each assignment. All of this demands considerably more than "just academic stuff" from students, as well as the teacher, which I'll turn to next.

The Teacher

In our fragmented, technologized, over-hyped society, we often surrender to "the cult of the expert." Often, though, we're far less needy of specialized training or advice than we're led to believe—a kind of learned helplessness. On the other hand, some professions suffer from the opposite perception, the "anyone-can-do-it" syndrome. The teaching of writing (and teaching in general) have long been cast into this category. When people decide to write about their own traumas, regardless of their reasons and motivations, an experienced writing teacher can help them reap greater benefits, at a much faster rate, than if they were to go it alone. The younger and more novice the writer, the greater the need for a professional instructor.

A few people, though, will feel no need to seek out a professional teacher of writing. I closely studied Lucy and Kate (see Chapters 3 and 5) precisely for this reason: they were mature experts, who instinctively and quickly turned to the page after experiencing their respective traumatic experiences. It's also true that a basic, preliminary research decision is whether to study novices or experts. I chose the latter because they could model behaviors that could help everyone. By the same token, most (but not all) of the writers in Chapter 4, "Seven Writers Composing in Word and Image," were also professional, experienced writing teachers, albeit in earlier-career stages than Lucy and Kate, whom I studied separately, after they independently chose to write about their experiences. The writers explored in Chapter 4 expressed few reservations about exploring trauma through writing.

Experienced, professional writing teachers are needed to help students and others navigate personal traumas for far more reasons than I can note here. First, many people will reasonably argue that teachers should *not* take on the role of psychologist or counselor. While I clearly understand this position, I also disagree with it, mainly because teachers are not displacing such professionals. I always include a "counselor on call" in my courses, though, fortunately, I have never had to contact them. Second, teachers are the ones "there" all the time, they know their students well, and are called upon to dispense "counseling" on the spot, many times each day, without consulting anyone. It's always been part of the job.

I believe teachers should face their students' traumas head-on for many other reasons, several of which appear throughout this book, including the fact that the kinds of thinking and writing involved demonstrate the same qualities of critical thinking as traditional academic writing. (In the pages ahead, you'll see this demonstrated many times.) As well, the written page is where the subjective meets the objective. We write about trauma encased in our own subjectivity. We must "run hot" as much as we can in order to generate all the details and sense of the experience. At the same time, we begin to "run cold(er)" because the mere act of putting down words begins to "objectify" them. After that, the more they're revised, the more distanced the writer becomes from the prose. When the text is read and responded to by peers and teachers, more steps are taken *away from* the trauma itself, as it recedes a little further into the background as a more natural part of our internal landscape.

What may be more important here is that these alternating cycles of subjectivity/objectivity occur almost simultaneously or close to each other in time, thereby making them more immediately relevant and applicable for us to begin perceiving our traumatic experience in different ways. I believe this process may become more meaningful for writers than widely-spaced oral discussions with a counselor. Of course, this process can further develop writers' sense of rhetorical flexibility, which can serve their future thinking and writing. In short, a writing class (also a safe environment) just may be where the rubber best meets the road: when the intangible trauma meets the visible words on the page, combustion is more likely, as one feeds the other.

Writing about trauma, then, occurs in cycles of subjectivity and objectivity, hot and cold. Experienced writing teachers are well familiar with these alternating cycles, though they don't necessarily occur consistently, nor are they of equal duration. We are deft at reading and writing processes that must run hot and perch up close to us, when fluency and ideas, through the gush of words and images, dominate our internal universe. On the other hand, we are equally deft at distancing ourselves, at running colder, when we revise and edit. For these reasons and more, we can help students with their trauma and writing at the same time.

Truth in advertising: teaching writing about trauma is not for everyone. You have to feel the need, and you have to feel confident. Such teaching takes courage, even a kind of gall, which often comes with experience, when you know you've worked with enough different writers and texts to know that writing really does work. In this section, then, I offer some basic advice about the roles of teachers.

Preparing to Teach Writing about Trauma

Many teachers who choose to focus on trauma in the writing class will be well-prepared to do so, even though their backgrounds and terminology will somewhat differ from others. Nonetheless, I feel strongly that the following five elements be seriously considered when teachers prepare to help students mend ruptures in their lives.

Understand General Semantics

First, instructors should thoroughly understand and be able to apply the basic principles of general semantics. Hayakawa and Hayakawa's *Language in Thought and Action* (1991 or later) remains the best introductory source. The over-arching principle is expressed in the semanticist's mantra, "The map is not the territory; the word is not the thing." You can also think of it as, "intensional orientation vs. extensional orientation"—the world out there vs. the world inside our heads, i.e., our *representations* of reality.

For example, before soldiers go into battle, their inner consciousness may be full of patriotic movie scenes, song lyrics, and texts that glorify war. As Twain would say, they may be full of "gunpowder and glory." However, when these soldiers actually step into a real battle zone, their idealizations of war can starkly differ from actuality. As Johnson (1946) and others have explained, such idealization can lead to frustration, which in turn can demoralize us. The internal constructs formed in words and pictures can be way different from outer reality. In terms of trauma, over time, one may "abstract from" the original experience certain elements that can exaggerate the actual event. One problem here is that traumatic events can reside inside us, frozen in time, and not change. The process of "recovery" via writing is to begin changing those frozen elements into different, more realistic, or more flexible ideas. A related concept here is the *Is of Identity*, a term that describes an unchanging or frozen sense of who we are as a person. The problem is our labeling of people in specific points in time, and then assuming that reality is unchanging—that those labeled will *always* be what they were branded. Here, *is* denotes or implies a state of being that lasts forever.

For example, one of my students lied when his mother asked him if his brother was a drug-user. This student's younger brother had been arrested for marijuana possession. My student carried guilt about lying to his mother for several years, so he at least somewhat represented his identity to himself as a liar: "John *is* a liar"—not in that one conversation, but for all time. As well, he and his family regarded the jailed sibling as a drug addict: "Rob *is* a drug addict." The facts, though, were that John was not a liar for eternity. He lied to his mother once, yet the simple word, *is*, labeled and froze him forever in that state. Nor was his brother Rob a drug addict forever (if he ever was).

A related concept familiar to writing teachers also applies to this same student, *context*. I learned through John's writing that a good portion of the guilt he carried was connected to where his trauma occurred, a small, conservative rural community in the Midwest. John and Rob's parents felt especially shamed by Rob's arrest because "everyone in town knew about it." He and his family therefore felt isolated and looked down upon in their community. The best teaching approach was to convince John to "enlarge his context" by researching the history of minor drug arrests in different locations in America, as well as overseas. I believed he would come to regard his brother's arrest as "not such a big deal" if he were to view it through a wider lens.

The *ladder of abstraction* is another important principle surrounding how we may think about past trauma. Writing teachers seem to spend much of their careers telling students to "get down to specifics" when encountering lofty generalizations. The bank teller who habitually described a robbery she experienced as "nightmarish" needed to dissect or partition this abstraction into smaller pieces before she could begin to deal with it a bit more rationally. Following is a series of questions (and the student's responses) that was made by the teacher and this student's small writing response group, all focused on the central question, "What *exactly* made the trauma nightmarish?"

> "Was the robber holding a weapon?"
> "Oh yes!"
> "What kind of weapon was it?"
> "A gun."
> "Did you actually see it?"
> "Well, no, but he was holding it in his sweatshirt pocket."
> "So . . . he could have been holding a pen or just using his fist?"
> "Well, I guess that's possible."

You get the idea. Other semantics principles are equally important as those summarized here, especially *either/or* language and thinking, our habit of seeing the world in polarized terms; the differences between reports, inferences, and judgments, as well as between denotations and connotations; and advertising and propaganda techniques, such as repetition and association. If your students are also working with actual images (see Chapter 4), these principles can also apply to visual renderings. You may also want to explore some basic tenets of Gestalt psychology and semiotics.

Select Readings that Weave a Web of Connections

Another important consideration is deciding what students will read and why—texts that they can link to other texts, as well as to their own and their peers' writing. I use books that very clearly provide essential information about writing and trauma in organized and accessible ways, such as Louise De Salvo's (2000) book noted earlier. I also use Anderson's and McCurdy's anthology, also noted earlier, because it is more academic in tone and demonstrates the variety of professionals who seriously study writing and trauma. I also use a number of separate articles and excerpts that focus on insightful details about language and trauma. All or most of the readings should be discussed in class, so that students can draw some lines of connection between four types of texts: 1) academic and research; 2) literary nonfiction that focuses on the author's traumatic events; 3) their own writing; and 4) their peers' writing. This is a challenging task, and I don't "test" students on their ability to solidify such links. I trust they'll do so in their own ways. It's best if such links arise as a natural outgrowth of discussion. Also, an even larger amount of synthesizing occurs when students create the final "Collage" project (see the syllabus).

Emphasize Fluency, Freedom, and Flexibility in Writing

Donald Murray (e.g., 2003), Peter Elbow (e.g., 1998), and many other scholars place fluency at the necessary heart of any writing course. Generating language will never be more important than it is in writing about trauma. If your students are unfamiliar with freewriting, you should model it for students on the first day of class. I ask students to assign me topics and I list them on the board, select one, and then use an overhead projector or smartboard to compose aloud, including all kinds of questions, hesitations, false starts, stumbles, and occasionally coherent phrases or lines. I ask students to take notes on the kinds of things I do, such as re-reading, asking myself questions and answering some of them, and going off-topic. What's important is to keep going. This is followed by my emphasizing that most writers flounder like this. Again, for novices, freewriting should be practiced at every class session, for increasingly longer amounts of time. I begin with three minutes and gradually increase it to 10–15 minutes. Especially with trauma, writers should work from abundance.

Students should have utter freedom in the types or genre of writing. They typically write in narrative form. This makes sense, given their familiarity with this genre. But they are never restricted to narrative or any other pattern or format unless the assigned project requests it, as some do. In most cases, after students make informal lists or "cluster" diagrams, freewriting and narrative rule the day. If students express difficulty with an assignment, the first thing I tell them is "try writing it as a poem"—or news report or graphic short story, or other genre. Students are also free to abandon the "assignment" and approach the task in any other way.

Nudge Writers to Break the Chains of Chronological Order in Writing

Given these established freedoms, I also want students to break the chain of chronology that's usually imposed by the narrative form. A hallmark of literary nonfiction, getting student writers to "move about in time and space" is one of the hardest things to teach (see, for example, Fox and Lannin, 2007). However, disrupting a traumatic event's time sequence can be very important for re-seeing and re-framing traumatic events because such events tend to "freeze" in our memory as a cause-effect chain. The student bank teller described earlier may in part blame herself for the robbery because the thief entered the bank soon after she unlocked the main door, a few minutes before she was supposed to. This sequence is cemented into her festering memory of the trauma, but, in reality, her performing this daily chore was very likely unrelated to the robber's actions.

Responding to Writing about Trauma

Undeniably, the small peer response group should be an integral part of any writing about trauma course. All of its virtues—providing a variety of perspectives and types of advice; clarifying the nature of the paper's topic; showing emotional support for the writer's experience, as well as her paper—are intensely needed when writing about trauma. While the syllabus provides guidelines for students (see Appendix A), they are equally useful for teachers. Because my students are experienced teachers, they know how to prioritize and phrase their comments, delivering them in ways that allow their peers to be fully receptive. Of course, the nature of the topic steers most students into adopting supportive stances toward their peers. However, if your students are novices, you'll need to model how a group should respond, as well as provide them initial guidelines (especially see Elbow and Belanoff [1999] and guidelines from the National Writing Project). After your class gets rolling, sit in on peer sessions (trying very hard *not* to speak!) and record examples of helpful and specific comments. Then, reproduce and discuss those notes with the whole class.

Differentiate between Written Comments on Students' Papers and What You Speak Directly to Students

Especially in a writing and trauma class, students will often imitate (in content and expression) the kinds of comments you make about their writing. In stark terms, if you regard yourself as more of a "talker" than a "writer," then save the most sensitive comments for speaking to the student, preferably out of earshot of others. I'm more of a writer than a talker, so it's easiest for me to write the most important and/or sensitive comments. This decision also applies to the student in question. If I view the writer as shy or defensive about his writing, I'll be sure to write my comments, but will engage him in less important conversation, in hopes that we can, in the future, speak of weightier matters as well.

Empathize with Students' Writing. Always.

Even though you're all in a writing class, and writing is important, it's even more crucial to first respond as a human being. As the course gets rolling, you'll be able to focus comments on style, word choice, organization, metaphor, etc., but this should never occur prematurely. And when it does occur, it should always include the human-to-human response. Even late in the course, I've found myself so "blown away" by the prose that I am unwilling (and unable) to respond as a writing teacher. And I'm fine with that. Empathic comments should avoid clichés and be as specific as possible to the paper's content. One obvious way is to recall a similar situation you may have experienced or know about.

All of this being said, it's possible to overdo empathy. Striking the right balance is both art and craft. When students take a risk in their writing and read your comments, they first need to hear a sense of safety and acceptance in your voice. They need to know they are on solid ground. This is often accomplished through the human-to-human response and some mention of the paper's strengths. Once students realize they are in safe and accepting territory, then they are better able to read more specific comments about the writing itself.

Navigating Typical "Gaps" in Students' Writing about Trauma

Just as in any other writing course, when you engage students in writing about trauma, you'll have some firm ideas about what you'll want them to do. When their writing doesn't deliver, it's hard to call these "mistakes" or "errors," because (again) of the sensitive nature of this course. That's why I use the term, "gaps." This fairly neutral term emphasizes the text, not the writer. Sometimes, with hardly a brief mention (or none) the gap will be addressed in later writings; this is one reason I prefer to use 10–12 relatively brief projects.

Nonetheless, there's a stable of productive ways for speaking or writing back to students. It should be a natural reflex for you to ask questions that may not have occurred to the writer, or which are simply ignored. The most common question I ever ask is "Why? Why do you think that? What made you think that?" In this class, "correct answers" are irrelevant. Rather, students' thinking and reasoning must become visible, brought to light, so that we can *do* things with it.

The writer's peer group will initially ask about "small" omissions and missing or vague practical information. Often, though, you'll need to prompt or model for students how to ask more sensitive questions by demonstrating this when writing responses on their papers—or asking the "hard" question when you sit in on a peer group session. Group members may all be thinking the same thing you are, but feel too hesitant to ask such questions as, "You say at the beginning of your paper that you were 'emotionally and physically paralyzed' at your friend's death, and I can imagine how you must've felt, because you two had been through so much together, for so long . . . but later on, you say that you quickly left the hospital to meet friends at a concert. . . . Maybe you should explain that?" In short, teachers will sometimes need to break the ice that goes into deeper water. The good news is that once this occurs, students usually go even deeper.

Sometimes writers will devote too much time to "setting the stage," providing too much background detail. Here, you'll need to determine whether these are good writers merely "writing from abundance"—or if they're avoiding the traumatic issue (a more serious concern dealt with later in this chapter). Sometimes writers are unaware that they're doing this. Also, they may be very new to writing about trauma. Even "personal writing" may be so foreign to them that they can't get started. (Personal writing and composing about trauma are very exotic birds for my international students, but they have been more receptive, more quickly, than American students.) Regardless of the reason for too much background, we can help students by sitting down with them and outlining their paper with a simple list. Next, ask the writer what these details are adding up to. If their reply is vague, try teasing it out in clearer, more definitive terms. When even this doesn't succeed, I've asked the writer to make a single declarative statement about *exactly* what the trauma is she wants to pursue. This may elicit another vague response, but it could be a start for another round of questions that narrow and specify the generalities. An option is to slightly change tack and ask the writer to complete a "lead sentence," such as, "The trauma I wish to explore involves the following people: _____; _____; and _____." It may be easier to proceed to the issue by starting with specific individuals.

With the unusual verbal and visual projects I assign, students can become "stuck" for countless reasons. It's often more efficient to divert them to another writing or task until the freeze softens. Another approach is to ask them to change gears and write in a different form or genre: "Try writing this as a fairy tale or news report." Or, "try saying this the way a sports announcer would say it, if she were describing a dramatic, game-winning home-run." Or, "Forget about the written part, and just do the visual part first (even using any media), and then we'll talk." A last resort is to invite the stuck student to avoid the letter of the assignment altogether, and instead, address only the spirit of the project. Students know that I always want them to try my assignment first, but if it just doesn't work, they always have the option to abandon it and do their own thing. The next stage is small-group and teacher feedback, but my students know that it doesn't stop there. *Revision awaits.*

Revising is even more important in this course than in "standard" writing courses because writers need to view their renderings of trauma in many different ways, over an extended time. Final revisions are due right near the end of the course, and they must also submit all previous drafts. I want students to think of writing about trauma as a very long cycle of deconstructing and re-building their traumatic experiences. They need to know that *revising* means far more than mere *editing*. In this course and all of my other writing courses, I sometimes require students to write the same content three entirely different ways, what I call *reformulating*. I tell them that writing about trauma demands rhetorical flexibility. I then ask them to select which of the three is most effective (and sometimes, the most effective is comprised of parts from all three). Another reason for doing this is to help writers see quality, in very concrete ways. That is, many writers cannot imagine how to judge a single piece of writing, i.e., how to improve it. However, most writers can indeed choose a single best piece from three pieces. Here, the vague notion of "making my writing better" becomes concrete, as writers can *see* three options and choose. My refrain is, "Don't make your writing better; just make it different."

Finally, when writing back to students or talking to them, lest we get too absorbed in the details of difficult experiences and the millions of points involved in composing, we have to remember that all such concerns should be aimed toward connections, solutions, resolutions, reconciliations, or whatever it takes to calm the inner seas within us.

Negotiating Serious "Gaps" in Students' Writing about Trauma

The first gap I want to focus on occurs *after* students are well into articulating their trauma through a variety of visual and verbal projects: their reluctance to engage in secondary research, to investigate "researchable" elements of their experience. I firmly believe that students need to expand the first circle of their perceived woundedness because they often think and feel that, "I'm alone in my trauma." When I began this work, I expected that students would be eager to learn about issues within a broader context. However, I learned that I have to push most students toward even simple Internet searching, and as you noted in my project's descriptions earlier in this chapter, I sometimes require it. This reluctance is interesting to me, for when they do indeed integrate relevant secondary research, they benefit from becoming a smaller fish in a larger pond. One guess is that writers become so wrapped up in their trauma, they find it hard to extricate themselves and focus on more impersonal information. However, this is precisely the reason for requiring secondary research—to move students away from their particular circumstances.

Another significant gap is student writing that "tells more than shows"—a familiar but fundamental hurdle in any writing class that we want students to jump cleanly. The advantage here is that a common refrain in the textbooks and articles I use is that there are psychological health reasons for writers to be specific and detailed about their traumas. "Disclosure" has been well-studied. I often have to write comments in the margin, such as, "Can you 'explode' this moment into details?" (Lane, 1992). Or, you can point to a professional piece you've recently read in class: "Remember how Foy (1999) goes into such detail about preparing his son's casket? Can you try that kind of detail here?"

A more difficult gap to deal with occurs when writers don't clearly identify the issue at hand. They don't explicitly state what it is. One student kept writing in circles about a childhood house, she and her sister playing in the yard, and on and on. In such cases, I've been forced to ask the writer to state exactly what the trauma is in one sentence. Of course, there are different reasons for such avoidance, including the fact that the writer thinks she is ready to write about the event, and wants to, and tries to—but never hits the proverbial nail on the head. She was just not ready to engage this memory and needs to hear that it's okay to try something else. Of course, it's possible that this writer needed to see our counselor on call, but there were no other signs of depression or anxiety to warrant it. If students just cannot state their memory in clear terms, I suggest they find another event, one that might even be less traumatic. I make it very clear that for class purposes, we have to define trauma as existing on a *continuum*, from most severe on one end (e.g., death, violence, terminal disease) to least severe on the opposite end (e.g., an argument with a neighbor). Also, while I like for students to settle down with one experience and write several different pieces about it, they are free to "try out" other topics as well.

An equally troubling gap occurs when the writer *somewhat* addresses the issue, but keeps avoiding it through diversions into humor or sarcasm. In one such case, after a few papers when this issue became obvious, I recall writing something like, "Writing about trauma can often use some lighter touches, but in order for them to really be effective, they need to contrast with a serious treatment of the event, and I'm not sure I find this here, yet."

Maybe the most troubling gap to address occurs when students say, "I just don't have any trauma in my life; I can't think of anything that I need to 'heal' from." In the case with "Claire," who appears in future chapters, I suggested that she not define "trauma" in its darkest terms, but think of it as existing on a continuum—that she was free to write about less intense issues. She tried that and was still dissatisfied. She ended up taking an "Incomplete" grade for the course but did indeed complete the work after she had counseling.

Retaining Your Sanity

Teaching writing about trauma requires strength and durability. To succeed in this course demands that you engage in intense empathy with students and their texts, at the same time that you intensely instruct. It's demanding, mentally and emotionally. Veteran teachers often present themselves to students as human and approachable, yet maintain varying levels of "distance" as each situation demands. Even so, outside of class, conversations and interactions can echo in our thoughts, can get to us (see the "coda" at the end of this book). However, there are a few ideas that can mitigate these occupational hazards.

My habit is to ask students to write an informal reflection after they've completed each project and before I read it. I ask them to write about how they feel about what they wrote and what was especially difficult and satisfying. I typically read these first, which helps me read their projects more efficiently and with greater understanding. For me, this order is more efficient. Reading these reflections also informs me of what I should and should not worry about. That is, our concerns should be grounded in what *students* say, not what we think they might be thinking. Such brief reflections help everyone stay grounded.

Another helpful approach is to talk with trusted colleagues about what you're doing and what you think about it. Writing (surprise) can help you puzzle out what seem to be entangled issues about the class dynamics. Sometimes, just before I head to lunch with a trusted colleague, I'll make a brief list of what I want to bounce off the sounding board. Similarly, after the end of class, I immediately jot down a few key words or phrases of what I want to say to a student at the next meeting, lest it gets swept up in the whirlwinds that blow across good classes.

A more subtle way of keeping sane during this class is to read accounts of trauma written by superb writers, such as Joan Didion's *The Year of Magical Thinking* (2007) or William Styron's *Darkness Visible* (1992). Such reading, as it informs, has ways of reaffirming the deep value of our daily work.

There may be times when you sense that your class *really* needs a break and would benefit most by doing something less related to the course, or even totally unrelated to the course. (I have never felt this way, because my classes are three hours long, which typically includes students meeting in small response groups, which have a way of finding their own release valves, evidenced from occasional bouts of laughter.) If I do need a "soft" break, I will arrange for the class to meet in an art museum or gallery and ask students to look for artists who somehow communicate deep sadness and joy, and to think about how these artists accomplish this.

Finally, if a class needs a serious or "hard" break, I'd suggest what an English Majors Club once recommended—play board games. I thought board games sounded like a terrible idea but grudgingly went along with it. I did, though, realize it was near the end of a busy semester and the members, high-achievers all, were burned out. So, one night, we sprawled on the floor, playing Scrabble or Connect-Four or some other game that demanded little attention. This allowed us to *not* talk at all, or talk only about the game. The conversation got slower and quieter as we continued. And you know what? That was the single most relaxing time I had ever spent in any school. More importantly, we came to know each other much better.

The Study

In 2007, I began the research project of working with "literacy experts," one by one, people who had chosen, completely on their own, to write about their traumas. I collected reams of data on fourteen people, but only two of these cases are presented in this book. I soon found that I had to "invent" certain approaches and methods if I was to learn as much as possible about people and their composing through trauma. The following items summarize the methods employed for this study.

Research Design

This project employed a modified case study approach, from 2007 through 2012. Because I am not aware of any researchers who have delved into the specific rhetorical and composing practices of people who engage in writing about trauma, the case study method was the most natural approach for two reasons. First, writing itself is a highly complex behavior, and second, because dealing with a serious trauma adds yet another layer of complexity.

Pilot Study

The second time I taught a composing about trauma course served as an unofficial pilot study for the current project. Rebecca Dierking (2012), completed an excellent dissertation on students' experiences in the course, "'Writing Down is a Way of Letting Go': Individuals Using Writing to Return to 'Remembered Wellness.'" While this course included an equal emphasis on imagery, Rebecca primarily focused on students' writing. Please see Rebecca's study for more information on this version of the course.

Selection of Participants

I wanted individuals who would be considered "language and literacy experts" by most criteria. The "expert vs. novice" is a common choice made by researchers, depending upon what they want to learn. I wanted to study people who knew what they were doing when they composed about trauma, especially from the writing and language perspective, a view that is seldom addressed. I also chose language experts because they would be comfortable with "meta-language," or, language about language. I reasoned that such veterans would likely better articulate what and how they wrote, as well as why they wrote. Lucy, for example, was selected because of her rhetorical flexibility in addressing multiple audiences, her writing abilities, and her range of thinking strategies. Please note that "language and literacy experts" can be found in all walks of life. However, I sought people who had much experience articulating and solving problems in many facets of language and literacy, typically through their own writing, teaching, and editing

Because I wanted most interviews to be conducted face-to-face, I approached people that I knew on a limited professional basis, as well as some who were recommended to me, but whom I did not know. A few people, I knew relatively well over several years' time.

I wanted to focus on experts who *voluntarily* engaged in writing about trauma, so I only selected participants I deemed to be veteran professionals, using the following criteria: 1) holds a Master's or preferably PhD degree in English, Education, Literacy, or Language; 2) has published articles and presented at professional conferences in one or more of these fields; 3) has successfully taught a variety of language-oriented courses for at least ten years, at the secondary and/or college levels; and 4) has served as external consultants to various agencies. Most participants had received various awards for their teaching. After securing my university's research board approval, I extensively interviewed fourteen individuals, through 2012. Nine participants in this study were middle-aged females, ranging from 45–65 years old.

Each person contacted agreed to participate. Four participants lived in other states. One person dropped out of the study due to changing jobs and re-locating. It is important to emphasize that four participants gave me *total and complete access* to their public and private journals, letters, and emails that they had not even shared with their spouses and families. Had Lucy and Kate not been so trusting and open about their private writing, I could never have learned as much as I did. I am truly indebted to them. It's also important to note that all participants (except for those enrolled in my classes) had *freely chosen to engage in writing about trauma long before I asked them to be a part of this study.* Finally, you may find insufficient details about the lives of the participants, because it was crucial to protect their identities. As well, the names of all others have been changed. These procedures apply to most research, but anonymity is especially important for the sensitive material involved. (Lucy is the only person who wished me to use her real name.)

This study also draws upon a second group of participants, comprised of graduate students selected from my composing about trauma courses. I judged these people to be language and literacy experts, albeit at earlier career stages than my primary group. These students were experienced teachers from the USA and abroad. Their average age was 35. They all held master's degrees in English and/or English Education. Several were advanced doctoral students.

INTERVIEWS

Before I began interviewing, I participated in a professional conference, "Writing and Wellness Connections" in Atlanta, Georgia, attended by a few English teachers, but mostly counselors, medical doctors, and psychologists. I distributed a few samples of writing about trauma (collected over many years) and asked them to respond: What did they see in them? Were the authors sincere? Were they really trying to understand or deflecting blame? I also asked them to evaluate or respond to a set of questions for my own research. These activities helped me to further refine my questions and approach.

Before I scheduled personal interviews, I sent each participant a letter or email in which I described my purpose, procedures, possible research questions, and general information about writing and trauma. This letter included the following definition of writing about trauma:

> "Writing about trauma" must be interpreted broadly—as any kind of communication that focuses on *any* kind of traumatic experience—any experience which harms, worries, fears, saddens, scares, or makes the writer anxious; any experience which creates feelings of violation, dissociation, isolation, alienation, confusion, depression, or inferiority.

Some topics that are often written about include, but are not limited to, the following: death of a loved one; suicide; alcohol or drug addiction; divorce and other forms of separation; gender orientation and confusion; disease and illness; relationships with parents, children, and siblings; Post-Traumatic Stress Disorder (PTSD); cultural and racial bias; rape; and all forms of physical and psychological abuse.

DATA COLLECTION

Interviews were conducted in person and by phone. They usually occurred in my office and in complete privacy. Several times and in different ways, I assured each participant that they could choose not to answer any question and could terminate our interview at any time if the topic became too emotionally taxing. I tried to make each interview a conversation, a kind of dialogue, so that the participant would feel at ease and elaborate more than she might otherwise do. I never tried to "take over" or monopolize these "conversations," but to function as a subordinate partner and sensitive listener. I believe that dialogues are co-constructions of reality, built by interviewer and interviewee, and that this may be taken as a limitation of this study. However, the topic and research context of this particular project renders this approach crucial. I audio-recorded each interview, while simultaneously scribbling notes as fast as I could without distracting the interviewee.

Prior to the initial two-hour interview, as a means of "easing into" the topic of each participant's own writing, I sent them two samples of such writing, completed by two different and anonymous writers—one by a young woman and the other by a teenage boy. We began the first interview by talking about these samples before we moved on to discuss his or her own work and experiences.

Also before the first interview, I asked participants to select a few questions that they felt comfortable talking about, selected from the list of questions they had received weeks earlier. These questions were organized for participants into categories, with examples of each. Appendix B contains the complete list of questions that each person received at least two weeks before our first interview. Questions are grouped into the following categories: Introduction to Potential Questions; Overall Perceptions of Writing and Trauma; Genre and Medium; Global and Local Connections; The Craft of Writing; Voice/Persona in Writing; Audience; Teaching, Learning, and Writing about Trauma; and What Questions Do You Have?

I assured each participant that these questions were merely a guide and that they should in no way feel obligated to any of them—that our interviews were about what *they* wanted to say. Even though this large number of questions can seem overwhelming, and even though each interviewee only selected a few questions to begin with, I believe that the simple act of scanning through all of the questions gently induced participants to thinking about their own writing in broad terms.

Before we began the initial interview, I felt it necessary to remind participants of two items in the guidelines they had earlier received:

1. They can stop our discussion at any time, for whatever reasons.
2. They can deviate from any topic or question at any time, and if so, I will not pursue their reasons for doing so.
3. They can delay responding to any question.
4. They can expect follow-up questions, such as, "Why do you think that?" and "Can you give me an example?"

Each person was interviewed an average of three additional times, each session lasting 60–90 minutes. When responses did not include the writer's reasoning or motivation, I consistently followed up by asking, "Why do you think that?" "Can you give an example?" Also, follow-up questions and responses occurred several times with each participant, usually via email or phone. See Appendix B, Research Questions, for a complete list.

Participants provided me with complete copies of their public and personal writing. Public writing includes web site postings available to a large number of friends and family members, college course materials, and published articles that the writer identified as relevant to her writing about trauma. Lucy, for example, supplied approximately 250 pages of journal entries, email messages, and web site postings.

DATA ANALYSIS

When given a personal journal, I first made a copy and then returned it. I did not want to lose such a possession. I also have a habit of writing on whatever I read. While interviewing, I took quick notes as I talked with each writer, trying to jot down those topics that I judged to be important at the time. I soon transcribed each interview after first listening to it all the way through. I consulted my during-interview notes as I listened to the recording and as I transcribed it. These notes served as a kind of marker for places in the recording that I wanted to pay close attention to. I would next match my handwritten notes against the spoken version, as well as the transcript. When talking about an intense trauma, it's not unusual for people to speak softly, and if I asked them to speak louder, I feared it would interfere with the moment at hand. Therefore, I sometimes had to re-play recordings several times, and even ask for others to verify what I thought I heard.

With written materials, including hand-written journals, I read through them several times, adding questions and notes as I went. After each cycle of reading, I would write a brief note to myself about what I saw as tentative categories. With successive read-throughs, some categories changed, some expanded by subsuming other categories, and some categories broke into smaller, more specific ones or became more refined. Once in a while, a category was tentatively removed (but not entirely discarded, in case its characteristics surfaced later, even in another context). The ultimate, surviving categories appear throughout this book (e.g., connecting, balancing oppositions).

I devoted much time to the first case study, Lucy's, which provided a kind of rough template for looking at successive writers and their work. This helped me to get started with a new participant, though I of course had to go different directions due to the extreme uniqueness of each writer and her particular trauma. In short, Lucy's profile shares some similarities with Kate's, but the fact remains that they are very different people with unique thinking strategies and other approaches.

The critical lenses with which I initially viewed all of this data are necessarily varied due to my long experience and background. First, I strive *not* to approach any text, spoken or written or rendered in images, with any preconceived notions. (Remaining as receptive and open as possible is one of the serious joys of qualitative research.) Nonetheless, I regularly employed several critical lenses, which I'll summarize in no particular order. My analysis typically proceeds by looking at data through one lens, which then can suddenly switch to another, and sometimes include more than one lens at a time. This is why I constantly take notes during this process. My habit is to work with a handful of lenses and to "shift gears" as the unfolding data warrants. Later, during listening to recordings, transcribing, and taking notes, I try to review all data for all interpretive possibilities.

It was impossible for me *not* to view my data in terms of my past readings from the literature on trauma and narrative (e.g., Brand 1994; Charon 2006; Husain, 2001; Pennebaker, 2002). Such readings served as a kind of background or context. For lenses that operated more in the foreground when reviewing data, the most influential in this study were James Pennebaker (e.g., 1990), Charles Anderson and Marian MacCurdy (2000), Jessica Singer and George H.S. Singer (2008), and Louise DeSalvo (1999). For more specific lenses—critical thinking, language and meaning, and imagery, several sources were most helpful for each category.

Early on, I viewed the data for basic qualities of critical thinking. Lev Vygotsky's (1986) influence on my conception of language and thought undergirds much of how I viewed this data. While many scholars have labeled and described how we think, from Jean Piaget (1962), to Daniel Pink (2005), Lee Odell's (1999) categories focus on written text and serve as an excellent synthesis of various tools that I often relied upon for this project's data (see "Appendix C: Assessing Thinking in Writing," adapted from Odell). Of equal importance here is the field of modern rhetoric, including the roles and functions of audiences and readers, as well as issues of discourse analysis, especially the works of Kenneth Burke (cited in Enos 2010), James Britton (1975), James Kinneavy (1980), James Moffett (1992), and James Paul Gee (2010). Cognitive psychologists who value the interactive roles of language and imagery, such as Allan Paivio (2001) and Stephen Kosslyn (2006) had a major impact on how I look at thinking, as have the sociological perspectives on media, thinking, and language, articulated by Marshal McLuhan (1964) and Neil Postman (2005).

Also, when analyzing language and meaning, I employed principles of general semantics, from the larger "map/territory" analogy, down to more specific elements, such as two-valued thinking and the use of qualifiers. One principle, the *Ladder of Abstraction* (e.g., Hayakawa 1990), was especially useful in observing how (or if) writers and speakers connected generalities to details and examples. Wendell Johnson's *People in Quandaries: The Psychology of Personal Adjustment* (1946) provided significant insight into the "language of maladjustment." Other useful sources included Lakoff and Johnson's (2003) work on metaphor. Also relevant here (and overlapping with thinking in writing) are fluency in producing discourse, including the more subjective notion of "voice" in writing. The work of Peter Elbow, beginning with *Writing Without Teachers* (1973), along with Donald M Murray's, *Learning By Teaching* (1982), and Ken Macrorie's *Writing to be Read* (1986), were especially influential in my understanding of voice.

When analyzing writers' internal imagery and their uses of actual images and electronic media, the field of semiotics provided the basis for my thinking, especially the work of Umberto Eco (1978) and Robert Scholes (1985). The ambitious collection edited by Anees Sheikh (2003), *Writing about Trauma and Images: The Role of Imagination in Health,* was a treasure-trove of resources for me. Also, the Gestalt psychologists, especially Rudolph Arnheim's *New Essays on the Psychology of Art* (1986) was extremely persuasive in convincing me of the primacy of visual thinking. Howard Gardner's *Frames of Mind: A Theory of Multiple Intelligences (1982)* and Vera John-Steiner's *Notebooks of the Mind: Explorations in Thinking* (1997) have helped me to value and identify all types of thinking and experiences across a variety of disciplines and contexts.

When I completed a first draft, revised it several times, and was reasonably satisfied with it, I then sent it to the participant and asked her to read, respond to possible misinterpretations, and correct any misinformation. I also requested any general comments. They readily complied and I integrated all of their changes and suggestions into the draft and returned it to them for a final check. Several times throughout this extended period, I shared drafts with colleagues, advanced doctoral students, and professionals who attended my conference presentations. In these instances, as well, the identities of participants were always protected.

THE SHIFTING ROLES OF THE RESEARCHER

Throughout this period, I sometimes felt the need to note my own shifting roles as investigator. Novel or unusual kinds of research sometimes require novel approaches. These roles often had a "Jekyll and Hyde" or dualistic quality to them. While my observations on these shifting roles are purely subjective, I offer them here to alert future researchers of what may be in store for them.

First, during interviews and afterwards, when I was listening to recordings and reviewing participants' writing and my own notes, I often felt like an objective researcher. No problem here; this is what I strive for. However, especially when writing and revising my notes, I sometimes felt like I was "reducing" or "atomizing" issues that were literally larger than life—that I was shoplifting life's mysteries and miracles, then squeezing them into little marching lines of subjects, verbs, and objects. All the while, my gut reminded me that life is not this simple. And my gut is still correct.

Often, because I had known several of the participants ahead of time (to widely varying degrees), I felt like a concerned friend. This role felt natural to me in this context, sometimes to the point that it seemed that other researchers would need to have some relationship with participants in order to obtain the level of trust that participants invested in me. The main benefit is the honesty and depth of responses I received from participants, enabling me to learn things that I could never have learned, had their great level of trust not been bestowed. However, this benefit also made me feel like a priest hearing confession—and a phony priest, at that. More disconcerting were the times I felt like a "Peeping Tom," or worse, a "pimp," hell-bent on exploiting the tragedies of others. While these nauseating, ugly feelings did not arise often, when they did, they made me doubt, albeit briefly, the entire project.

At the end of the day, I view these roles—good, bad, and indifferent—as an occupational hazard. Of course, like the fluctuations inherent in the mind of any researcher, these shifting roles can distract us, as well as make it harder for us to situate or contextualize our results, which may further pull us away from objectivity. I feel certain that the best "interview" possible, for any researcher and participant, is nothing more than a good conversation: friendly, respectful, co-constructed, and mutually enlightening. The huge majority of my interviews, I'm happy to say, were like this.

Overall, this project worked as well as it did because all of us believed in the quiet power of the humble word and image. The only thing we believed more deeply was that the word and image could help those who have yet to realize this power.

3 Lucy

> *Not only did I privately recite narratives or storylines of hope, read narratives of hope, and envision narratives of hope, I had to publicly tell my own new narrative. I had to tell my story over and over, out loud, as a way to gain some control over it. Like wrangling a monster to the ground. My disease was so big and overwhelming, I had to find a way to incorporate this new narrative into the existing life I had been living—the 42 year old Lucy, mother of two, professor without terminal cancer. I had to hear my voice, the one I knew, the one that has been narrating my life all along tell this new part. Whether at a department meeting or in class, I told them. Whether it was relevant to the class or not, and as self-indulgent as it might have been, I needed to speak it.*
>
> —Lucy Stanovick, unpublished memoir, 2012

Introduction

When I first met Lucy in my university office twenty years ago, all I can remember is that she was one of the easiest people to talk to that I'd ever met. She was smiling but not in any artificial way, relaxed, straightforward, and laughed easily—the word "easy" keeps coming to me whenever I think of her natural, thoroughly disarming manner. Her way of talking carries over into her written voice, regardless of her purpose or audience. Within minutes of first meeting her, I knew she was someone that I would enjoy working with in our doctoral program in English Education. There was no mistaking her bright, perceptive mind. I knew instantly that students and future teachers would benefit from knowing and learning from her. I have never been disappointed.

Over a ten-year period, I served as Lucy's academic advisor as she completed masters and doctoral degrees. During this time, she and her husband John and two small children bought a home outside of town and grew Christmas trees. Lucy worked closely with me on some favorite projects: helping me to organize a conference I called, "Music and Language as Meaning-Making," which featured author William Zinsser and the legendary jazz duo of Dwike Mitchell and Willie Ruff. At an elementary school, when Ruff demonstrated *The Hambone*, Lucy enjoyed it as much as the rapt children in the audience.

She traveled with me to some rural schools and helped me interview students about the "Channel One" commercials that they had to view as part of their regular school day (see Fox, 1996). She proved to be a skilled and perceptive colleague, as usual. Her PhD dissertation focused on the roles of popular music in the lives of young adults, exploring a powerful text that most people overlook. Among her many insights from that research, Lucy found teenagers, including my daughter, who were disappointed—even angry—when they discovered pop singers who did not write their own material.

Lucy had long since taken a faculty position in another state when she was diagnosed in April 2008, at age forty-two, with Stage Four Metastatic Breast Cancer. At that time, I had just begun planning this book, even though I had taught and researched writing about trauma for several years before her diagnosis. When I heard this news, I knew I wanted to talk with her in detail about her writing, when the right time came. In the fall of 2008, when I first broached the subject of my planned study, fearful that I was being too clinical or detached, she immediately saw the need and the value of it, especially for other people. Over the next four years, I collected notes from several hours of recorded interviews, many e-mail exchanges, and a couple of face-to-face meetings at professional conferences.

In an e-mail message, Lucy's own perception of writing about trauma somewhat reflects Charles Anderson and Marian McCurdy's (2000) nuanced treatment, which I had sent her (see the "Introduction: An Unfinished Furrow").

> When you say writing as healing—what am I healing? It's not like I am going to heal or be on the mend—so I guess what I am healing is my . . . spirit, my identity—how to integrate this new

aspect of my life that has caused a rupture in who I was, how I saw myself.

On two occasions, Lucy confirmed what other researchers (e.g., Pennebaker 2004; DeSalvo 1999) have noted: that initiating and writing about trauma can be upsetting, but Lucy keeps writing, " . . . because I *know* it will help in the long run." As a language expert, Lucy knew that she would "come out better at the other end." She also knew that other people would likely give up before they had given it much of a chance. About all of her writing for healing, Lucy concluded that she was "lucky from [her] training to be able to do this, versus more non-verbal people who cannot."

Lucy's writing about trauma takes three main forms. The first one she calls "emotional"—the private kind of writing she does for herself and for close friends, "just to get it out," to unburden herself of worries and anxieties. The second type she calls, "rational." This is the public kind of writing she does for the *Caring Bridge* website. This organization describes its services as "free, personalized websites that support and connect loved ones during critical illness, treatment, and recovery." It allows family and friends of patients to read updates or *posts* about their medical treatment and other news. It is efficient in that Lucy can write one update about how she is doing, and her subscribers are notified with an e-mail. They can then access the site, read her entry, and write back for Lucy and all of her other subscribers to view. The third form of her writing—and the one she engages in the least often—is her "professional" writing, such as her report for a grant agency. While Lucy defines these forms as being very different, they sometimes overlap, such as when she blends the emotional and private prose with the rational and public writing. Lucy characterizes these types of writing: "Some of them are directly related to the cancer, and some . . . are *because* of the cancer, but they're not *about* it. . . ."

Lucy's Emotional/Private Writing about Trauma

For most people, including Lucy, the bedrock of writing about trauma is emotional, expressive, and private. However, Lucy, also like many others, did not write—*could not write*—in the immediate throes of shock:

> You'd think once I was diagnosed with metastatic breast cancer that my private writing would increase tenfold, that I would use

> it as a way to make sense of this situation. But it didn't. I was so in shock that I didn't know what I felt; I had no words. The fear was so raw, so big, that I could not even begin to name it for fear of it breaking me into a million tiny pieces.

After a few days, though, she began writing because her background and experience told her that this was the right thing to do. The following three excerpts are from one e-mail Lucy sent to a close friend, PK, in December, 2009, and one that she labels as "emotional." PK is also a writer fighting a life-threatening disease, and maintains her own *Caring Bridge* website. I will discuss this single message in three parts—in the same sequence as the original passage—because each part reveals different qualities.

> PK: I know I haven't posted on caring bridge and maybe this is some of what you feel, but I think what I feel and think these days isn't for public consumption—don't want my kids to read it. I feel really down. Being on the second hormonal treatment already really has me thinking I'll go 16 or 17 months on each and then have to switch, which gives me ~5 years. It sounds so morbid, but I just cannot help it. A woman I know with stage 4 colon cancer and all kinds of surgery is now "no evidence of disease" and I can't even talk to her. Another woman at work looks great, stage 4 something, and my friend tells me, "She just has to do two chemos a week for the rest of her life. She looks great," to which I respond, "yes, but how long is the rest of her life?" My friend wasn't really up for my "downer tone." I am surprised to see her as being so strong and honest and a straight shooter, but when it comes to my cancer, she cannot talk about it—she tells me, "You'll be the exception," and I just look at her. I told her I wanted to start reading about death and dying and she named some scientific stage crap, and I told her no, I'm talking philosophy, and she could talk about it for a minute and then just changed the subject. Part of that tells me, wow, she really cares about me—this is affecting for her, it is hard to talk about, and that makes me feel warm and touched. But, it also surprises me. So, working is really hard for me—I just do not care. I love being in class with students, my gen ed class is my favorite class this semester, but all of my admin responsibilities I could care less about.

Lucy refers to this letter as "emotional." Such close-to-the-self messages are intended only for a very few readers and sometimes even exclude family members, such as parents, children (as she notes here), and spouses. This writing, like nearly all of Lucy's writing, shows an active, thinking mind. For example, she qualifies her assertions: "maybe this is *some* of what you feel, but I *think* what I feel. . . ." She writes with precision, using direct quotes from specific people and citing specific numbers, such as "16 or 17 months on each." She reveals several oppositions or tensions in her writing, such as, "It sounds morbid, *but* I just cannot help it" and " . . . to which I respond yes, *but* how long is the rest of her life?"

She shows how her emotions directly change up and down, from feeling "warm and touched" in one sentence, to feeling "surprised" in the next sentence. Lucy later pointed out to me that "surprised" here was really a euphemism for "pissed off." On one hand, she "loves" her class, but on the other hand, she "just doesn't care" about administrative duties. She even allows herself to utter what S. I. Hayakawa and Alan Hayakawa (1990) call a "snarl" phrase, "scientific stage crap," in which we literally hear some anger. This phrase also serves to *name* complex phenomena in a colorful, condensed way, as does her phrase "downer tone."

Such *emotional* writing is commonly known as *expressive* language—the kind of language in which we think—to ourselves and to trusted others (Britton, et al., 1975). This type of active, intense, focused writing allows Lucy to more efficiently *empty* herself of what is causing anxiety. Many of Lucy's word choices are positioned low on the rung of S. I. Hayakawa and Alan Hayakawa's "Ladder of Abstraction" (1990): If the writing is specific, precise, and concrete—as this one is—then it represents an accurate, more detailed map of the writer's reality—a closer *match* between what she perceives as accurate actuality or *real life* and how she represents it to herself and others. Positioning oneself closer to reality, I believe, helps reduce her sense of disconnect. As well, making the details sharply visible means they are more clearly laid out on the table, so they can be manipulated and dealt with—including merely abandoning them for a while.

On a deeper level, this writing demonstrates two important assertions, albeit indirectly. First, Lucy communicates that the conventional scientific belief systems or *ways of knowing* are privileged in this context—but they should not be. For example, she is at odds with the woman who notes that another cancer patient is receiving "only 2 chemos a week," and that she "looks great." Lucy's unease here resides with the emphasis on a scientific remedy and one's physical appearance, both of which, she indicates, add up to a shortened lifespan. As well, she dismisses one type of scientific discourse as "scientific stage crap."

Second, and most importantly, Lucy communicates an overall sense of discord created by her cancer, pinpointing specific ways in which she is at odds with how she relates to other people and situations. How others expect her to feel is not what she feels. Her cancer has made her *different* or *unique,* and her writing about it is one of the precious few ways that she—or anyone—has of making sense out of this difference, of righting the ship so that she is more like other people. She knows that PK will agree with her, because PK is close to Lucy's own self, in essence saying, "They are not me—and we are not them—so we are alike." This writing allows Lucy to integrate herself with another person, even though that other person is not present and may not even respond.

The Roles of Imagery

The specificity and concreteness of Lucy's language, noted earlier, is a product of her nature and habit—of her love for language and literature, which led to her teaching career, and of her practiced ways of visual thinking—of imagining still or moving *pictures in her mind.* As a literacy expert and experienced teacher of language, she is, of course, fluent in verbal thinking, or thinking in words. However, we have learned over time that verbal and visual thought processes are not easily pigeonholed as one or the other, but that sometimes, one may dominate (see, for example, Fleckenstein 2009; Paivio 2001; John-Steiner 1997). Mental images can be activated by our memory, perceptions, and sensations, as well as by our everyday experiences, including what we read, write, view, and talk about. In short, mental images can be powerful in writing for healing purposes, as Lucy's following entry demonstrates.

> This was last Wed:
>
> I'm sitting in the chemo room. I always look around, try to size everyone up. What stage? What kind? How sick? Today there is a woman, 39—I overheard her recite her birth date to the nurse. She is with her sister. She wears a scarf, indicating she has lost some of her hair, but otherwise, she looks good and healthy. She talks to Tam, the nurse, introduces her sister who is

from Florida, and says that her brother will be coming from New Mexico next week to do chemo runs with her. I think she is in an earlier stage than me. I get annoyed when they make friends with the nurse and try to find out everything about their treatment, like this is an exotic journey, one she is already imagining telling her family and friends about years from now around the holiday table . . . oh, remember when I had cancer? Part of it I think is because in her case, there is a beginning, middle, and end. The treatments are finite. She can say when they will end, and an end of the treatments can become synonymous with the end of the cancer. I don't have that. It galls me: her sister just took a picture of her in the chemo chair: in one hand she holds up her store bought cup of tea, and with the other she makes a peace sign and smiles to the camera—like she's at a party. One for the scrapbook: When mommy had cancer. Her friends will call her strong and when her scans come back clean, they will say she beat it, and she will walk the relay for life with pride, a survivor, in every sense of the word. I become reclusive here. I don't want to know the nurses. I don't want to belong here because my stay here is temporary. I don't want to make friends. This is not what I want to do with my life. I don't need to know with great clarity what they are putting in me or what it does—I feel healthy. I am doing well right now. That is all I care about. I know I can't begrudge her; I know I am being hypocritical, contradictory, and crabby. But at this moment, in this place at this time, this is what I felt. It just hit me wrong to see her take a picture.

While this is an *emotional* entry, it was, nonetheless, made in a relatively public venue, the *Caring Bridge* website—more on this overlapping of genres later. Much writing about trauma contains clear oppositions and tensions that are somewhat resolved in the final paragraph. Lucy's emotions here are clearly linked to observable events, a highly desirable quality of writing for healing because it avoids the vagueness of *moaning and groaning* for no discernible reason. Overall, Lucy's discourse rejects the current general belief in the courageous and proud cancer survivor. To Lucy, the act of taking a photo of the patient, holding her hand in a *V* sign, is too much like the celebratory quarterback dance in the end zone of a football game—or at least a common high-five slap of hands.

She seems to feel the clichéd routine of it all, sensing that such falseness trivializes the uniqueness of such illness, of *her* illness.

The people and place that Lucy observes here—the *external images*—seem to be directly recorded and create a sense of immediacy, putting the reader there in the room with her. This use of the present tense is effective for healing purposes because it forces the writers—not just the readers—to *directly confront* what is bothering them—no hiding behind past tense or passive voice. Also, Lucy's use of some very short sentences helps to convey immediacy: "I'm sitting in the chemo room." As well, her repetition of certain sentence structures work to place readers at her side: "What stage? What kind? How sick?" All these techniques quicken the pace for readers and the writer, further ensuring their involvement and immersion in the story, important for healing because they deepen our symbolic *identification* with the narrator and events. In literature, this is most important for readers. But in writing about trauma, it's more important for writers.

Lucy's highly specific language is most powerful for healing purposes because it enables our direct confrontation with the issue at hand. In opposite fashion, writers who rely upon generalities and high-level abstractions are either unaware of how to *get specific*, or they are resisting the very notion of writing for healing. In Lucy's imagery, we not only view the scene more sharply, but more slowly, as the action is *slowed down:*

> . . . in one hand she holds up her store bought cup of tea, and with the other she makes a peace sign and smiles to the camera—like she's at a party. One for the scrapbook: When mommy had cancer.

This slow motion allows us to better absorb it, to process it more completely. But, that's not all. The image further works by becoming metaphorical: "like she's at a party." Next, the image is *speeded up*, with the projection of what happens to the photo being taken, as it becomes an artifact in a scrapbook, viewed by the patient's child. This manipulation of imagery—depicting reality up-close, showing its movements, slowing it down, speeding it up, comparing it to something else—demonstrate a writer exercising firm control over her language and thinking in order to directly face and deal with her challenge. Lucy is not *time-bound* in her writing about trauma; she freely shifts from present, to past, to a hypothetical future. These skills are *automated* or fluent for most literacy experts and serve them well when writing about trauma.

As effectively as Lucy manipulates these images in reconstructing the scene that upsets her, imagery can also be a double-edged sword, turning downright scary if it embodies our absolute-worst imaginable thoughts, as it does for Lucy in the following excerpt from our conversation.

> RF: Talk a little bit about those more private writings that are NOT on Caring Bridge.
> LUCY: Like, what they're about?
> RF: Whatever you want to offer.
> LUCY: These are about John and the kids . . . and uh . . . and sort of . . . and way more directly . . . they are um . . . they are um . . . . Okay. . . . So, these are about being afraid of, um . . . not being able to . . . you know . . . you know, like not being around . . . just being sorry I won't be around. . . . So, it's more that family mode, emotional life. . . . One I had written about having this image . . . telling them I won't be around. . . .
> RF: You said something about images?
> LUCY: Yeah, like I get this image in my head . . . a scenario. . . . You want to know what the image is?
> RF: Sure.
> LUCY: I get this image in my head, this scenario, or whatever, of being close to death, of lying there with them, crying, of telling them I'm sorry a lot, that I'm so sorry that I won't be around. . . .
> RF: . . . You should know, but I'll say it anyway—anything you don't wanna say, don't say. We can skip it—that's no problem.
>   . . .
> LUCY: I don't care if you don't mind if I get a little emotional.
>   . . .
> RF: No, I'm fine. My focus is on you . . . I'm fine. . . . Do you recreate this image in words? Or did it already exist in your mind? Or is it playing out as you write?
> LUCY: I think I had the image in my head, until I pretty much recorded it in writing. . . .

I make it a practice not to quote directly an interviewee's backtracking, repeating, hesitations, and circularities—unless I think these actions connect to the point at hand. I believe that here they are relevant because they underscore the difficulty Lucy had—that *anyone* would have—in confronting their own horrible image with words that do not and cannot come easily. It was terribly difficult for this clear-headed, grounded, unsentimental woman to do this—to face the unfathomable sky.

Lucy's internal imagery is powerful indeed. It seems saturated in personal meaning, condensed, and highly charged. Confronting such imagery with language—to name it, to unpack it, to gain a measure of control over it—represents the greatest challenge for any writer. The tragedy is that many people can never do this. Lucy does. She reflects on this point:

> I think I'm lucky from my training because I know that people want to capture that [their feelings about trauma], but if they don't have any training in writing, it could end up clichéd and general—and you know it means something to them, but it doesn't mean anything to anybody else. . . .

Writing, then, helps Lucy cope. We know that writers' skill levels are connected to their confidence levels. That's why it's sad and frustrating to think of those people who desperately need to write about their trauma, yet, due to their lack of skill and/or confidence, may flounder and too-quickly abandon the whole enterprise.

Lucy's Motivations for Emotional/ Private Writing about Trauma

Several factors seem to motivate Lucy to engage in emotional writing for healing. In our conversations, she stated that she wrote out of "panic and fear." Other motivations included the fact that she simply wanted to *do* something, she wanted to maintain her sense of agency—to act upon the world, to avoid being the *victim*. Another motivation is a natural one for many writers: She wants to leave something for her children; she wants them to know what she's doing, thinking, and feeling.

As noted earlier, maybe the most compelling reason to engage in personal writing for healing is merely to "get it out" into the light of day, so that the thought's pressure or weight is reduced. Getting a thought out increases the rhetorical distance between writer and idea, so the idea can be viewed more objectively, making it less scary. Also, as external, visible marks on a sheet of paper or a computer screen, the ideas are easier to grasp, delete, elaborate upon, or transform in an infinite number of ways. An idea held inside of us too often feels like a brick—frozen and one dimensional, trapped in its present form. But once we "get it out," it becomes more like a fistful of clay—malleable, more likely for us to reshape it. A brick in our head can only take up space and weigh us down. Warm clay in our hand not only feels better, but also molds into different shapes.

Following is the second part of this same e-mail message quoted earlier, from Lucy to her close friend, in December 2009:

> So, tonight, Katie and I are cooking and talking. Can't remember how we get on the subject—I think talking about a YA novel and I ask her, If you could know you were dying in two years, would you want to know and what would you want to do. She says, yes, she'd want to know and immediately says she'd want to "sky dive. Then go to Europe." So we talk a bit and she says, "ok, mom, how about you? If you knew . . . well, you already kind of do know," and I said that I would want to be with her, nick, and john all the time. I would want to pull them out of school and just be with them. She was like, "Mom, come on, that is dumb, what would you want to DO." And I started to get teary, and she was so surprised. "Mom, are you crying?" and I told her, "Well, Katie, this isn't in the too far future," to which she scoffed—as she should. I don't want her to walk around worried. And she gave me a hug and told me she loved me, and it felt so good. And then we just changed the subject, which was fine, and then when nick came down, I was able to laugh at the absurdity of Katie's question to me—I told nick what she said, and we all kind of laughed. . . .

In a later note to me (January 2012), Lucy explains why she felt compelled to recount this conversation to her close friend:

> I think I felt compelled because journaling was not as fulfilling for getting out the private stuff. I also know, as a writer, that I will not remember events, anecdotes, and I know that those are the prize, so I use PK as a friendly, non-judgmental ear. I can get these quick stories out, know I am writing to a real audience, without having to go totally public, and provide context, etc. PK and I go way back, 7th grade, and we wrote notes to each other all the time, wrote a song together, so we already have this very intimate relationship.

In Lucy's account, she worries about how her children are processing her illness and more importantly, how—or whether—they are prepared for a future in which she may not be there to protect them. Because this message focuses on an intense moment with her children, Lucy directed the writing toward her friend and not her husband because, as she indicated to me, she viewed it as too upsetting for him.

At bottom, Lucy initiates the conversation because she wants to take care of her children—she wants to know that *they* know what the possibilities are. This conversation is emotionally traumatic for Lucy because she seems caught unaware that her daughter does not truly grasp the situation of her mother's illness. Her daughter's focus on travel and skydiving starkly highlights her youthful innocence. At this moment, I sense the chasm suddenly opening up, widening, between what Lucy believes and what Katie understands to be the case. And the sheer poignancy of it all overwhelms Lucy to tears. This *rupture* or disconnect between what Lucy may have thought she knew about her daughter's perspective—and what her daughter revealed at that time—motivates Lucy to seek understanding in "getting it out."

As well, a second, related rupture or disconnect underlies this writing: On one hand, Lucy wants her children to be informed and prepared for what her illness may bring. On the other hand, she does not want her children "to walk around worried." This writing may partly allow Lucy to negotiate these oppositions or tensions, mainly by recounting her talk with Katie to her son, Nick—and her naming the situation as "absurd." However, as Lucy verified later, the "absurdity," she notes here is for reconciling her *own* disconnect, as well as for that of her children's.

Lucy's Relationship to Readers of Her Emotional/Private Writing about Trauma

The final paragraph of Lucy's December 3 e-mail to PK follows. Here, Lucy explains her need for a very trusted and "close" audience or a reader, that is, one whom she knows intimately and trusts completely. In communicating with such readers, writers regard them in the same trusted ways as they consider their spouses, parents, or children, but may not necessarily choose these family members. In her note to me that prefaced this e-mail, Lucy described PK as, "a dear friend of mine who is suffering terribly with MS."

> I dunno, pk—I just need to get these thoughts down and I can't just write in a journal with no audience—no real reader, so thank you so much for being on the other end—I don't need

> you to fawn over me or even really respond—I just need a safe, knowing place and you are that place for me. I just don't think caring bridge [a public, interactive web site for people suffering from disease or trauma to communicate with friends] is the place—I mean nick and Katie read that—do I really say I have been so melancholy lately, so convinced that I am not going to be a long-liver, that the impending doom feels like it is getting heavier—whoa, this is getting melodramatic—

Lucy had told me in a conversation that she *wants* to write similarly private messages for readers on *Caring Bridge*, but that she just does not consider it the right venue, because she does not want to "overly upset people or freak them out." She wants to "take care of the people she knows" who are reading her posts on this website. Her message in this ending excerpt shows that personal writing "for the self" can sometimes need a real reader, as long as that reader is similar to, and close to, the writer—or, as Lucy stated, the reader is "completely anonymous." Although such writing is freed from the constraints of more public writing and is not subject to editing or self-censorship, the final sentence, nonetheless, indicates that Lucy is aware of an external reader, as she deftly uses humor to deflect what may be too intense for her reader, as well as for herself.

I'll end this section by quoting from the very beginning of Lucy's e-mail to me, explaining what she was sending and why she was sending it to me. It speaks to Lucy's overall feelings about this writing to PK in particular, and seemingly confirms her overall belief in writing about trauma.

> Hi Roy—not much time right now for small talk, so right to it: last night I wrote an email to a dear friend of mine (PK) who is suffering terribly with MS. We share stories and thoughts. I have been feeling really low lately and carrying it around with me like an extra weight and not really knowing what to do with it. I knew I couldn't write on caring bridge (I talk about that below). So, I wrote this email to her last night around 9:30, and I gotta tell you, unexpectedly, I went to bed feeling so much better and woke up today with such a lift. I always know intellectually that the writing will help, but I am really knocked back by how much better I feel just by unloading this, and if you think about it, there is no logical reason—I didn't get any new news

about my health, everything is still the same, so it is the writing that has helped me heal a temporary broken spirit. Thought you might be interested—do with it what you like . . . hope all is well with you—saw Brenda Randen—had no idea about her diagnosis!

And part of my reply to this note:

Am so glad the piece you sent somehow 'worked' for you. I don't understand it either, except for the fact that life is so unfathomable and writing is slightly less so—all these neat little letters in logical lines provide some illusion of order and control. But it's more complicated than this!

Lucy's Rational/Public Writing about Trauma

Lucy described her writing for healing as comprising two different categories: "emotional and rational." Most of her rational writing is done for a more public audience, the *Caring Bridge* website—often referred to as CB—for patients who want to keep many people informed of their illness, by making periodic entries. Friends or subscribers are notified when a new entry has been made and they can access it at their leisure. Mainly, this approach benefits everyone, especially the patient, who is relieved of writing numerous individual messages. Further, this type of public writing for healing takes at least two forms—the rational entries for the website and, to a lesser extent, the writing about trauma that's more *professional* in nature—those pieces that have a more utilitarian purpose or goal, including reports, articles, and speaking and writing responses back to her students' writing.

Lucy's Writing for the *Caring Bridge* Website

Lucy was diagnosed on April 1, 2008, and the *Caring Bridge* journal website or blog was created on April 22, 2008. After four years of writing (April 2012), she had completed a total of sixty-seven entries, roughly seventeen per year or one entry every three weeks.

> LUCY: I *want* to write these private things for an audience . . . but it's weird because I know these people and I get immediate feedback. I feel this weird responsibility to the people who

read CB. I don't want to overly upset people or freak them out.... Once in a while, Nick and Katie read them and I don't want to freak *them* out!

RF: So, with your more public writing on CB, it's more for the readers, more for keeping a stiff upper lip?

LUCY: At the beginning, I think I actually *did* have that stiff upper lip, because I was in so much shock.... But now, day to day, I'm fine, as far as a stiff upper lip.... I don't think that CB is the right place for private stuff. I know that CB is a blog, but it feels different. The last one I wrote, people were like, "Oh my God!" in response—that immediate feedback is kind of weird. I want the old kind of blog, where I don't get reminders every time I post something, to have not so much responsibility on my part. It's just weird.

RF: After you write a public entry on CB, what does that do for you? How does that make you feel when articulating things in a more "objective" and rational way?

LUCY: They remind me that I have cancer. They make me aware of that because, to look at me, I'm fine. I don't feel bad. I was re-reading it and there's a lot of repetition about what my treatments are. And in the beginning, I *had* to say it, I had to articulate it. I needed to say it—*a lot!* It was a way to get a handle on it, a way to take control. My writing also helped me to raise a lot of questions, in a very practical way. I was never angry, like the people who say, "I'm so mad at my body!" I never felt that way. I was in this weird calm and it felt good to let people know that my head was okay.

There are obvious tensions here: Lucy wants to write for these readers, but she does not want to feel obligated to them. She wants to be truthful, but she does not want to "freak them out." In one of our conversations, Lucy spoke of how she is able to "teach" her readers on this website. This is a very natural response, given that she is a professional "teacher of teachers." Her desire to teach here is also fueled by what she has learned—that metastatic breast cancer is under-funded and little understood by the general public. Of course, her entries on *Caring Bridge* also teach us how to deal with what we cannot control.

More importantly, her public writing seems to help her become *orderly* in dealing with her cancer, raising an interesting question. Because she feels an obligation to her friends, she keeps a consistent journal for them to read—and because she does not want to freak them out, she carefully chooses her words and tone, to assure them that her "head was okay." Here, I cannot help but wonder if the *measured* and *rational* writing she does on CB is merely a recording of how she feels? Or, does this rational writing—this *tending* to her readers—help her feel more emotionally stable? Does this tailoring of a message for others, in itself, help keep her ship balanced? I would say it is some of both, especially given her elaboration on how the journal enhanced a feeling of calm.

> LUCY: in the beginning, it felt very good *not* to be alone, to say some things over and over again. To be able to write the positive news from the doctor . . . was very good. By saying it and writing it, it made it more a part of me, so that I could believe it more. It created order for me, because I did have doubts about the treatment I was on and I was really scared, so saying it over again, I went from "I want to believe this," to "I *do* believe this." What was especially frustrating was that there was very little I *could* do. Just taking medicine (vs. not taking chemo), there was nothing to do—so the writing took care of my nervous energy.

Organization of Writing for the Caring Bridge Website

After three years' worth of writing for the CB website, Lucy well-knows how typical entries are organized. She notes that they are "like essays" that begin with some note from personal experience, which acts as a "trigger" for the reason for her posting. She prefers that her entries have a specific reason or event, such as when old friends visited from out of state or when she met for a few days with women friends from college. She then ends the journal with "a reflection of where my head is now." She added that, "over time it's become more boring—but I think it's important that people know I'm moving, that I'm okay."

Here, Lucy comments on what people write back to her on the website.

> I don't ever answer responses on CB, 'cause I'd spend all my time writing people back! However, she added, "If people wrote me back individually in the beginning, I would write them back. .

. . I feel better for getting certain things out of my head. The writing on CB is more obligatory. That sounds bad, doesn't it?

RF: No. It sounds perfectly normal to me.

Mixed Genres of Writing for the Caring Bridge Website

While many entries are indeed organized in the way Lucy describes, I should also note that many entries consist of a range of genres—from the objective tone of purely informational writing, to the emotional tone of subjective, personal writing. These two modes can slide effortlessly, from one to the other, or they can *erupt*, juxtaposed, just a few paragraphs afterward, or even within the same paragraph.

> Another Party4life is in the books. We raised close to $13,000 that night alone, and once we get final numbers from the mail-in checks to support Party4Life, we think we are close to $35,000 for the event. That is amazing. Despite the torrential downpour that would not let up, it was a great time. I would say there were close to 200 people, and as long as you stayed under the pavilion, you didn't get wet. I know it was a bit comical moving the basket raffle tables in . . . and then out . . . in . . . and then out. Thank you to everyone who donated food, time, money, and talents. Thank you to everyone who came and partied with us and stood as supporters of me and what the Lucy Fund is trying to do. You can check out pics and even some video.
>
> We stole a few days at the shore right after—and it was just what I needed to re-coup. My brother and Julie have an amazing place on the bayside that they lent us. Two nights we crabbed off a small pier, and caught the stew out of them, as John would say. And a family vacation wouldn't be complete without John losing a game of Hearts.
>
> I've been kind of out of it lately. You could say it is all the planning for P4L [Party for Life fundraiser] and then you could say that after p4l, the letdown brings you down. Nicholas said I've been stand-off-ish and quick to get angry, and we had a couple go-arounds. Last night, I had my "this is how things are going to run this year" talk with Katie and Nick—they are going to do what I say, when I say it; they are going to pick up after themselves, they are going to ask before they go and do

things, they are going to keep lines of communication open. And then I went in my room and cried. I had no idea why. John came in and asked if I felt better. I didn't. I don't know what it is, but for the last few weeks, I've been crying and just kind of angry. So, he left and I got thinking about the kinds of things I was getting mad about—things I can control (or think I can control).

So I went out to the nook, told all three I knew what it was, and I told them: "I know what is bothering me: I feel out of control, like I can't control the cancer, and so I gravitate toward things I can control and that is housework, that is Nick and Katie, who I think I can control. I have to tell you everything now; I have to teach you everything now because I may not get another chance. I have to prepare you for being adults, because if I don't say it now, it may be too late. Ever since I had to change drugs, I have felt this way. I don't know if the new drug will work, and even though I am three years still here, it feels like time is starting to tick faster toward the end of a finite line. Maybe it's that Nick is a senior and I feel like we are drifting apart, maybe it's that today, at chemo, she had trouble getting a vein, and I winced at the idea of needing a port, and once I get a port, I'll never not have a port, maybe it's that I don't know how any of you feel about the cancer or if you even think about it . . . and you don't need to tell me, that is fine, but that's it. That's what I think is bothering me."

And it's all just tumbling out, mixed with tears and just lying there in the middle of us. And they all just looked at each other, and I said you don't have to say anything, and they didn't. I went back to my room, and John came in with a tentative thumbs up, "Feel better now?"

"NO! God, no." I don't want to have to say any of that to them. I don't want to complicate teenage-hood, which is tough enough, without adding my terminal disease on top of that. I don't want to feel this scared. I don't want to have very real images of my last days flash through my mind, uninvited. So, I just laid there. And, if you were writing some blockbuster movie, they'd come in together and each take a spot on the bed, and we would talk, soft, loving talk and cry together til we started laughing about something, and it would fade out with nice, warm fuzzy feelings. But in my real life . . . Nick had three hours of homework ahead of him, so he got started on that, Katie turned the TV on and John did bills. And you know, I think that is fine. There is no script for any of this, and you can't say how people should react in the moment. I pretty much dropped a bombshell right in the middle of the room. I know they heard me, and I know in our own ways, we will be there for each other and we will talk. I came out and watched a documentary on the making of *Jaws* with Katie, and I made sure to kiss her good night and we told each other we love each other. John gave me a back rub later, and Nick asked what I needed him to do this weekend, and I gave him a kiss goodnight.

This entry clearly shows the *rational/public* form in its first paragraph focused on explaining the Party for Life and then, after a transition paragraph, moves to the more emotional/private mode, becoming more intense as it progresses. Two important points must be made here. First, such categories as *public* and *private* writing are arbitrary constructions imposed by people like me who are trying to organize information! Below their surfaces, they hardly exist in real life. We should not expect such neatness when meaning and emotions and family and healing are bubbling in the same stew. Second, writing for healing is necessarily *associational*, in that one random topic, detail, word, or image can *set off* another point or story. Lucy wisely does not edit out these so-called, *tangents*. Doing so would defeat one of the main reasons for writing about trauma—disclosure and release, not to mention discovery.

After about four years of making regular posts on the *Caring Bridge* website, Lucy did not seem to be receiving the same benefits from this public writing as she had in the past—though she continued making them. In an excerpt from her unpublished memoir Lucy sent me on July 19, 2012, she stated,

> I was getting tired of the public writing and my own perceived pressure to reassure everyone I was "good" and "thankful." I was writing these crafted essays that I made sure had some humor, some emotion, some information, and maybe even a little message. It was getting boring.

These pressures, along with the predictability of how her public messages were organized, led Lucy to focus more on writing to her close friend.

Here, Lucy articulates her dissatisfaction with her public messages on the *Caring Bridge* blog:

> I felt limited with the blog through no fault of the blog itself. It was my perception of its function and its boundaries, and it was my own, illogical sense of how audiences respond. It is like if you write a book or memoir, you have space, you have pages and pages to tell the back story, to fully explain a thought, or to more roundly present your life. With a memoir, the reader knows he is in for the nit and grit. But with the blog, the space just doesn't allow for that, and I think readers are expecting something different. If a blog entry went on for pages and pages, readers might be like, "This is not what I bargained for. I don't have time to read all this."
>
> Sometime in 2010, I was chatting with . . . the researcher we give our fundraising money to, and we were talking about a Lucy Fund e-newsletter we were starting; he suggested I write what it is like to live with metastatic breast cancer. I told him I more or less do that on Caring Bridge, but his words kept banging around in my head—"what is it like to live with mets breast cancer?" Sometimes I am reluctant to write what it is like—who will read it? Will I scare people? Will I sound like a melodramatic diva? (That is funny—a breast cancer diva.) But then I run into people like a dental hygienist or a librarian who say things like, "You'll beat this in no time" or "my friend had breast cancer last year," like it was a bad flu or minor surgery or house renovations that are now done. And I think, "You don't even know what stage IV or mets is." They don't even know enough to ask about stages unless they've had someone in their lives go through direct experience of a cancer diagnosis. And it's not their fault. That's how our mass culture talks about cancer—we like the "cure" and "survival" and "good kinds" we can battle and destroy to feel safe. That's how we talk about most diseases. Our national attention span isn't long enough to handle the nuances. I didn't know there were different kinds of M.S. til my friend PK was diagnosed and she educated me. And I can't get all huffy and indignant if I keep my mouth shut. So, I see that there is use in writing about what it is like to live in this nether world.
>
> The story of having stage IV breast cancer is that life goes on, but it changes everything, and blog entries just didn't allow

the room or the depth to get into it. I needed to find a different genre, a different audience, a different purpose. In came PK.

Both Lucy and I would be the first to assure readers that *Caring Bridge* provides an exceptionally positive and powerful service for everyone. After time, though, it may have its limits, depending upon the writer, so I view Lucy's frustration here as a natural one in this context. I also view her return to private and emotional writing as forever natural—especially with a dear and close friend, like PK—as forever needed. In Lucy's words, "PK became the merge of the public and private. She was a real time audience (public) reading the uncensored me (private)." Opening the valve completely with a real reader is the bedrock of writing through trauma. It has been and will be forever natural.

LUCY'S PROFESSIONAL/PUBLIC WRITING ABOUT TRAUMA

Lucy's *professional* writing for healing is the one she engages in least of all, as would be natural for most people. The fact that she has done it at all attests to her flexible approach to what constitutes any given genre, as she knows that no genre is "pure." This type of communication is typically intended for more public readers—those she is not as close to on a personal level. Such writing is intended for transactional or work-related purposes—to get something done. Lucy's integrating her illness into such forms represents a non-traditional approach, though one that has gained credibility in the past few decades due to an increasing acceptance of *literary nonfiction*. This type of writing includes communicating with her students about why some of their assignments (which integrate "healing" into certain academic genres) need revision to better address their intended audience. Other forms included in this category are sections of a grant report, descriptions and explanations of her fund-raising efforts, a book proposal, and her encouragement of her husband's and son's writing about her cancer.

LUCY'S EXPANSION OF THE TRADITIONAL BOUNDARIES OF WRITING ABOUT TRAUMA

Lucy told me that after her diagnosis, "there was enough going on that I could avoid professional writing." Still, she wanted to do it, so that her children "could point to it and say, 'that's my mom.'" The following passage, "Shifts and Changes," was written for grant proposal reviewers of The National Writing Project. As the director of her site, Lucy explained that "each of the [assistant] directors wrote a paragraph about how my diagnosis has affected how we run the site, how we see the site." This is Lucy's contribution:

> April 1, 2008 I was diagnosed with Stage IV breast cancer. My God, I was 42—none of us knew what this would mean—treatment, quality of life, longevity. I remember one of the first things Leslie said to me was, "You are still the director." What she meant was no matter how much or how little I could do, the cancer didn't mean I had to step out, wholesale. So we'd take it one day at a time. But for the immediate time, I had to step back—I was going to lots of doctors, having lots of tests, and feeling a great need to be home—with my family. Because of the cancer, I couldn't do everything, and so I learned how to not be at every event, every meeting, but still be the director. Leslie and Sue met with the leadership team and the cancer gave everyone the opportunity to see their individual role as vital to the continued growth and success of the site. It made the site less about me in my own head—and I think this is how it should be. It let us all see that it isn't Lucy's, Leslie's, or Sue's site. Delegating and mentoring is easier for me now. Prior to the diagnosis I worked frantically, in my head—making decisions on the fly and wondering what did it matter if I didn't tell Leslie, but now, the cancer has slowed me down and I realize that decisions and division of work isn't about personalities, people, or power, it's about the site. The cancer has helped me see that the work I do isn't about me, it's about the site, about ensuring its success long after I am gone.

Once again, in this piece, Lucy blends genres: the emotional and private with the rational and public. Her illness is directly tied to the public work at hand, as delegating and mentoring site leaders has long been an important goal of the National Writing Project. Lucy also wrote about her cancer for the organization's newsletter. Most importantly, about such writing, Lucy said, "Leslie asked me to write about cancer," *but it had to be about something else, paired with something else* [Italics are mine]. As discussed earlier, this *pairing with something else* helps us gain fluency with private and emotional writing. I believe that it helps in a similar way with this public writing, but it seems that Lucy's decision was likely more influenced by considerations of audience and purpose—that she had to have a reason for breaking the conventional separation between private and public discourse.

This public piece was loosely revised from a *freewriting*—written quickly without editing or stopping—that Lucy had composed earlier. She found the initial draft to be therapeutic, but slightly less so in revising it. She also noted its additional benefits. It allowed her to collaborate with her two colleagues, enabling her "to think about the site in a different way and [her] relationship to the site in a different way."

Another way that Lucy expands the conventional boundaries of writing for healing is that, somehow, she has motivated her family to write about the same and similar issues. Her son, Nick, wrote a college-application essay about a person who has influenced him—his mother. It was published in the electronic newsletter of the *National Foundation for Cancer Research*. His writing is lean, direct, clear, and powerful. It compares his own experience to a film he recently viewed, which seems to function as the *other thing*, which helps writers address trauma and will be examined in the pages ahead. Nick makes it abundantly clear that he has learned vivid, strong lessons from his mother's approach to her family, to him, and to her illness.

Lucy's husband, John, who always refers to himself as "Mean Uncle John," has also written a few entries on her *Caring Bridge* website. One of John's entries begins, "A rough day yesterday. We put Gunner down." Gunner was the family's cherished bird-hunting dog, and the rest of the piece is a tribute to him, crafted in direct and unsentimental language, such as the following excerpt:

> Gun really loved field hunting for geese and pheasants. None of my hunting buddies will ever forget the year the geese were thick at Eagle Bluffs in the late season. Because of the deep snow on the ground, we simply laid among the decoys with a white sheet over the two of us. His head either peeking out of the sheet or on my chest waiting for the geese to arrive.

In several of her own entries, Lucy mentioned John's consistently "even-keeled" mind, ready to acknowledge that things may not be as bad as they appear to her and offering specific reasons why he believes this. A few years after Lucy's diagnosis, John experienced his own life-threatening illness but is now doing fine, as he notes in this excerpt.

> I know Lucy and I are both thankful to still be here. Lucy often writes about hope. I got a very brief glimpse of how her mind works when I was in the hospital. I had never really been that close to death before. All I kept thinking was—what about the kids—I have got to be there for them. Kids need at least one parent to bum money off of, right?

Of course, humor can be an escape from reality—but it can also serve very practical purposes by innocently *taking the edge off* of a serious situation, consequently making the message more appealing for others. In one entry, Lucy describes how she showed up for treatment one day and was informed that she could no longer receive the drug, Doxil, which had been helping her. The company's supply was gone, so they had to begin a new drug. Lucy was surprised and crushed:

> So, I cried for twenty minutes or so in the chemo chair, the tears leaking out on their own. I used the pillow to cover my face. I felt like I was ten years old again, hiding behind the security of my big soft pillow. You know, in chemo rooms you all face each other; the chairs are pushed against the wall and they all face the center, so I could see folks through the crack of my pillow stealing sideways glances at the woman with the pillow over her head. The nurse didn't know what to do. She offered me a doughnut, which I thought was pretty funny.

Lucy and John continue to see humor—I suspect they reinforce each other in this regard. They wisely integrate it into their writing, when many people would not consider doing so. Overall, people who successfully and consistently write about trauma do not do it alone but with strong support from friends and family—a strong support that flows both ways.

Lucy's Response to Her Students' Professional/Public (and Academic) Writing about Trauma

In her university class, "Writing about Young Adult Literature," Lucy described one assignment for her undergraduates as being a form of writing about trauma. By extension, her responses to their writing constitute an indirect form of her own writing for healing. Young Adult Literature is a genre aimed at middle school through high school aged students. Such fiction typically includes plots, characters, and themes that such students can connect to—separation from parents; the main characters' quests for independence and their own identities; substance abuse; bullying; interactions with the opposite and same sex; sports, and so forth. In one of our conversations, Lucy explained how her students' writing addresses personal as well as academic objectives:

> In Young Adult Lit, all of their writing is writing about healing. I ask them to write about the coming of age moment they identify with and use their own story as a comparative text. A lot of them end up writing about issues that are unresolved for them. One wrote about her father's death, her father's alcoholism, his public and private identity. You have to be prepared to deal with this as a piece of writing, for example, adding details or organization, because it's a piece of [academic] work . . . If a student comes to me with a draft and he or she is writing around it, I tell them it's not good writing: they've got to supply details and take the lid off.
>
> The feedback I get is that this was an incredible experience for them. I use Tom Romano's (2000) different genres, so one student made a life-sized door covered with words. The other side of the door was covered with red paint as blood and kids screaming. It is shocking. The writing she did from that was explaining the creation of this door. In this writing, they try to reconcile a split they have had in adolescence. A lot of them want to share it because it becomes a way of reclaiming their own voices!

After Lucy obtained permission from her college students, she sent me a few sample papers. Their topic was to write a comparative essay between themselves and S E Hinton's classic novel for young adults, *The Outsiders* (1997). A major theme of this novel, set in the 1950s, is bullying, as it plays out in a socioeconomic clash between rich kids, the *Socs* or *Socials*, and poor kids, the *Greasers*. Lucy's students told her that this was the first time they had written about this topic. The following excerpt from one paper compares the writer's experiences with that of the main characters—Ponyboy, Darry, and Johnny.

> Kids are cruel. That's an understatement. Kids are the Gestapo, they are meaner than the Nazi's, and they travel in packs. I was so alone, but always surrounded. I was surrounded by people that inspected me, and then made fun of me every time I made

a "wrong" move. I remember sitting in the middle school cafeteria and I had these hunter green shorts that had a lot of belt loops. They were decorative, I guess, and I had missed one. It was as if I had peed my pants. I sat there as they taunted me that I couldn't dress myself, and I was retarded, and I was ugly, and I stopped listening after a while. When the mortification wore off, the anger dug in. I felt like someone was whipping me in public. Still, to this day, as an adult, I double-check my belt loops. I know those kids don't remember that day. I never see any of them anyway, but I remember, and I don't want to risk something like that happening again.

I used to have nightmares that I was on fire and no one would put me out. They all stood around pointing and laughing while I begged for help. Ponyboy might have felt isolated but he had family and friends that would help him no matter what. Darry gave Johnny and Ponyboy a gun and all of the extra cash he had to help them get away. I've never had friends like that. I don't know what it feels like to have that kind of backup. I transitioned from the middle to the high school hoping that I would find friends and solace. In ninth grade things were at their worst. I was throwing up before I got on the bus in the morning, and I was usually so defeated by the time it came to the afternoon bus, I just put my head down and walked out to the lions that were going to eat me, if not that afternoon, tomorrow afternoon would suit them just fine.

I started to make friends with the older kids once I got to high school. And by friends, I mean boys. I used all that I had to get their attention and once I had it, I twisted it to my advantage. Now, all they did was call me a slut. At least that was closer to the truth of what was going on. When they called me stupid, ugly, slow, and fat, I couldn't embrace any of that. But I embraced slut, just as I would later embrace "thug" and "the bad girl" later in high school. They thought it anyway, so why not reap the benefits? I was alone. The guys that I paid attention to had cars, and always offered to drive me home. My need to escape the bus and be driven home by older boys led to a "date rape" at fifteen. When no one believed what had happened to me, I wasn't surprised. People had been ignoring or hating me for years. Why should things suddenly change?

We can only hope that this student continues to *escape* her previous life and her feelings about it, that she continues to view her past with this sense of *objectivity* and distance, so that she can get outside of it and, further, manipulate the trauma in positive, constructive ways. This excerpt demonstrates several characteristics of effective writing about trauma. First, she specifically *names* or *calls out* those words and actions that hurt her the most: "fat," "ugly," "retard," "stupid," and "slow."

Second, this identification is not in black and white, either/or terms: She *qualifies* the level of damage inflicted by three of the names, "slut," "thug," and "bad girl," stating that "at least that [being called a "slut"] was closer to the truth of what was going on" and "they thought it anyway [that she was a "thug" and "a bad girl"], so why not reap the benefits?" Her placement of quotation marks around the term *wrong* also communicates that she is reading her map of reality with some finer distinctions. Such qualification seems painfully honest and maybe leads readers—and especially the writer—to believe the truth of her other assertions. Third, this writer, like with Lucy's writing cited previously, uses imagery skillfully. One way is through her use of metaphor and simile: Her classmates are "Nazis," "Gestapo," and wolves or predatory animals in that they "travel in packs." Her missing a belt loop was treated as if she had "peed her pants."

What may be most significant about this excerpt and others that explore writing for healing in *comparative* ways is the function of *the other thing* in the comparison—in this case, *The Outsiders*. When we write about our own experience, our own trauma, we tap into our *inner stream* of memories, images, associations, and perceptions. Writing directly about what is going on in our heads is an intense experience because it is a direct transaction, unfettered by anything else: it is just the writer and her thoughts appearing on the page or screen.

In Lucy's earlier writing about her fellow cancer patient being photographed in the chemo chair, that woman served as Lucy's *other thing*. The presence of some *other thing*, such as a book or a film we are comparing ourselves to, or a description of what we are viewing, helps *ground* and *anchor* those feelings being tapped from our internal reservoir; they help deflect or reduce some of the intensity that necessarily occurs when we write about highly-charged feelings. Similarly, when Lucy responds to her students' academic writing for healing, she frames her remarks as instruction to improve a piece of writing, not as a therapist addressing a patient but as a reader trying to understand. Here, the other thing becomes the academic task-at-hand. These *other things* assist us in getting it out.

Because of the additional *layers* of complexity involved in working with students, their thinking, their writing, their revision, and their interactions with others, it is hard to determine the degree to which this work may directly influence Lucy's own writing for healing purposes. In simple terms, her students and their writing can serve as *the other thing* or a comparative element for Lucy to view her own situation. It is also true that responding to students' writing—or anyone else's prose—is similar to reading literature, because we are able to identify with the fictional character. In the following excerpt from our conversation, Lucy discusses one student's writing for healing:

> I wonder if he did that. It ran through my mind all the time. I wonder if he lived and if he felt awake and then, you know, I wanted to ask questions, but then in the next paragraph, *I'm over what he did to me and I don't think I ever bring it up to him* [italics are author's], I guess on one hand, I don't believe that she's over it, because otherwise, she won't have all these questions. . . .

In this passage, Lucy seems to slide into her student's words unconsciously, shifting her point of view from first person to third person. She begins by talking about a person described in the writing in the third person (e.g., "I wonder if *he* did that"). Next, when Lucy paraphrases, "I'm over what he did to me and I don't think I ever bring it up to him," she speaks from *that writer's point of view*, as Lucy, in effect, becomes the writer. In short, responding to others' writing can be an act of empathy, of putting yourself in another's shoes, as Lucy does here. This imaginative act of identification, of briefly transferring our self into that of another, can serve as *the other thing*, helping us understand our own issues, if even vicariously.

While this example of how her students' writing may have influenced Lucy's own writing about trauma, I wondered if there were more explicit links, so I asked her. This is her reply:

> Holy shit, Roy:
>
> This completely got away from me. Sorry bout that. Attached is the piece I wrote for my YA lit class.
>
> I had been writing "end" pieces for my classes on and off. I was thinking of what I could write and then it hit me that I was

having my own coming of age moment. A lot of the students didn't know that I had been diagnosed—it had been a year. I was nervous and tried hard to think critically, like, is this melodramatic? What is my motive? But then I thought that this is the only life I know, these are the only experiences I have. I'm not good at making stuff up. I wasn't writing it to upset anybody; I was writing in essence what I had been asking them to write about during the semester (sans connecting it to any novels). I also wanted to show them that I wrote, too. That was important to me. Last day of class we have a read around; they all read what they like most from what they wrote during the semester (got that from you). I read last, and I remember one girl, when I was done, she goes, "Damn, Stanovick." It was pretty quiet and I felt kind of awkward, so tried to just say, hey, you know, it's cool, just wanted to share that, have a great summer. I got a few hugs, and it was fine. . . .

Here is the paper that Lucy wrote for her students, *Coming of Age*, which she read aloud to them:

We spent a lot of time talking in class about coming of age, and I remember one day saying that our coming of age moments don't stop; they continue to occur. And then in my mind, I thought, hmm, I had a major coming of age just last year. I lost my innocence in terms of how I thought my life would play out; I was naive and thought that hard things only happen to others, that I would spend my life being a bystander, a sympathetic ear, one degree removed from any real hardship.

But then, last year, I was diagnosed with stage IV breast cancer. Out of the blue. I can remember saying to John months before, "Just for the record, I have a slight pull of a muscle right here in my side." We would do that all the time—go on record so later we could say, "Let the record show that I knew. . . ."

I can remember sitting in Anne's office, April 1, after hours—she called me back to her office after a chest scan that was supposed to show pneumonia, and she looked at me and said, "Lucy, it's not good. It looks like cancer. And it looks like its spread." Huh. It was like it bounced off me. So weird. I would always tease Leslie about getting sick every other week because she was too careful about her health—no caffeine this, no fat that, heavy on the bran and homegrown garden style tofu. I bragged about my inherited iron gut. I began to think that the privilege I enjoyed growing up even made its way into my health—my wealthy grandmother lived til she was 93, my own parents are still alive, for Christ's sake, I am a doctor's daughter. All six of my family are perfectly healthy. But in another part of my brain I was starting to get worried: no one gets through unscathed, something happens to everyone; look at my sister in law—lost her sister, father and two dogs. What would it be for me? I always thought John would go early, and I would have panic attacks thinking that something might happen to one of my children. It just never occurred to me that it would be me.

You have spent this semester writing about moments that have played a major role in defining you, but do not define the totality of you, and I have long believed in the power of writing to reclaim the self. I have been touched and moved by your stories. I have laughed and welled up and punched my fist in the air right along with you. This is my story about an event in my life that has played a major role in defining me, and it hasn't been all bad, and it does not define the totality of me.

What I've tried to do with this piece is represent the inside and the outside. My all-time favorite song is Seasons of Love from my favorite play, RENT. The song is about measuring a year in the life, and it asks, is it 525,600 minutes (the total of minutes in a year), or is it something else? Love, laughter, tears, midnights, sunsets, cups of coffee? I have figured that of the 525,600 minutes of this year, we have spent 2700 minutes together. And I wouldn't trade them for anything.

Lucy's Teaching of *Voice* in Writing

Throughout these pages, Lucy's voice rings true and strong. It's hard to miss. Lucy has long valued writers developing their own voices—that sense of a real human being, a unique spirit, behind the written words. Lucy has worked hard to teach voice, but maybe no harder than she did with her own son, as she relates in this excerpt from her unpublished memoir:

> Nick is a skilled writer, too, but he likes a real, public audience. After his 7th grade basketball season, he wrote a two-page

speech about what the season meant to him and a few choice memories for their end-of-season dinner. We knew then this kid was well beyond his years. Then it was time for the college essay and the prompt was to write a narrative about someone who has influenced him. He wrote a perfect five paragraph essay about me that said little more than in general that I had stage IV cancer, that he wanted to be like me, and that he has learned that no matter what comes your way, you have to keep going. Of course, it was nice that he was writing about me, but you know, the teacher in me, thought, "Well, sure, pick the easy one: my mom has cancer."

While reading it for him, I made numerous marginal notes, prompting him to tell more, explain this or that, get more specific here or there. He was bewildered. Instead of answering any of my prompts, he wrote a new introduction, one that included stats about women with stage IV breast cancer and left the rest the same.

"Nick! This is like a dry academic essay. It has to have a voice."

"Mom, how can that not be my voice? I wrote it!"

The bitch of it is that I have taught voice over and over again, but when it comes to my own kids, I can't seem to explain anything. I would try and give him examples but he was kerflumoxed and starting to get mad. He wrote yet another one, and I almost thought, "Just forget it, Lucy," but I tried one more time: "Nick. Thousands of kids' moms have breast cancer. You have to make your essay stand out, make them remember it. Right now, there is nothing to remember. You need to include your voice."

"Mom! How is it I get A's on all my writing? Everyone is not like you. I don't know what you mean by 'voice!' We don't learn that!"

I left and came back and started to cry. "Nick, I'm not crying because you are writing about me, which is very nice. I am crying because you say you don't know what voice is! You have been taught to write with no voice. Thirteen years of school, and yes you get A's, but you have been taught and rewarded for excluding your voice. For just filling in a formula. You don't even know what I mean by a writerly voice." He just shook his head. So typical of me.

He left it alone for a couple of days. Then in the car one day, it hit me:

"Nick! Remember when you told me about that movie you watched about the mom who dies of breast cancer and that you didn't expect to cry? What if you started your college essay with that?"

"You mean start it like that? Tell that story? Well," he snorted with relief, "I can do that." And when we got home, damn if he didn't pound out the following essay, as is:

I seldom cry at the end of movies. There are two movies I can think of: Sounder, when I was a little boy, and the other, a more recent film, called Family Stone. I didn't go into the movie expecting to cry, and even half way through the movie I still had no idea I would be crying at the end. But the last few minutes of the movie completely caught me off guard and hit close to home. The premise of the movie is irrelevant, and all I truly remember is that the movie deals with the family's struggle with the mother's cancer. Every year the family has Christmas together, and the last scene of the movie shows the first Christmas without the mother. Yeah, yeah so the movie ends with the mother's death, and I probably wouldn't have cried if it weren't for the fact that I, too, will experience the same event. My mother has cancer, and while she lives today, I do know that one day she won't be here for Christmas, or my birthday, or to see me get married and have children. I, too, will experience the eerie feeling of having lost something so familiar and routine.

The family in the movie dwells on the fact that the mother isn't there, but I believe that when my mom dies she will still be with me. Right, she won't be here in body, but she will definitely be here in spirit. She will live through me. I will be the same type of parent she is—I will strive for top goals like earning a Ph. D. and getting a job that I enjoy. I will tell it how it is and never sugar coat things, like how she tells me I played badly during a game or how my writing is subpar. I hope my mother's qualities will show through me because she is a hell of a person.

The fact that she has cancer hasn't changed who she is, she simply lives with it. I feel like her battle embodies what all people should learn: Sometimes you're hit hard with adversity, and you find out what type of person you are by how you tackle that adversity. My mom has tackled it head on, and is now living her fourth year with Stage IV breast cancer. She fights by living her life normally; she stays up late with a glass of wine, or takes our dog for a healthy walk. I hope my encounter with the first Christmas without her is far in the future; I don't want to feel the pain the children in the movie felt. Until then, I am going to learn as much as I can from her because I want to be like her when I grow up. And when I am on my death bed, I hope I can look back and say I was half the person my mother was.

Issues Influencing All Types of Lucy's Writing about Trauma

The following sections define and clarify several elements that I've observed at work in *all* types of Lucy's writing, at one time or another. First, fluency is the simple act of generating words per minute, the practiced coordination of hand, eye, and brain. Process means the *stages* that one experiences in producing a piece of writing—from vague thoughts you may have while mowing the lawn, to the listing or jotting down of ideas, to revising and editing more finished prose. *Fluency and process*, then, are fundamental to everything else. Without sufficient motivation and time, there would be no chance for Lucy's writing to grow, no chance for her to think and shape and revise her perceptions—no chance to make sense of the unfathomable chaos of her life.

Second, *simultaneous differentiation and integration* seems to occur throughout Lucy's writing. Simply put, this means considering how you are different from other people, and how you are similar to them. Perceived differences, through the act of writing, may confirm the writer's individuality—or may lead the writer to change her perspective and somehow *integrate* these differences into her sense of self, in effect realizing that she "wasn't so different, after all."

Third, *tapping into the inner stream* is an old and venerated concept—and valuable metaphor—for our thinking. Accessing and manipulating our inner stream of consciousness assumes that we are thinking *all the time*—that it is impossible for us *not* to think. We can *witness* our inner stream of thoughts, *focus* it, and, maybe hardest of all, *suspend* our moving stream. Fourth, when writers transform genres, they seem to activate alternative perspectives, which can help their thinking. Finally, I was somewhat surprised at the extent to which these writers connected their own or *local* traumas with larger, global issues.

Fluency and Process

Underlying all of the writing, reading, and interviewing explored in this chapter is the concept of *fluency* in language. Whether we are generating speech or writing, fluency means that the speaker or writer can produce many words per minute. Fluency is fundamental to maximizing the effects of writing for healing because fluency in language is directly connected to our thinking. In short, our language modifies our thought; in turn, this modified thought changes our language, and on and on. Thought and language continually affect each other, spiraling outward as they grow. The more that we can articulate and clarify and think on paper, the more likely we can harness the powers of writing for healing.

Fluency also means that our language has a natural flow to it—that it is often free of tangled syntax, hesitations, and other types of garbled utterance. It does *not* mean that the person's words stream out *perfectly formed* the first time. Fluent writers have to revise, just like everyone else; they just begin from a more *advanced* position and work on different issues than the less fluent. With her advanced education, background, and experience—not to mention her natural talents—Lucy is a fluent writer. No doubts here.

The point is that much of fluency is *learned* over an extended time—through practice with many purposes, audiences, genres, rhetorical contexts, thinking demands, situational and psychological constraints, and revision. While writing is one of the most complex of skills, it is also simple in that it requires practice, just as any other skill does, from driving a car safely, to shooting baskets. Like playing basketball or driving a car, writers, too, must develop automaticity, gained through practice—which in turn increases confidence.

The central issue, then, for novice writers who would benefit from writing for healing is that they could soon become frustrated and give up. Why? Because they think their words somehow *fail*—that they do not reflect what they want them to reflect or that they sound immature or incorrect to the writer. In these cases, writers become overly halting, slowing down to a snail's pace, as they censor themselves *before* they generate enough material. People suffering extreme trauma spend a lot of time worrying, which is natural. But worrying preoccupies us, distracts us from creating and shaping meaning. Lucy describes one technique, which helped her schedule worry so that it would interfere less with her writing and other activities:

> A cancer survivor and work colleague advised on one of his posts back to me that "if he needed to worry [he] told himself he could do that tomorrow; he could carve out a part of tomorrow." That helped so much. Worriers often feel like if they aren't worrying, then they are dropping the ball, they will miss something. So they must worry all the time. Setting a time aside is a mind trick—it allows me to say to myself, "Ok. I am going to do my worry. I even have it on my calendar, so I know I have that taken care of, and I can do something else right now." I know it sounds crazy, but it works for me.

There are few healthy or productive reasons for not writing. These mistaken notions of what writing is and what it should be—upon becoming visible on the page or screen for the first time—brings me to my next point, *process*.

We know from decades of research (e.g., Emig 1971; Flower and Hayes 1989; Murray 1982) that writing does not spring, full-blown, perfect from our first utterance. To get the writing we want, we have to "re-see" it, re-think it, re-view it—revise and reformulate it. This is the natural process that writers go through, often many times over again. *Freewriting* is first-draft writing: It is sloppy, contains grammatical glitches and misspellings, rough, circular, ego-centric, tentative, and often contradictory. First drafts also contain much thinking, because such *sloppy* language is the same kind of language many of us use to think *in* and to think *through*. Initial attempts at writing clarify and solve problems, paving the way for later drafts to qualify assertions, elaborate solutions, question, hypothesize, and speculate.

The writing process is not a microwave oven—it is more of a crockpot: Ideas have to be thought through slowly, sorted out, elaborated, refined, focused, and revised. Process and revision are crucial for writing for healing: The more we work at our writing, the more control we usually feel. These two concepts, fluency and process, are often difficult for those new to writing or for non-writers to internalize. This is a natural response because they have often viewed writing in a *one-and-done* way, similar to building a table, reasoning like this: If I have already made it, why should I construct *another* one?!

SIMULTANEOUS DIFFERENTIATION AND INTEGRATION

James Moffett (1992), William James (1974), and others have clarified a basic thinking process—one that I believe we *cannot help but do*—"simultaneous differentiation and integration." In one sense, to differentiate is to focus on differences, to break a whole into parts, and to analyze these parts. The opposite process, to integrate, is to put these parts back into a new or different whole, to synthesize. These complementary processes are inherent, not just in how we think and process life's changes, but also as a force throughout culture—a basic dichotomy reflected in art, literature, and even nature itself. Consider the following pairs of elements: night and day; light and dark; yin and yang; emotion and reason; tension and equilibrium; complexity and simplicity; life and death.

In simple and practical terms, *differentiation* means accepting or learning how our self *diverges from* others, while *integration* means learning how our selfhood is *akin to* other people or ideas. In short, we are constantly reflecting, consciously or unconsciously, how we are unique and how we are different. When we encounter a serious physical, psychological, or emotional trauma, our sense of self, our core, is shaken and thrown out of whack: We find ourselves no longer the same person we thought we were. This trauma differentiates us. Consequently, some change and readjustment is needed, as we seek to negotiate this rupture, this change, and integrate it into our *new* or re-shaped identity.

This basic process is fundamental in defining who we are, as well as in *healing* or *re-defining* or re-shaping our sense of selfhood. As I have noted throughout this chapter, Lucy has specifically engaged in differentiation and integration through her uses of the *other thing*—some other object for purposes of comparison. Rather than dwelling exclusively on *just* the traumatic issue, she places it next to some other object, event, text, or person, which seems to help—and enlarge—her thinking. This process seems inherent in nearly all of the writing and speaking that Lucy does throughout this chapter. Her following comment supports this assertion:

> I was just re-reading *UpDrafts* (Fox 2000) [Author's Note: Lucy had contributed a chapter to this book] and reading about identity and differentiation and integration and the cancer differentiated and so writing is a way to integrate, so my sense of self isn't broken, and that is the way I could see it as healing. Hmm,

> what if you couldn't see yourself, or what if I couldn't see myself with cancer; what if I couldn't accept it? How that would suck! I guess some people react that way. I actually feel very lucky that I didn't—not lucky to have cancer, but not to feel so irrevocably broken. . . .

Of course, writers do not have to be consciously aware of this basic force, the movement of separation and unification, in order for their writing to work for them, though this awareness could help their overall understanding of their writing, in turn encouraging them to continue.

Tapping into the Inner Stream

Writing through trauma depends upon our tapping into our inner stream of thought and language. In short, a physical and/or psychological rupture in our lives throws us out of our otherwise normal state of equilibrium. The surest way to fix things is to tap into our inner life, to get as much out as we can, then explore it and make logical and reasonable adjustments—and then put the pieces back together into a new or different whole selfhood.

Of course, there are several ways for us to tap into our inner stream— that ever-flowing river of heart and mind—of images, words, sensations, reasoning, perceptions, memories, and emotions. Creative people do it all the time: in music, art, drama, sculpture, dance, and other creative activities. However, in his book, *Coming on Center: English Education in Evolution*, Moffett (1992) articulates how reading and writing remain the most intense, focused, and integrative ways of accessing our inner stream. Writing and reading, Moffett believes, are the purest and most direct way, because, unlike, say, painting, we do not have the other thing—the half-finished canvas in front of us, to act as an "intermediary" or as a kind of "way station" in our transactions. Moffett further notes that,

> Reading and writing are not necessarily superior to some of these such as musical performance or martial arts, which certainly preclude mind-wandering or obsessing, but reading, writing, and meditating induce and sustain concentration to an extraordinary degree *on the inner world itself.* (157)

Writers do, though, have the visible words on the screen or page, which are a form of this *other thing*, but there seem to be differences between words as the other thing and a painting, a sculpture, or a piece of furniture under construction. With painting, for example, we tend to focus on the canvas for longer periods of time and in different ways due primarily to its commanding and tangible form.[1] On the other hand, we tend to view visible words differently, as more ephemeral. Visible words seem to *dissolve* or flow more quickly back into our thoughts—which, in turn, evoke new and different modified language, as the process rapidly spirals. It's important to note here that tapping into our inner stream also changes the inner stream itself, eventually modifying, or *expanding* our thought patterns and perceptions, which is crucial, of course, for purposes of writing for healing.

Practitioners of meditation and others who focus on the development of our inner speech and thinking processes (e.g., Ornstein and Naranjo 1977; Moffett 1992; Kabat-Zinn 2011) describe three basic ways for tapping into our inner stream: *witnessing* the inner stream, *focusing* the inner stream, and *suspending* the inner stream.[2] Briefly, witnessing the inner stream is becoming aware of our flow of thoughts, images, and sensations—of slowing down to hear ourselves think. Focusing the inner stream involves actively directing it, concentrating it in some way, as we alter, select, and manipulate our thinking. (Suspending the inner stream is examined in the next section.)

This type of introspection seems similar to Mihaly Csikszentmihalyi's Flow Theory—discussed in more detail in Chapter 5, "Kate." When we engage in pleasurable yet challenging activities, we can become so intensely engrossed that we lose awareness of time and our physical surroundings (Csikszentmihalyi 1990). Engaging in the pleasures of a flow experience, Csikszentmihalyi demonstrates, helps us develop a more integrated and complex self. Here, the author clearly distinguishes between "pleasure" and "enjoyment." "Pleasure," on one hand, is associated with little effort or attention on the seeker's part—no more than, say, eating a chocolate truffle. "Enjoyment," on the other hand, demands focused attention and deep concentration. Its reward is a sense of accomplishment and productivity.

Such enjoyment is what often happens to writers in the act of writing—or reading. They find it so enjoyable that language may become their life's work, as it has with the people explored in this book. They see language and writing as worthwhile and permanent, unlike the far more ephemeral "pleasures" that quickly dissipate. This enjoyment in creating—and re-creating—ourselves into more complex beings is the active ingredient in motivating literate behaviors and in constructing meaning, regardless of the form it takes. Of course, this is *not* to say that those who write for purposes of healing are having a peachy time doing so, but they *trust in the process* sufficiently to see them through. Both Lucy and Kate stated directly that such in-flow and deeply absorbing writing usually resulted in such feelings of enjoyment.

Suspending our inner stream means silencing it, turning it off, and discarding the *buzz* of thinking inside our heads, so that we can become clear of it. Of course, witnessing, focusing, and suspending our inner stream are not tidy, distinct categories, but useful for understanding writing about trauma. Lucy seemed to show evidence of these three types of accessing her inner stream.

Witnessing Her Inner Stream. In responding to a student's writing for healing, Lucy stated, "It may have started the healing process because she voiced it, which is really important." Several times throughout our conversations, Lucy mentions the importance of "voicing" the issue at hand—of naming it as a first step. Here, acknowledging the existence of a phenomenon by merely naming it or "voicing" it is how she witnesses her inner stream. You must slow down the fast blur of life before you can name anything.

Focusing Her Inner Stream. Most of the previous excerpts of Lucy's writing show an active mind at work, as she harnesses her lived experiences: manipulating her language and thoughts, as she compares, contrasts, defines, analyzes, synthesizes, and dissects. In the following passage, she describes the family dog, Gunnar.

> Getting the good scan results has helped my spirits immensely. When I get depressed or when I am having some physical side effects from the chemo, I tend to think, "Ok, this is it, there is only one way to go from here." So I am amazed when I come out of a funk or my body rebounds. We have a 12 year old dog, Gunnar, who is starting to ail—his one leg has atrophied and one eye doesn't work (I posted two pics of him). But, man, in his day, he was a barrel chested beast of a dog (beast in a good way). So full of life and muscle. Now he is thin and drags his leg around and if we don't line the wood floors with swaths of rug, he is left hostage in whatever room we last attended. When it began, we would think, Ok this is it, but then with some cortisone pills, he bounces back. Not totally. To most other people, he looks like he is in pretty bad shape. But I look at him and

> think "thank you, Gunnar, for showing me the way." It really feels like he is my mentor in living and dying. He is allowing me to experience it with him. I have so much respect for Ole Gun. The way he still smiles and wags his tail and gets the hop in his step when we go out. I don't see him as pathetic. I don't feel sorry for him. And I tell my family—I will look like him one day and I don't want to be pitied or feel pathetic.

Here, Lucy directs her attention first to herself, then to her dog, then back to herself, each time selecting which details to include and how to construct them. She chooses to quote one of her thoughts aimed at the dog, selecting the details of his smile, tail, and the hop in his step. Her language moves from the general and abstract: "respect," "pathetic," and "mentor in living and dying" to the specific and concrete: "cortisone pills," "barrel-chested beast of a dog," and "line the wood floors with swaths of rug." In creating the entries for the *Caring Bridge* website, Lucy observed that they "made me feel calmer . . . made me think, 'What *do* I think?' and helped me redirect my thoughts to what's most important . . . and even beyond clichés. You can only say, 'my family's important to me' so many times." Lucy's more public writing for healing, then, helps her focus her inner stream—prioritizing, connecting, and communicating in a more tempered way.

Another way to focus the inner stream is to use information from external or secondary sources that help writers position themselves within the *larger* context of their trauma. Such objective information can include facts, statistics, chronologies of events, and interviews with experts. Integrating secondary-source information with our personal writing helps to convince us of a simple fact that is all too easy to be obscured when writing for healing—that we are not alone, as Lucy describes:

> I have articles I really like and I write about why I like them. Also, repeating what doctors and nurses say about treatment options and their effects is another way of placing me into a larger context, which gives me confidence, so I don't feel alone. It also gives me a sense of credibility; I know how to talk about it. I verify what doctors and nurses say and compare one doctor against another. I have two doctors that I see and I compare what they say with each other and with other sources. The doctor's resource librarian sends me articles about relevant topics.

The BCmets.org list serve includes conferences, articles, and all kinds of resources.

Suspending Her Inner Stream. Suspending the inner stream is the opposite side of focusing it. Particularly for writers, the force and rush of thoughts can be exhausting. A truce is periodically needed. Silence can be clarifying and restorative in itself. In response to my question, "How do you turn your mind off?" Lucy wrote:

> What do I do—I think I read or watch TV—it usually happens at night, when I am trying to fall asleep, my brain will just run and run—the quiet of everything doesn't offer the distraction. I guess I go to story—I want to be in someone else's story—that is the best way to get out of mine. Other things I do—like drive or clean—those help me think, or those are times I am really thinking, even exercising . . . so I have to have something that draws me out of me, and that is stories—the only other thing is watching my kids play basketball—I get totally absorbed in their games—which are definitely stories! I remember the day I was diagnosed Katie had a playoff game and we went—John was the coach—and it felt so good—I felt weird and diff but I could lose myself in the game. . . .

TRANSFORMING GENRES

During the time frame of this study, Lucy had transformed some of her initial writings for healing into poetry, into an actual dialogue with her oncologist, into a reflective essay, and into a brief informational writing. As discussed in the previous section, when she focused her inner stream in certain ways. One important way of directing our inner stream is to funnel our initial freewritings into different forms or genres. Mixing and transforming one genre into another is a classical but seldom-used way of (re)focusing our inner stream, even among literacy experts. Its chief value resides in the relatively nuanced ways it can modify our perceptions of the original content.

Following is an example of one initial, raw writing Lucy composed about four months after being diagnosed with Stage IV Metastatic Breast Cancer. She made few substantial changes to the first writing, when she revised it the following day. However, she also highlighted certain parts, as I've indicated here with italics. Nearly seven months later, she transformed this prose into a poem.

Revised Freewriting (August 29, 2008)

Not sure how to say it all—feels like the numbness and adrenaline has worn off. I do think that is what happened. I got diagnosed and my adrenaline kicked right in—tried to fight off this monumental weight, like lifting a car off a child, but that can be sustained only so long. It was as if I was high. I don't think I was in denial, but just feeling so awakened by this major change in my life, and now, it is every day—I feel like it consumes me more, I get scared more, like fuck, I don't want to go yet, not that I will, I am on a website with all mets gals and some have been living 10 years, some with very few side effects, but I guess it is like any process, I am in this place, where it seems pretty f-ing real, and I just can't picture the end—*to imagine never coming back, never ever seeing the kids or john again—it is like a black void in my head, that is how I picture it.*

I do pray and my relationship with god is in its infant stage, but I do well with asking god to be with me, not to take the fear away but to be with me, to help me keep putting one foot in front of the other. I think about it, and I am not even suffering, I mean women are really suffering, in pain, with all sorts of complications, so I feel kind of guilty even sounding so morbid. Is that from my healthy dose of TV drama? I guess it is in one way: my head can say death is inevitable, and I suck everything I can out of each day, but the truth *is I want to be here, I want to be grandma, I want John to be grandpa and me grandma, and have our farmhouse and have grandchildren waddle over around the pond and Katie run after her little ones and Nicholas patiently pick one of his up—what that must feel like to see your children grow up and have children of their own—*must just beautiful, like to breathe it all in, to see it and want to capture it, and now I can kind of see another reason people write—I mean *how do you hold on to all that is so precious and so fleeting at the same time? How do you hold on to that sunset or that perfect dusk night or making pancakes while Nicholas does dishes and Katie does the puzzle, and we each, in our own space rock out to Donna Sommers' Last Dance. Painters and writers and musicians—I think that is* *what they are trying to do or that is what they are capable of doing even if they don't realize it.*

It's also a way to take oneself out of the ego. That it isn't about you writing and your ego; it's bigger than that, it is connected to god and community and appreciation, and that what we have is so precious, it sounds so cliché but precious in that fragile and strong and breathtaking and out of body way.

This unvarnished piece is typical of Lucy's live-wire thinking. It contains several metaphors and images. It expresses oppositions. It curses as well as qualifies, running from one extreme to the other. She speculates, hypothesizes, questions. Her images of the future become more vivid and intense as she goes.

Poem of February 24, 2009, Transformed from Revised Freewriting of August 29, 2008.

How do writers, painters,
I
Stave off
The black void?
The inevitable unimaginable?
How do writers, painters,
I
Capture desire,
Heart-squeezing want?
I want to be here, to be grandma and grandpa
At the farmhouse with green fields, yellow tall grass waving
Pond water crystalline, flickering sunlight
And grandchildren waddling over, just out of their mother's outstretched arms—
My Katie, arms flailing, giddy laugh
My Nicholas, tempered walk, long bend down and gentle scoop of his youngest
Rests him on his hip, looks at us, and smiles.
How do the writers, painters
I
Hold on
To the fleeting, the perfect, the
Nights
Of making pancakes, while

> Nicholas does the dishes and Katie works the puzzle and we
> Each in our space, rock out
> To Donna Summers
> Last Dance?

Lucy selects the images and what she sees as the most important elements of the free write, and she puts them into sharper focus as a poem with short lines. Poetry forces emphasis and compression. She has added more detail to key images. By interspersing "I" with "writers, painters," Lucy sets up a tension—however unfounded—between what they do and what she hopes to accomplish. A secondary opposition—and a more poignant one—is the image of her family members being individuals, doing their own thing—as well as doing it *together*. We talked about this transformation of genres and its effects.

> RF: In your writing about trauma, what does recasting it into a poem do for you or mean to you?
>
> LUCY: For me, it makes it more of a public piece and I think the free write or the narrative is sort of the journal. . . . From my schooling and training I learnt what a poem can do, so try to capture one moment out of that . . . taking it from that journal to something that someone else could get something from. . . .
>
> RF: Okay for another audience—but does it do anything for *you?*
>
> LUCY: Yeah, it's fun for me to do, and it felt like I had accomplished something. Those emotions that I had in the poem, I felt like, "Okay, I have that now."
>
> RF: You mean you now had something that was. . . .
>
> LUCY: Permanent.
>
> RF: Yes, permanent—and something more grounded, more artful?
>
> LUCY: Well, yeah. I think the freewriting is useful. I have to do it to get something out, but the poem for me feels like I don't have to be forgetting that emotion that I had or those images that I had in my head, because now they're in the poem. The free write . . . I don't know . . . it's kind of messy to me, because in the free write, I wasn't sure yet what I wanted to say.
>
> RF: Okay. So putting it into a poem makes it clearer or sharper?
>
> LUCY: Yeah, and then I can share it. When I finished the poem I think I revised it even again a little bit, so the poem is a way

for me to share it with my family or whoever. That's the way for me to communicate some very deep feelings.

RF: When you do the poem, does it expand or elaborate your ideas or compress them?

LUCY: I think it elaborates. What I like about it is that in the poem I can focus just on this image I have of me being a grandmother. It forces me to play that sort of vision out and everything that's around it.

RF: Okay—so it does *both:* the poem compresses and focuses, but also allows you to elaborate?

LUCY: Yes.

Connecting Local with Global Concerns

I had been reading about a conference focused on global issues, such as environmental degradation, poverty, and social changes brought on by rapidly changing technology, when I decided to ask the people I was interviewing if they ever connected their own, personal traumas to larger, more global issues. I did not expect that these literacy experts—being finite, local, and human—would have much to say about such a connection. I was wrong, as my conversation with Lucy illustrates.

RF: Do global issues or huge news events impinge upon your writing for healing in any way?

LUCY: I do feel a sense of urgency. Writing about fear, emotion, joy—there's a connection between the things I write, such as emotions and fears and joys that have come along with being diagnosed with a fatal disease, getting that out there I think there's a connection there, but there's a disconnect now, which allows us to perpetuate wars and social injustice . . . and things like that. The voice in my head is much louder now regarding things like social justice. . . .

RF: Tell me about the link between what you write about and social justice . . .

LUCY: I think that what I write about is how issues of agency, of voice, of recognizing fear have always been interesting to me but are way more, much more clear to me now. Those are the same issues as social justice, especially in the schools. So, if I'm talking about agency, of letting go of thinking I can control the disease, that I can fix it—if I let go of that—I'm actually in more control in another way. And that's how I think about teaching. . . .

In the dominant culture we've been taught to think that we CAN control things; the Teacher Ed program here teaches our students to be scared—so fear is their frame of reference. My point is that students are taught that they can control every aspect of the classroom, so they don't have to be scared of getting fired or being called in to the Principal's office. So, I can write about fears I've dealt with in having cancer and see a direct connection to how teachers and pre-service teachers are behaving.

My sense of urgency is so clear to me now, the issue is so huge. Teachers are taught that they are inadequate. It's taught in that there's only one way to do it, that they need lesson plans. And if that doesn't work out, then it's the teacher's fault.

Last night in my class we were talking about this fear and a student said, "What if I get a parent that calls?" and I said, "You want a job with a guarantee that a parent will never call?!" They're not taught in methods courses about having any kind of professional identity. They are not taught to explain to parents "This is why we did what we did."

Lucy definitely links her own fears to the professional fears of her fledgling teachers, realizing that they both need a greater sense of agency, of knowing that *they* can and should act upon the world, not just suffer their way through life as victims. This linking of local and personal to the global is also evident in Lucy's writing and the resulting poem explored earlier. There, she connects her own situation to community, to writers and artists, and to God.

I can only surmise that writers who somehow link their own writing about trauma to other people and issues beyond their own boundaries are helped in at least a couple of ways. First, as earlier noted, the connection places them into a larger context where they have to sense that they are not the only person fighting the good fight. Second, when the larger context is at least somewhat developed (e.g., Lucy reads some medical research articles recommended), the chances increase that she may hit upon new ideas, new questions, and new perceptions. Third, exploring the more objective language of outside sources can serve to temper or counter-balance our "up-close-and-personal" writing for healing, which can subtly influence or soften our intense prose.

Conclusion

In one conversation, I asked Lucy about "oppositions" in her writing about trauma. What she said is a fitting conclusion for this chapter:

> I do see oppositions and conflicts and tensions in my writing. I do see that and I think they're helpful. The [main] opposition is negotiating the cultural norms about how one "should" behave—and trusting myself. And the benefit of writing is that every time I write, I become more confident. If I don't do this, it would be debilitating!

In her easy, casual way, Lucy taps into what, ultimately, may be the single most powerful reason for anyone to write anything: making a mark on a page to clarify yourself, to trust yourself, so this cycle of growth can begin again and again.

4 Seven Writers Composing in Word and Image

In the previous discussion, visual thinking and imagistic language played fundamental roles in Lucy's composing about trauma—from motivating writing, to generating ideas; from tapping into her inner stream of consciousness, to casting ideas into metaphors. Now we turn to how writers "up the ante" by also interacting with actual, physical images. When these are added to the mix, thinking and writing can become even more combustible. This chapter, then, contains brief portraits of seven writers using visuals in their composing through trauma. All were enrolled in my graduate course, except for one middle school student and one junior high school student, whom I worked with separately.

In "Healing Images: Historical Perspectives," Anees A. Sheikh (2003) illustrates how pictorial images (like language) have long demonstrated "healing":

> The ancient literature of numerous cultures abounds with accounts of spectacular cures resulting from the imaging process. These accounts are now being corroborated by a growing body of clinical and experimental evidence. The effectiveness of mental imagery in the treatment of a wide variety of problems has been documented (Epstein, 1989; Naparstek, 1994; Sheikh, 1983). These include: obesity (Bornstein and Sipprelle, 1973), insomnia (Sheikh, 1976), phobias and anxieties (Habeck and Sheikh, 1984; Meichenbaum, 1977; Singer, 1974); depression (Schultz, 1984), sexual malfunctions (Singer and Switzer, 1980); chronic pain (Jaffee and Bresler, 1980; Korn and Johnson, 1983; McCaffery and Beebe, 1989), fibroid tumors (Pickett, 1987–1988), cancer (Hall, 1984), and a host of other ailments (Sheikh, 1984, 2002; Sheikh, Kunzendorf, and Sheikh, 1996).

I've long been convinced that images, whether we receive them, send them, or think in them, constitute the most basic unit, the DNA, of our personal and professional lives (e.g., Fox, 1979, 1994; Fleckenstein, 2003). This is equally true in how they can help us demystify trauma. (For a more detailed discussion of imagery, please see "Other Symbols" in Chapter 1.)

Since the early 1980s, I've taught a wide variety of writing courses, along with courses in the teaching of writing, literature, language, and media. Long ago, I created a writing prompt called, "The Snapshot." I asked writers to select a family photo that was somehow meaningful to them, an early attempt to integrate visual and verbal thinking with pictures. I asked writers to identify a visual element within the photo, such as the arm of a friend loosely draped around another person, or how one person in the photo was apart from the others. Next, they were to use this visual element as a springboard for explaining a larger theme, such as a deep affection that turned out not to be what it appeared or how the *separated* person in the photo actually became socially isolated later in life. This was before the days of computer manipulation of text and images, so students used a copy machine to reproduce the photo within their papers.

I kept using this assignment because it helped writers demonstrate excellent connective thinking and writing. Back then, my purpose was not primarily therapeutic—though if that also occurred, great. Rather, I wanted to help teachers and others to recognize and develop their students' cognitive abilities, especially those of analysis and synthesis. It served this purpose well.

In the early 1990s, Lori, a graduate student, was heading to Los Angeles to work with a friend over spring break in an inner-city school. She asked me for ideas in teaching "at risk" inner-city, middle-school kids. Computer manipulation of imagery was now more common, and I had been thinking of asking students to alter or manipulate a photo so that it would portray what *should have been* the truth, not what the camera had actually recorded. At this time, I was reading and learning more about "writing as a way of healing." I naturally merged this study with my lifelong work in visual and media literacy and re-named this assignment "Fixing the Photo." I suggested to Lori that she try this assignment with the students she planned to work with. Lori returned and showed me her results. Following is how one student, Juan, responded to these activities.

Juan

Juan, a middle school student, wrote about the altered image—how and why he made changes to his original photo.

Figure 4.1. Juan's Fixed Photo. Source: Lori Wilson (pseudonym)]

Juan's Writing about His Fixed Photo

> The original picture has a blue background and is the right color with the three people. The character relationship is they are all cousins by law but they are aunt, uncle, and nephew by blood. The way they are close together shows an effect that they are related. I think this is one of my favorite pictures because I like all my cousins.
>
> A thing I changed in the picture was the background and added black and white scribbles. I changed the background because it's crazy like the way they are related. I added the lines to show that rape was involved with the relationship because of the mother of the brother and sister. The white lines represent that the person that was hurt is living a healthy life, and the black

is to show kind of, like her life was scarred. The effect that the scribbles have is the relationship. I think this revision has made the picture different in a big way.

Another thing I changed was the way they are put; I put the brother and sister away from the baby. I changed the way they were put to show they live far apart from each other. I also put an inverted colored picture in the middle to show they have a hard time communicating. I think that has a big effect, because it changes the way they are limited to communicate. I think this was an important revision because communication is big with a family relation.

Juan knows how to think and how to express himself in language. First, he well knows that his original photo, as a kind of *map* of reality, does not match his actual world or territory—a basic principle of general semantics. While Juan does not provide sufficient detail for readers to untangle the legal and familial relationships he notes, he likely understands this complexity himself. His thinking is highly *relational* in terms of space, color, and time. He evaluates these relationships, including his conclusion that some of the individuals do not communicate well with each other. Juan also uses black and white colors as symbols and an inverted image to communicate larger issues or conclusions. He synthesizes, referring to these relationships as "crazy" and provides evidence for his assertion—that the people are "cousins by law but they are aunt, uncle, and nephew by blood."

The types of thinking strategies Juan uses here have long been described as necessary for academic success. However, Juan's school had completely given up on him. He seldom came to class and never completed assignments, except for this one, which somehow caught his interest. I like to think that Juan somehow benefitted by imposing this bit of order on his life. Eventually, Juan's altered image and brief writing became a kind of "tipping point" for me, so I designed a new graduate course that fused writing and images—and sometimes, music and video—to address trauma. The remaining writers you'll meet in this chapter were enrolled in this same graduate course, offered occasionally over the past ten years.

The graduate course focuses on three basic processes: (1) exploring psychological and/or physiological wellness; (2) using spoken and written language to explore these issues; and (3) creating and manipulating internal and external imagery in tandem with using language. The writers here are also language experts—experienced teachers and writers, who completed a series of assignments in which they addressed a particular physical, mental, or emotional trauma or issue of their choice. Two of the writers explored in this chapter are not language experts—at least not yet. They are students I've added in because of how they responded to the same assignment as the graduate students. One is a middle-school student, and the other is an eighth grader whose teacher (who was enrolled in my graduate class) and parents encouraged her to write about her family issues, using the same prompt as the others.

The heart of the course consists of ten assignments I designed specifically to engage my graduate-level college students in using writing and imagery, in equal measure, for purposes of healing—about one project each week. Students had to actively manipulate imagery in different ways, just as we manipulate written language. These assignments allowed writers a lot of choices within a framework. The assignments were revealed three at a time, so that future assignments would not influence their work on the current set. These assignments included "Synesthesia," "Entrance into Another World," "The Monster and the Angel," and "Conversation across Time." (See Chapter 2 for details of assignments.) The college students also read relevant books and articles, such as Louise DeSalvo's *Writing as a Way of Healing* (1999) and Michelle Payne's "A Strange Unaccountable Something: Historicizing Sexual Abuse Essays" (2000). Other readings included literary selections that focus on trauma in some way, such as an excerpt from Maya Angelou's 1969 autobiography, *I Know Why the Caged Bird Sings*. Readings were often followed by oral discussions and informal writings.

As a safeguard, I always listed the name and contact information for the counseling psychologist *on call* for the semester. We never needed to contact these kind volunteers. Students regularly met in small response groups to review each other's writing, focusing on strengths, weaknesses, and possible revisions. I also provided written and oral responses to each writer.

I told students on the first day that formal grades were off the table; they would be graded on active participation in discussing reading, completing all writing and imagery assignments, which would not receive a formal grade, a necessary ingredient in this unusual instructor-student relationship. In short, I could not ask people to write about their fears when they might be afraid to say something. Although the following writers are very different people, they quickly harness word and image for purposes of facing their own important issues.

Minji

Minji, a student from South Korea, focused on an important "lost love" for the assignment called, *The Monster and the Angel*. Eight years earlier, as a college undergraduate, Minji experienced a serious relationship with a young man she worked with at a pub. He entered the army and, upon release, broke off their relationship by not returning her phone calls. Minji is a very bright, poised, and serious young woman who was deeply hurt by this sudden termination.

The Monster and the Angel assignment asked writers to compose a letter to their personal "monster"—a traumatic experience or issue, as well as a letter to their "angel"—a very positive force in their life or the best "counter-point" to their monster. It was important that writers *physically re-construct the image of the monster into a completely new image of the angel*, so that they could be immersed in the transformation via composing with several senses, not just written words. Following are the instructions for this assignment.

- As prewriting for this paper, please list the major issues that severely depress and frustrate you (or, you can use the list created on the first night of class).
- Next, select *one* of these and write a letter to this "monster" OR write a poem TO this monster or ABOUT this monster. Next, create or find an image of the monster you wrote to, and place it into a PowerPoint slide.
- Then, take the image of the monster apart, piece by piece, and reassemble it to depict your new "angel"—or some other creature that is far more benign than your original critter. *You must physically and actually take apart the pieces and re-arrange them into something more friendly and positive.*
- Finally, write a piece that explains, analyzes, and reflects on this experience.

Minji's Monster and Angel Assignment

Following is Minji's poem about her monster and her image of the monster. Appearing next is her monster re-configured as an angel. Following that is Minji's written reflection on her work.

> Cruel Beauty in the Red Thorns
>
> Red, the blood
> Coming from your words like a needle
> Red, the blood
> Coming from your smile like a spear
> Red, the blood
> Coming from your promise like a bar in a prison cell
> Red, the blood
> Coming from your love like a thorn on a rose
> Why do you disguise love in red
> Piercing my mind
> Bleeding my mind
> If you would kiss me forever

Figure 4.2. Minji's Monster: *Bleeding Thorns.* Source: Minji (pseudonym)

Figure 4.3. Minji's Angel: *The Heart of an Angel.* Source: Minji (pseudonym)

Minji's Written Reflection on Her Monster and Angel

The theme of my poem is basically about change. People change and so do their behaviors, sayings, promises, and their mind. In the monster picture, each bar refers to each thing that people change.

I described how this monster is hurting my mind, as if it is stabbing me with a delicately sharpened knife. That is why the monster has many thorns. Each point refers to a thorn stabbing and hurting my mind and memory. And the color of red indicates the bleeding from my mind caused by each piercing thorn.

It was not hard for me to create this monster. Interestingly, the red monster with thorns was an initial image that came up in my mind when first thinking of a monster. I visualized it as an explosion, with each thorn piercing and hurting my mind.

Then, I reformed the monster into an angel of a heart. The heart is my symbol for love. I cut the monster into pieces and re-arranged them into a heart with an additional full heart inside. I tried to use each point to link, one by one, in order to disguise what it was originally. I did not want anyone to get hurt from these points, because I know it is really heart breaking and painful. Connecting the points together, I came to have the outer heart frame at the end. I especially tried to face the sharp points inside, so that again, no one, including me, would get hurt from them. So I put the six points together facing the center of the heart as if each pair of the points was holding hands together. I meant this part to show reunion and togetherness.

I had a wish that our relationship would be a full-hearted love without any breaks. So I placed the full-hearted love inside of the big heart. Each thorn came to make the big heart frame. In the frame, I visualized that he and I were holding hands together. Under this idea of togetherness, I imagined we could have the full heart of our love.

I realized that I was still imagining, "What if we were not separated from each other?" And this imagination made it possible to reconstruct the monster to the angel of the heart. Overall, my re-arrangement included hidden meanings of love, reunion, no harm, togetherness, protection, safety, and fullness. I acknowledged that these were the wishes I had hoped to see in our relationship, what it looks like, and how my memory of him remains positive in my mind.

When Minji shared her writing and images with her small group, I was impressed with how she engaged in the whole process. (I sat in on a different group each class and did my best to remain silent, but this guarantee was not foolproof.) I asked her to "write up" exactly what she did and what she was thinking while she did it. Her response follows:

I made several copies of the monster in case I made mistakes. Sitting at my desk and cutting the monster into pieces, I was thinking how to reform the monster into an angel. The first thing that came to my mind was that I was uncomfortable with the spikes and the points. I did not like those because their sharpness seemed to hurt me even though it was just visual and nothing that would hurt my mind in reality.

I was playing with the scraps, especially the spike-shaped pieces, thinking how to make them into a shape that was not harmful and dangerous. Once I tried to make a big circle connecting the points with each other. Then, I came to have a dodecagon shape left at the end. I just put it inside of the circle. Suddenly, I thought that the dodecagon could be heart-shaped if I cut it in a smoother way.

I pulled out another copy of the monster and cut it into pieces again. I also thought to recreate the big circle into a big heart shape this time; the little heart inspired me to create the big heart. I tried to link the points with each other again, making the big heart frame. While making the heart frame, I visually imagined that he and I would hold hands together. This image finally made me have the three pairs of two spikes—each point was a hand; the symbolic image of holding hands together shows reunion and togetherness. Then, I put the little heart inside of the big heart I recreated.

Once, I tried to cut the little heart in half and put each half on each side. It looked like ears at first, but I meant to have them as wings of the angel. However, I realized that I did not like cutting the little heart in half, because it seemed to symbolize separation to me. Also, having wings was not satisfactory either, because I thought having the wings would symbolize flying. The big heart seemed to fly away if I put wings on each side, which would never happen in reality.

Finally, I decided not to cut the little heart in half, rather to keep the original heart and put it in the center of the big heart. I liked how the big heart was made and how the little heart was placed. Also, I liked seeing how each point was smoothly connected with the others; therefore, the spikes did not look dangerous or hurt anyone. I was satisfied with the meanings I put in the angel that imply protection, safety, stability, full-heartedness, reunion, and togetherness.

The simplicity and elegance of these images do not hint at the interplay between Minji's verbal and visual thinking processes. In all, this project helped Minji crystalize this issue, one she had been addressing, in different ways, as the varied assignments requested, throughout the course. The poem seems to serve as a kind of "launching pad" for the two images, and once she is immersed in physically manipulating the pieces of the monster image, she seems to move beyond the poem—which is one of the reasons to add imagery to language in the first place. They can help writers to think in different ways, to move in new directions, than if they had remained in the "verbal tracks" already created solely with words.

Her poem seems sufficiently effective and interesting—but not as intriguing as her visual monster and angel. The "cruel beauty" in the title is a promising opposition in the title, but it's ignored until the final line. The short lines and stanzas, as well as the similes, add to the feelings of sharp, cutting pain—the internal made external. This decision communicates but also objectifies her feelings, gets them out and visible—the power of self-disclosure. However, at least in Western culture, red, blood, knives, and thorns are clichéd expressions, though this may be less true, or not at all true, for Korean culture.

Nonetheless, I didn't pretend to understand everything in her poem and in her written reflection on her images. Here are some intriguing observations about Minji's work:

- First, she made "several copies" of her monster in case she made mistakes. She planned to compose from abundance, not from slim pickings, a good move that experienced writers know. Her fear of "mistakes," though, was possibly more of a cultural influence—that there must have been a right and a wrong way to go about such an open-ended project.

- Second, sitting at her desk and cutting the monster into pieces allowed her to physically disassemble her monster but also allowed her time to think—specifically that she was uncomfortable with the spikes and points of the image, because they (rightly) suggested harm. She noted here that she felt this way, even though she realized they were mere shapes made of paper—an anchor to reality. Minji's realization of the dangers of sharp things steered her toward creating something more benign—she wanted no one to get hurt in all this messy issue of lost love. This, I view as a kind of turning point, given her apparent anger at the deceptive young man in her poem.

- Next, the dodecagon led her to think of a circle, which in turn led her to think of a heart shape. And both shapes more directly reflected her desire that nobody be harmed by sharp angles and points. The small heart inside the large heart led her to think of her and her friend holding hands together. In her words, "three pairs of two spikes, each point was a hand." I didn't see what she stated, but I *did* see the bottom of the heart looking like two hands encircling, cradling everything inside—an inventive, powerful *hidden* image I would not have noticed had she not explained it when speaking and writing.

Would Minji have arrived at such thinking just through writing? I don't know. But what I appreciate most is that she indeed arrived at this kind of protective stance, that she did not really loathe the guy for standing her up, eight years earlier. This was a turning point for Minji because she had focused on the issue all semester, quietly showing anger and feelings of betrayal for her friend's "disguising his love in red."

Anne

In contrast to Minji's subtle and cerebral approach, Anne, a veteran junior-high English Language Arts teacher, is crystal clear and definitive, even in her open-ended, informal, exploratory writing. Anne chose to focus on body image to address the same assignment, *The Monster and the Angel*. Anne also chose to write a poem about (and to) her monster. She also used her computer to manipulate words and images. Although I preferred the more *physical* approach of actually tearing up an image and re-constructing it in some different, more positive way, Anne well succeeded.

Anne's Monster and the Angel Assignment

Following are Anne's poem, the graphic Monster she created, her graphic Angel, and her written reflection on all of them.

That Figure

Where have you gone, that figure from old?
We fit in with everyone
and never felt we were big.
But times change. Now you are told
that you are someone
who needs to eat fig.
Lose weight, slim down, we'll mold
you so you aren't a ton.
Why can't you be a twig?
Mom said, "You don't look like gold.
All will make fun.
Why do you want to look like a pig?"
Sometimes I feel like I could fold,
just disappear and be done.
Would she do a jig?
Then, I look beside me, I don't feel cold,
I feel the love of one
who loves me more than trig.
I will break the mold and shine on my own.
The beauty I have within will blind.
They won't wonder why she isn't
but instead insist she rocks that body.
I don't have to fit that figure.
My muscled thighs and blue eyes
can commandeer a man's heart
and keep me feeling loved.

Seven Writers Composing in Word and Image 137

Figure 4.4. Anne's Monster. Source: Anne (pseudonym)

Figure 4.5. Anne's Angel. Source: Anne (pseudonym)

Anne's Written Reflection

> This was the image I was kind of going for, my Angel. For so long my mother harped on me about losing weight and being more like her (never a day over 118). One year I lost over a hundred pounds and passed out in her arms at 125 pounds. After a day in the hospital, she continued to pressure me to keep losing more.
>
> A month later I met the man who I would marry, in a lot of ways my real Angel. He taught me to love myself. He gave me permission to be who I am, as long as I am healthy. Through the years, I still battle with depression about my weight. I remind myself, I am healthy and I am happy and I am loved. I have to learn to face the fact that I don't have to fit the mold of the female figure. I enjoyed writing the poem and taking apart multiple copies of the original monster to make my Angel on slide 2. I'm me World. Learn to deal.

In this lucid style, Anne wrote about four issues throughout the course: (1) feelings of never fitting in with her peers; (2) her body image, fueled by an overly critical mother; (3) her inability to conceive a child due to a medical condition; and (4) a rape during her college years. I did not feel like she was addressing too many topics, because she so intelligently matched issues with assignments, as well as articulated her ideas so completely yet concisely.

Like Minji, Anne's poem seems of secondary importance to her illustrated monster and angel. First, as I told Anne when she read it in class, it is reminiscent of Sylvia Plath's poem, *Daddy* (1981). Anne, though, was not familiar with Plath, so there was no literary influence. Stanzas 3–5, using a direct quote from her mother and the question, "Would she do a jig?" showed the most resentment or anger, which was then resolved with a description of her husband's unconditional acceptance. Overall, inserting the words of her poem inside of the two figures was Anne's most creative decision here, in that she emphasizes that *all* human bodies are mere outlines and shapes, concealing the thinking, feelings, and language residing within them.

I would not do justice to Anne's courage unless I also showed how she addressed an issue she had never discussed—her rape. Following is her response to an assignment that asked writers to directly recount their issue in a third-person, reportorial, just-the-facts style.

The college freshman had never paid for a concert ticket in her life. However, for this concert, The Greatest Rap Show Ever, her father couldn't get tickets. So, she and her friends purchased tickets for this December 1991 concert.

They dressed up, took photos, and went to the show. After enjoying the show, they went to the hotel next door where more music was going on. She and her friends, aged 17 to 18, met a group of boys, aged 17 to 21. They saw them again. After hanging out this time, the group seemed to couple off.

She found herself with a young man named Rob. He was a student in a different town. The two hit it off. During the course of the break the group would hang out.

She returned home one weekend in March without her car and her parents knowing. She stayed with her friend, Andrea. Then, Sam, whose college was about forty minutes away from hers, offered her a ride. They didn't get to his apartment until late and he asked if he could drive her home the next morning. She agreed.

That night he raped her. She said no. He wouldn't stop. He forced himself on her. He held her down as he tried to force his penis into her mouth. She tried to shake her head back and forth and say no. Eventually he got angry and moved off of her. She didn't know what to do. The blood, the feeling of violation.

She went to the restroom. Another one of Sam's friends, one she had met before, looked at her with an apologizing eye. It was like he knew what happened to her. The shame she felt was too much.

She slept in a ball all night. She sat in the back seat the whole way back with S and his friend. Finally, she was able to escape the nightmare. She returned to her room, showered, and slept. She probably would have stayed there if she hadn't had to go to work.

All she could think about was the loss of her virginity at eighteen. The scare of what had happened. What could she do? She rode home with him. It was her fault for putting herself in that situation. She tried to talk to her sister about it but she couldn't bring herself to share the details. She spoke to Andrea, but again, couldn't really discuss the whole situation.

Her life of isolation began. It would take months before she could trust a man again.

While Anne *may* have mentioned this incident to her small response-group, I believe this was the first time she had *reported* her experience in a public venue; that is, to her group members and to me; the rest of the class did not see it. Brief paragraphs, short sentences, few if any wasted words, third-person, and *objective* tone, added up to a stark narrative, as requested.

In her final message about the course, Anne noted:

> I definitely feel like a different person as this semester winds down. I have come to grips with a very serious incident: forcible rape at age eighteen. I still have more to talk about it, but I definitely feel like I am in a better situation to have these discussions. What has happened for me during the course of this semester is that I have found myself discovering me.

JASON

Traumas come in varying degrees of severity or intensity, but trying to understand the severity of a particular student's trauma, and rating it by using a numerical value on a scale, is tricky if not impossible. If writers are in the midst of their trauma while they are writing, it's naturally more intense. On the other hand, even if a trauma occurred twenty years ago, like Anne's rape, the immediate "aftershocks" may have weakened over time, but the reawakened experience can remain severe. In Jason's list of possible traumas or "monsters" to write about, he included his sister, his father's health, his self-confidence, his procrastination, and his growing debt. He chose to focus on debt, a different kind of monster—seemingly less intense and severe, but maybe more subtle and insidious. Following is Jason's letter to his monster, Debt, a trauma that some observers might rank as less severe than many other issues.

> Dear Debt,
>
> I realize you may be questioning why you're receiving this letter. You didn't force yourself on me. In fact, I sought you out. You may even view yourself as the wounded party here. I'm writing to tell you that I don't really care how you feel. I sought you out because in order to do the things that I wanted to do in life, I needed your help. I wanted to get finished with graduate school

as quickly as possible and working to pay my own way would've put me back years. I figured that I would be able to pay you off in time and I still realized that I am indebted in order to pay you back. What I didn't realize is how sneaky and underhanded your practices are. You were not forthcoming with your repayment options, nor in working with me to suspend payments. When I ran out of my allotted deferments you refused to work with me and thus I am forced to sacrifice the very thing I've worked so hard to obtain. Coupled with my economic indebtedness is the realization that you will affect me for the rest of my life. I have to think about you daily and feel ashamed to admit how indebted I actually am. I have to worry that since I'll always be indebted that I'll be subservient to your wishes instead of those who will rely on me in the future. I hate you for this and I wish I'd never had the displeasure of knowing you. I will do everything in my power to pay you back, but I will not sacrifice my means of living in order to do so. I hope that lawmakers will intercede in our dispute, but I doubt they ever will and thus I'm stuck with you.

Dispassionately and forever yours,

Jason

Jason begins by explaining and clarifying why debt is a monster in the first place, even suggesting that this problem is his own doing. This is a classic rhetorical move: Early in his writing, Jason disposes of his opposition, refuting those "objections" that readers may have against his argument. Most of the time, the purpose is to answer and remove those doubts that readers may have, so they won't be distracted by them when the writer presents the evidence. Dispensing with our opposition can give us a kind of green light to become more specific (e.g., Jason notes that his repayment options were not communicated accurately). The green light of disposing of opposing arguments can also be a signal to ourselves to become more impassioned about our reasons. I can hear Jason's frustration grow more intense as he writes. It seems to peak when he realizes that this monster is a "forever" demon. In short, this green light allows more fluency, a basic ingredient in writing about trauma. His final hope that "lawmakers will intercede" is somewhat a product of our culture at the time in which Jason was writing—a few months after the presidential election of 2012, when the economy was center stage.

Figure 4.6. Jason's Monster

Figure 4.7. Jason's Angel

Here is an excerpt from Jason's reflection on the process of drawing his monster and angel.

> I took a white piece of paper out and started to think what my debt-monster would look like. I knew from my letter that it would have to be presented as larger-than-life and ultimately evil. It also had to be portrayed as something solid and powerful. I wanted to incorporate some image of money to symbolize its commitment to the all-mighty dollar bill. I took what I could draw of the bill and split it into two—angling them out so that they appear as wings. This would be one of the focal points, hopefully symbolizing how money somehow allows the monster to exist. Next, I drew the head. I didn't want this monster to appear human, so I gave it a demon-like skull with large protruding horns. The eyes are reptilian and black. I was going to give it (somehow I think of "it" as a "him") irises, but thought it looked

more inhuman without them. Also, it could represent how it doesn't need to see me. The body came next. Normally I'm not all that good at drawing muscles, but I wanted to convey how powerful this monster was and so I drew thick-corded muscles all over the body. Its hands and feet are laced with sharp talons—representing menace. I debated on (and ultimately chose to) incorporate a sense of scale by drawing a mini-picture of me. I also wanted to show how the monster controls me, so I drew it holding me on a leash. I think this symbolizes how beholden I am to this monster.

Deconstructing the monster was actually pretty easy. I simply cut it up into its component parts and played with how they should be arranged. I want to symbolize a loss of power or a switching of the dynamics—or, at the very least, to make my monster comical instead of menacing. When I cut its arms off, I immediately thought that that it would be funny to put the little person's arms in its place. The arms turned out to be too small to tape but I could use its arms in replacement. Now the little guy has these huge and powerful arms. Next I cut the wings off, metaphorically stripping my monster his source of power. Since my little guy is kind of floating off into space I thought it would be a good idea to make one of those into a cape for him. Now he's some sort of superhero! I took his feet and made them into arms and made his horns into legs. The monster looks disjointed almost in a puppet-like stance. I put the other dollar bill behind its head and found that it gave the appearance that it's asleep (which is much less menacing!)

I'm not sure I've arrived at any sort of conclusion on my frustration other than that I found conceptualizing it quite fun. I'm also quite proud of my representation. I do like how I turned the tables in my re-organization but am hampered by my realization that this isn't as easy to do in real-life. I've looked into my options and they are few and far between. I can just hope that something legally changes later on down the line.

Jason shows a lot of flexible thinking in his drawings and in his written description of how he created them. He begins his reflection this way: "I found this experience to be fun! I think partly because I like to draw and work with my hands." In creating the angel image, Jason wants it to be "comical"; he then describes it as the "little guy" and "little person," before finally adding a cape and referring to him as a "superhero." He ends by describing the experience as "quite fun." This language bestows a lively benevolence toward the re-constructed monster or "angel." Even though the visual and verbal work in tandem, Jason's artistic efforts trump the language part. It doesn't make any difference whether visual trumps verbal or vice-versa. The important thing is that they interact and the writer finds some balance or a measure of relief from the issue troubling him. In the last few lines, Jason kind of comes back to reality, stating that "turning tables" isn't as easy to do in real life. He's most correct. I do, though, detect a more tempered reckoning with his monster.

Cass

Cass is not a language expert—at least not yet. She is an eighth-grader at a Midwestern School. Her teacher is Stephen, a bright, energetic graduate-student enrolled in my course described earlier. Stephen noticed early on that he had some students who would definitely benefit from therapeutic writing, so he decided to focus on a few such students for his final research project. He explained the type of writing and imagery involved, including his own perceptions about his experiences in creating verbal and visual compositions for exploring trauma. After obtaining the necessary approvals from parents, he wanted a few of his students to write about the same assignment, *The Monster and the Angel*.

Cass's Monster and the Angel Assignment

Following is Cass's visual rendering of her monster, followed by her letter to this monster. Next, she explains her choice.

Figure 4.8. Cass's Monster: *A Marijuana Joint.* Source: Cass (pseudonym)

Cass's Letter to her Monster

Dear Marijuana,

Hey Marijuana, you may have never known me, but you definitely know some of my family. My Uncle Zayfir? Or how about my cousin, Shontelle? Well, either way my name is Cass and I have a few questions for you.

First off, why? That's my first question, why do you cause such pain for people? Why have you brought such trouble to my family? Why do you allow my uncle and cousin to be such cowards? Why do you give them a place to hide? No, actually, why does their salvation cause the people who love them to need salvation? Are you simply using them to get to us, so maybe we will fall into your awful "safety"? Is that what you do? Do you just recruit little rookies to get more people? You're like a worse version of a high school heart breaker! You are simply collecting jars of hearts. I think that's all you're really doing, and it hon-

> estly pisses me off! You are not getting your grasp on me or any of my younger cousins, that I can assure you!
>
> Forever NOT yours,

Cass clearly tries to understand the issue by asking her monster questions and trying to answer them herself, a crucial approach in writing through trauma. With language experts and novices alike, aiming questions directly at a visible monster—that is, putting a "face" on the enemy—can *free* us to write with a more confident *voice* and more *agency*, as we try to gain control of our own world. Also, putting a face and name on the enemy helps us generate more words, as well as connect our ideas more naturally and fluently.

Cass's mental wheels turn when she changes course after asking, "Why do you give them a place to hide?" She in effect re-directs her thinking by stating, "No—I really mean, 'Why does giving THEM a place to hide create a need for the people who love them to ALSO find a place to hide?'" Discovering this causal connection is a *movement* of mind, which helps Cass to understand the issue more clearly, placing it into a larger conceptual category, in turning affording her a greater sense of control.

Cass demonstrates effective thinking through some of her language choices in this brief piece. Because she is free to express herself, Cass tries out some comparisons. Is her monster most like a baseball recruiter scouting for "rookies"? A "high school heart-breaker," who attracts others by promising them one thing but never delivering? The freedom to cast about for comparisons leads her to her most original and vivid image—the serial heart-breaker, who merely collects "jars of hearts"—clinical specimens on a shelf for no rational or human purpose. I see this as a mature realization on Cass's part, that sometimes the universe makes no sense at all. Most importantly, I admire her looking it in the face.

Cass's Explanation of Her Choice

> Why did I choose a marijuana joint for my monster? Well, marijuana has managed to cause a bit of confusion in my life! You see, first we have the arrest of my uncle and his girlfriend. What happens when people with kids get arrested? Well, their children are given to the state, which then hands them off to a relative. Now, don't get me wrong—my grandma loves ALL of her

many grandchildren, but sometimes it can be a bit much for her and my grandfather to handle. Then there was my cousin (not my uncle who had been arrested) who decides, "I think smoking is fun! Let's get high and then get arrested!" She's just a genius, isn't she? This is why my family and I are now left to clean up their mess while they're off getting high!

In her explanation, Cass's anger and resentment fuses with her astonishment that anyone could behave in such inconsiderate ways. I also hear a dash of sarcasm that seems natural for any thirteen-year-old. Earlier in the school year, Cass had written about this same grandmother, who was not only left caring for her imprisoned son's children, but also coping with cancer and chemo treatments. These two simultaneous and interrelated traumas created far more stress for Cass than many children her age could bear. Wisely, Stephen, her teacher, recognized this need and enabled her to begin making sense of it all—not through counseling, but through realizing that Cass had a deeply-motivating need to express herself—in many ways, allowing her to at least begin the process of figuring things out on her own.

In fact, Cass had written about this topic in class on her own. Teachers often receive such writing whether they have asked for it or not. Stephen first learned about Cass's worry over her grandmother when Cass wrote about mustering her own courage to face her grandmother's serious illness, in an academic essay for a writing contest. In her essay, Cass compares the courage of Jackie Robinson, who broke America's color barrier in Major League Baseball in 1947, to the courage that she must rely upon.

Cass grapples with her family's drug abuse and incarceration, which leads to her ill grandmother's having to take care of her grandchildren. These twin traumas are visibly fused when she reconfigures her monster into an angel.

Figure 4.9. Cass's Angel: *A Breast Cancer Ribbon*. Source: Cass (pseudonym)

Cass transforms her monster, the marijuana cigarette, by cutting it, coloring it pink, and re-shaping it to look like a breast cancer ribbon—that familiar public symbol for fighting this disease. My response to Cass's revision even mirrors that of her teacher, Stephen: "It even gives me strength and hope for her . . . truly inspiring" (Personal communication, May 28, 2013).

Following is Cass's description of her angel.

> Well, as I said, my angel is a breast cancer ribbon. In October my grandma was diagnosed with breast cancer. All of my family still has yet to fully accept it. Even I had trouble believing it. It was not until my grandma lost all of her hair and was in constant pain from chemo that I fully accepted it. And yeah, I'll admit that I struggle with all of this. There have been times when I find myself alone crying, just so I'll seem "strong." Now that I've spilled my guts, let's get to the point: I struggle but I remember that the chemo that's causing her so much pain is actually saving her life, and that's why the cancer ribbon is my angel.

After describing her angel, Cass reflected on this experience. Her response, below, returns to her uncle and his drug use and reveals a tone that differs from her earlier anger and confusion. Following this is what she wrote when she was later asked to describe which writing prompt most helped her and which one did not. While she did not say, she returned to where she left off, describing the overall benefit of writing about trauma.

> Through this experience I have learned a few things. First of all, I thought I blamed my uncle for taking drugs as a way to get away from life. Now I realize that I honestly can't blame him. If I didn't know what the end result would be, I might give in myself. I mean, I know he knew what he was doing. I'd be in denial if I said I didn't, but I also know that sometimes life can get hard, and that all it takes is one small amount of weakness and you can fall and when you fall, it's hard to get back up. Second, I learned that when you sort things out and write it down, it's never as bad or as confusing as it seemed when it was all crammed in your head! . . .
>
> For me, it [writing] really helped emotionally. It helped emotionally because I got to focus on all my problems. I got to sort them through and have them organized and not clouded in my head, all swimming and pushing and beating on the sides of my head, all begging for room. All begging to be considered and to have their turn to be thought about . . .

For Stephen, her teacher, and for me, this final description of how writing helps is one of the best we've seen. If only all eighth graders realized this.

152 Roy F. Fox

Khanh

Khanh, a graduate student from Vietnam, is about thirty years old. He holds a full scholarship from his government to pursue a doctoral degree in English Education. Khanh has demonstrated a range of intellectual abilities in language education: from performing sophisticated statistical analyses of linguistic data, to creating graphic short stories, to therapeutic writing and imagery. He is ever-curious about most topics and always cheerful and open to new ideas. The first image Khanh created in the course focused on his friend, Han, who was suffering from cancer and died during the semester of our therapeutic writing class (This image is not included). Next, Khanh created the following three images for the *The Monster and the Angel* assignment: Figures 4.10, 4.11, and 4.12.

Khanh's Monster and Angel Assignment

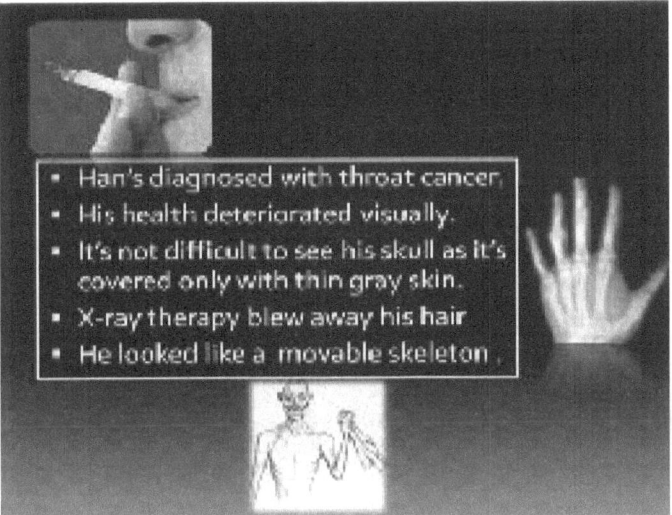

Figure 4.10. Khanh's Monster: *Han is Diagnosed.* Source: Khanh (pseudonym)

MONSTER:
A SELF-PORTRAIT OF MR. CANCER

Figure 4.11. Khanh's Monster, No. 2: *A Self-Portrait of Mr. Cancer.* Source: Khanh (pseudonym)

THE ANGEL: *MY LUCKY STAR*

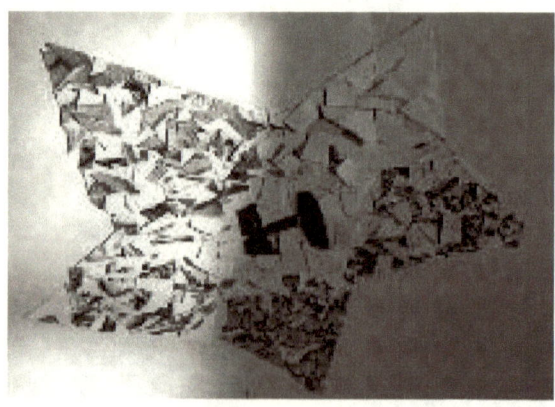

Figure 4.12: Khanh's Angel: *My Lucky Star.* Source: Khanh (pseudonym)

Students were also asked to describe their *movements* or changes in this transformation. Khanh's description, excerpted from his longer paper, follows (Fox 2011).

> Physically tearing (I tore) the monster apart into hundreds of pieces, and assembled them into a new, more positive piece that brought positive feelings. I could put the current monster aside, or let it out of my mind. I thought of the relationships be-

tween colors I would use to make a new image; I brainstormed positive and neutral ideas for the new piece, the content of the new photo; and I thought of how to make the most sense with the scattered pieces. I had an idea that perhaps my dead friend was enjoying his new life in some weird after-life world. And I thought of how to do some kind of tribute to him.

I came up with the idea of using colors (blue and red) and contrast (bright and darkness) to convey my message: the battle between the good and the bad (dragon and monster!). It's not easy to say who wins eventually. The star also represented hopes I had for the cure of such a chronic disease as cancer. The letter "H" was also an epitome of healing power of positive attitude/thinking/music my friend had, which helped him prolong his life. Plus, H was the initial of his name.

I moved from 'blaming Mr. Cancer' to 'accepting his intervention' as I believe in the coexistence of evil and good. Yet a more critical question arose: 'How to fight against it?' Maybe a combination of a good diet, sound plans of study, work, and recreation, and regular health check could be the answer. (93)

Figure 4.13 (Khanh's *Mr. Cancer Introduces Himself*) is Khanh's unique way of creating visually part of the written component of the assignment.

Name: Mr. Cancer
Interests: Killing people
Occupation: Rooting deeply into human beings to survive.
ID: + Octopus-like creature with numerous evil tentacles

+ The body is laden with nerves which often change their shape- hard to identify!
+ The deadly hyena head is often invisible, only appears in a certain period when the stomach is full of blood.

Figure 4.13: Khanh's *Mr. Cancer Introduces Himself.* Source: Fox 2011, 94)

Weeks after the course, I talked with Khanh about the creation of his *Monster and Angel* assignment.

RF: What influenced you the most in creating this piece?

KHANH: It was all motivation. . . . I was influenced a lot by the materials in the course. They helped me think more deeply, especially the assigned article about how to move from a two-valued orientation to a multi-valued orientation. Also, the list we did on the first day of all the possible issues we had in mind that we might write about. Here I realized that cancer was everywhere and that I had to face the problem, but I really didn't want to. Elizabeth Edwards has it, and so does the tennis player, Martina Navratilova.

I realized I had to face the problem. I had to visualize the enemy. It made sense that I feared something that I couldn't see. Giving [cancer] a face and a voice made it more explicit and multi-valued, making it easier to process. The "Mr. Cancer" piece shows a move from two-valued to multi-valued orientation. That is, the cancer image is two-valued and the star that I made from it is multi-valued. This project made it easier to process and get distance from it. I had to accept it *in my own eyes*. [Another influence] was that I wanted to do something for my friend, so that in the future I can return to it as a reminder. (94–95)

RF: How did you create this image of "Mr. Cancer"—how did you get the idea in the first place?

KHANH: I had to think a lot about it before I created it, because it's the enemy of both of us [i.e., Han, his friend who died during the semester]. My first idea was to use an image of a worm, because of the way they eat things. But they don't have tentacles or anything. I also thought about a movie that I saw a very long time ago about a very evil person. I also had read about an octopus in Sweden named Paul who was a genius because he predicted the World Cup soccer scores. But these were all a long time ago—and then I came across an image of an octopus on the Internet, so I used that, because it had tentacles, and Han had four tumors in his brain—a lot of tentacles attacking all parts of his body. Tentacles also reach out and affect his friends and family. And the hyenas are bad animals that cue other animals to eat—scavengers—killing and sucking blood.

RF: How did you create the star for the angel?

KHANH: Like the assignment said, I tore up Mr. Cancer and re-assembled it into the star, because Han's students thought he was a star. I placed myself into Han's situation.

RF: Why did you do the writing of the "Self Introduction" in this way?

KHANH: I wanted readers to gravitate to a familiar genre, to be hooked to the subject—like a driver's license, that shows the picture on the left and then information on the right.

RF: How do you feel about all of this now, several months after the course is over?

KHANH: The course helped me to see in different perspectives or lenses; to see in different directions. The thinking and approach were the main benefits—instead of just blaming and negative thinking. It helped me remember my friend and others. The course helped change my thinking orientation—to gain distance and put all emotions through a funnel to create things and demystify and deconstruct and reconstruct. I would not have thought of this unless I had this course. I've also recommended books on writing and healing and some of the activities we did to a special education teacher I met at the state language arts conference.

In this interview, Khanh also explained how the course helped his continued learning of English as his second language. He also noted that some elements of the course (e.g., objective reporting, different genres) "transferred" into other, more traditionally academic classes. Khanh seems to have generated most of his ideas, connections, and thinking through interacting with images, such as his idea of creating the introduction of Mr. Cancer as similar to a driver's license, bearing a photo and identifying information. His journey toward developing the dramatic image of Mr. Cancer bounced back and forth between images and language—that is, his reading about "Paul" the genius octopus—but seems dominated by imagery sources.

I was also intrigued by the contrast between his first image, focused on his friend, Han, and the much later image of Mr. Cancer. The first one is comprised of "stock images" or generic images found on the Internet. The latter one is drawn free-hand by Khanh, revealing his increased immersion in writing for healing—his greater sense of *agency* and desire for control in creating the image himself, so that he can more exactly capture his own perception of his friend's illness. In his bulleted description of the changes he experienced, cited earlier, it's clear that Khanh was delving more into specific visual elements to reinforce his writing, by employing contrast, shadow, color, and—not mentioned by Khanh—even clashing diagonal lines to indicate action.

Another contrast between these images resides in the language Khanh generated for each one. The language accompanying the first image is straightforward and reportorial—just the facts, except for a simile in the last line and a few descriptive phrases. In contrast, the language Khanh submitted with the Mr. Cancer image, in addition to the "Self-Introduction," was a poem (not included here)—an entirely different genre for him. By the end of the course, Khanh had learned to take risks in finding different genres to capture a different or more nuanced type of writing about trauma. Two years after the course ended, I asked Khanh to read this chapter to ensure my accuracy, as I have done for everyone. He had only one request on a post-it note: "Somewhere, if possible, please include this line, 'To Han—my dear friend. We will never forget you.'"

Melvin

Melvin came out of nowhere to be a student in my latest Therapeutic Writing class. In his early sixties, he had left a position to become a new university faculty member in physics. He had learned about the course from another faculty member and contacted me before the course began. He seemed motivated by a belief that he needed to improve his own writing. I quickly understood he was very sincere and would add a lot of depth and maturity to the class. I was not disappointed. For decades, I've spoken with all types of people who told me what poor writers they were. They are seldom as bad as they believe themselves to be, and this was the case with Melvin. He was a serious, dedicated, intelligent, and energetic writer, who always challenged himself.

During the course, he tackled several different issues, such as family relationships and history, but he focused on the extreme childhood abuse, both physical and emotional, inflicted by his mother, until he was able to leave home at age seventeen. For decades, Melvin suffered from flashbacks of this abuse. In a fascinating turn of events, he claimed that his flashbacks disappeared soon after he began writing about this trauma. I don't understand why or how this occurred, but I don't doubt Melvin's claim. In time, I hope to better understand this situation.

Melvin's Conversation across Time Assignment

Here, I will focus on Melvin's final writing of the semester, his response to my "Conversation across Time" assignment. I requested that writers include photos or visual renderings of the two speakers, to help them think of their writing as an authentic conversation of give-and-take. The visuals helped *concretize* the imaginary chat. Following are the directions given to class members, and next is Melvin's response:

Conversation across Time Assignment

1. Create a conversation, dialogue, or Q&A session between the current you—and the "you" of 25–30 years from now.
2. Label the speakers (e.g., "Me Now" and "Me Older").
3. Limit this dialogue to no more than 2 pages.
4. Place all or selected portions onto PPT slides, that show a visual rendering of each "you" (present and future) on each slide containing passages of conversation. The slides need not be the same ones repeated (though that's fine).
5. Finally, write a 1-page analysis-reflection on this experience.

Figure 4.14. Melvin's *Mr. Day*. Source: Melvin (pseudonym)

Mr. Day: My life today is as good as I could have possibly expected considering its successes and failures. Professionally moving from an aeronautical firm to teaching physics at the university has been the right decision, professionally and spiritually. I am challenged intellectually in areas of quantum mechanics that I quit paying attention to for the last 10 years. I also am expanding my experience and my mind by being a professor at a major university.

Figure 4.15. Melvin's *Mr. Silver*. Source: Melvin (pseudonym)

> Mr. Silver: Life did turn out better for us because of your last professional move. We stayed on at the University till 2022 when we retired and were granted emeritus status. I still have my old office in Fredericks Hall that I visit about once a week. Most of the staff from the teens are gone but I still enjoy seeing the students and talking to classes about the history of the physics department.
>
> You, Mr. Day, were so worried about such small items. You fretted over such small issues. You worried about student evaluations, Joint Review Committee reaccreditations, lesson plans, and a hundred other mundane issues. What you should have been concerned about was your relationship with your wife, children, grandchildren, and now great-grandchildren. The professional fate of your students should have come next. Most importantly, you needed a great passion to dedicate your

essence to. Nothing physical that you have done will still be around to be a memory of you. Only your family and good works will be a memory of your existence.

Mr. Day: That's easy for you to say 30 years from now when you can look back and see all that worked and didn't. The small things don't mean much as life is closing its door. But everyday issues are the stuff of reality for me today. The dog being fed, the grass getting mown, the homework assignment completed are the substance of what I do, and I am not willing to attack a large issue and ignore my day to day life.

Mr. Silver: Why aren't you willing to make a major commitment to a significant cause or project? What are you waiting for? At best, you are going to live to be 93 years old—30 more years, maybe plus or minus a year or two. How many of those years will you be healthy and strong enough to make a major contribution to anything? Today is the day when you should take what you are and what you know and commit to being something bigger and better than you have ever been.

Mr. Day: Honestly, I don't know of anything I would be willing to give up my life for other than my family. You know I dabbled in politics for a decade and was left cynical by the phony people and causes. I was dedicated to the Temple but that was just a building containing a different type of politics.

No, for me, family and students are the alpha and beta of my world. I no longer have dreams of greatness, only of making my time here a comfort to the ones I love and am responsible for.

Mr. Silver: Then there is no hope for you. I cannot be more than I am if you will not be more than you are. You can change history, I can only report it. If you choose to not attempt great feats, then greatness can never be part of your life.

If you are lucky you will die at 93 with your family about you. Your students will hear of your death, shake their head and maybe smile. They will murmur kind things about the "old man" and then your life will be over.

Mr. Day: Honestly, that sounds like quite a bit. My legacy will be my family and the students I have taught. There will be no statue or plaque, but my mind will be in my students, and my genes in my descendants.

When I introduced this assignment to the class, there were murmurs like, "God—I'll be so old!" At that moment, I thought of myself (age 64) and then glanced at Melvin (age 62), and immediately said something like, "That's if you're lucky—and yes, you 'get' to project into the future 25–30 years from now."

Melvin had written about some very tough issues over the semester, but he insisted this one was the hardest to do. I agreed that it would be hard for anyone who was facing retirement and those *whatever* years— Golden? Dwindling? Departing? Stepping-down? Going out to pasture? Seclusion? Last hurrah? At least to me, and I suspect to anyone in this age category—especially those of us who have suffered at the hands of "vaunted ambition"—Melvin addressed the central issue one finds at the threshold of retirement: "What's left in the tank, and how should I spend it?" Following is Melvin's written reflection about his conversation between Mr. Silver and Mr. Day:

> The basic existential question, "What does my life mean?" is of academic interest to students in college and even professors at universities, but it becomes a critical question when a man is at a tipping point in his 6th decade of life. Is it enough to live out one's life using momentum and inertia to continue one's path till death? Or do we have a responsibility to society and ourselves to continue to strive for greatness at every stage of life? This is a basic question I have chosen not to ask or even think about, now that I have a new job at a new institution, performing duties at which I am not fully functional. My current status is to maximize my capabilities to just get through the day, the week, the semester, and the academic year. I do not make plans for great accomplishments, as I did in my youth. In general, the occupation I am in is the job I wish to keep till I retire. Getting to retirement is the major goal.
>
> This is so different from the man I was 30 years ago. At 33, I was an up and coming scientist and middle-level administrator. My goal was to be the department chair of a midsized physics department. I was earning an advanced degree. I had a young family. I was involved in local and national politics. I was a man on the go with a bright future.
>
> Life happened and decisions were made, and at 60, I was Coordinator of a science department of a small college. I decided to throw the dice once more to be a Professor of Physics at a

major university. The question is, "Is that enough?" Is it enough for me to be the best large frog in my very small pond? Or do I still have a responsibility to maximize the remaining productive time I have left? I have no great passions, as I once did, to be a great man. To be a great scholar or leader of men is what drove me. Today my goal is to be successful in my tiny corner of the universe.

This project forced me to confront some of my greatest fears. What do I want to do with the rest of my life? Will my life have been worth living when it is over? When the counting is done, and my life is weighed and measured, will I have been found wanting? Do I have a moral responsibility to continue to attempt to achieve great deeds, even in the face of failure, because the pursuit of greatness is the only path to immortality?

And that is the key word, "immortality." No one can have physical immortality, but some have a type of spiritual or intellectual never-ending presence. Is what I'm doing enough, or do I need to start on another great quest? The current Mr. Day says it is enough. Mr. Silver says there is no sadder words than, "what might have been."

Melvin's "debate" here is well conceived, elegant in its simplicity. After a semester of untangling his childhood abuse, this assignment seems to have forced him to stand back and put everything in perspective (what the assignment was intended to do). I also think it's a mark of his growth that he does not explicitly decide which road he will embark upon. As I mentioned to him after class one night, I suspect he'll embark on another quest; it's just that he hasn't yet determined what it will be, because he's not finished with his present quest. If I had to place a bet, it would be on Mr. Silver.

5 Kate

> *Our deepest humanity is always about being able to see, to notice, to reflect on those connections. This is what being human is all about. I did not want to go to grief counseling, because these are the processes that work for me. Therapy is for people who don't pose questions to themselves.*
>
> —Kate

Deeply involved in her profession as a teacher and a writer since receiving her bachelor's degree in the mid-1970s and her doctorate nearly 20 years later, Kate has broad experience in language, reading, writing, publishing, and administration. In addition to having raised children, Kate maintains many interests, some of which overlap into her professional work and others which are more personal, including music, nature, science, and art. She has maintained a personal journal since childhood:

> I've been journal-keeping since I was a kid. In high school, when I had an interview to be an exchange student, they asked what I'd take with me in case of a fire and I could only take one thing. I told them it would be my battered blue folder with my writings in it. Letters functioned the same way—hundreds and hundreds of letters. When I was teaching writing, I kind of stopped for many reasons, *but* eased back into it over the last several years.

As a life-long writer, it was natural that Kate turned to words immediately after the worst moment of her life. Kate's husband, a successful professional in a different field, had recently died from head trauma when he veered his motor scooter away from a deer on the road. I never knew her husband. She introduced us once, when we met on a street, and I attended a dinner once with him, but we hardly talked. What I have learned about him in doing this project has made me wish I had indeed known him. The local paper described the huge crowd at his funeral service, where friends and colleagues spoke of his goodness, his decency:

- He was as good at guiding his kids through the woods, as he was at guiding his clients through the law.
- He was a rock that would land softly, or even roughly, in the water of life and caused a ripple that touched everyone in his life.
- Hank often remarked that camping was where boys go to act like men and men go to act like boys. He returned there periodically to smooth out the accumulated wrinkles in his soul

I did not expect Kate to volunteer her private journal to me for purposes of this study. I learned that she had never shared it with anyone else. Our first meeting occurred less than a year after her husband's death. She was hesitant and nervous when talking with me about her writing from this period:

> It is definitely not a question of not trusting you . . . I feel totally comfortable with you as auditor . . . but maybe in a couple months . . . I'll be able to talk about writing just fine, but I'm not *ready* to talk about this [pointing at her journal], but maybe in a few months . . . this is a pretty loaded thing for me . . . the meta-level is easy.

I realized that her allowing me to see this very private writing was a testament to several qualities—her belief in writing, her trust in the process, her belief in free inquiry and learning, her desire that maybe doing so could, in some small way, help other people. Most of all, I took it as a testament to her soft-spoken, innate kindness.

Kate's journal contains fifty-one separate entries, each written by hand, in pen, in a small, black, five-by-eight inches bound book with unlined pages. The first entry is dated April 10, 2008; her last entry occurred May 26, 2008. I only reviewed one journal; she certainly continued writing, filling up other small books. Her first entry details the busy, chaotic period, following the accident, full of people coming to her home, offering help, food, whatever they could.

Kate's Relationship to Readers of Her Private Writing about Trauma

Every entry in Kate's journal begins with "Dear Hank." They are clearly personal, private letters to her husband. Unlike Lucy in the previous chapter, Kate does not cleanly separate her writing for healing into categories, including the most basic division: writing for herself versus writing for others. Much of Lucy's writing about trauma was published on an open website, available to many people—those she knows, some more so than others. Kate, however, did not post messages on a public website or in any other forum, so she had no need to separate one type of writing from another. Nonetheless, the function of *readers* still operates in this very private context.

> KATE: Form and meaning are so intertwined—that's the thinking process. I'm too self-conscious a writer. Because I've been a writing teacher for so long, I never have a sense of an absolute private audience. I still have no faith in absolute confidentiality. For good or bad, there is the internal [reader] for anything I do.
>
> RF: So, because we've written for others for so long, we've internalized this habit?
>
> KATE: Yes. In terms of my sensibility I can be writing things that are very private, but I still feel an auditor. I don't mean it in the punitive sense, but at the same time, I think it's just the way it is. On one hand, I like to be free, but on the other hand, I know there's a reader.
>
> It's a very hard thing *not* to revise. It's embarrassing to me to expose myself without revising, even though there is an internal reviser working all the time. I've occasionally ripped out a page. I was trying to honor the history, trying not to manipulate that. The idea of honesty and sincerity is a premium thing.

Clear evidence within Kate's journal supports her assertion that she is *also* often aware of a reader, even though nobody has read her journal. In her first entry, she explicitly defines her purpose and audience, something often not found in writing exclusively for oneself:

> Well, enough of this initial ramble. What I hope to do in these pages is twofold—to continue to solicit your input on parenting (we're still parents) & to remember (to remember in whatever

order, whatever year) stories about you. I will be back. We love & miss you, Hank.

Here, at the outset of this journal, Kate seems to imply two *apologies*—to her husband Hank, her first reader, and to her other readers, whoever they may be. She first apologizes for her *initial ramble* and then, for her expected lack of precise chronology in her stories. Even her word choices "twofold" and "solicit your input" are more formal than we would expect in private, informal writing. While this *stiffness* soon subsides and is not present in most of the remaining entries, it may have served the function of just getting things started, of establishing a real and somewhat business-like agenda, a habit from her professional life.

Other clues point toward Kate's awareness of audience. She sometimes draws little icons of smiley faces to indicate—to a reader—that she is joking. She often crosses out phrases and sentences, making them completely undecipherable to a reader—versus not caring because no one else would ever see it. She sometimes revises words and phrases in an effort to be more precise. In a small script, she often inserts language that provides finer distinctions or qualifications into her passage. In one entry, after she crosses a phrase out, she labels it as a teacher would: *mixed metaphor!* A few times, Kate seems to address her husband and herself, as well as other unknown readers: "My last entry would be incoherent to most readers, but, upon reading it, I understand every word of it myself. Keep it?" This awareness of audience continues until the final entry, with Kate identifying, by name, each of Hank's relatives who attended his memorial service—people well-known to both of them. When I asked Kate *how* she thought of or visualized her audience, she spoke with conviction:

> I have no *one* concrete 'other'—but I was conscious of the possibility of a child finding, reading—like if a deer collided with me all of a sudden! I have no sense of *absolute* privacy. . . . I am the first reader BUT . . . Hank is part of *me*, part of my identity, my history, my way of thinking. . . .

People who write about trauma can do this effectively, whether they neatly separate their writing into intended-audience categories, such as private, public, immediate family, professional, or whatever. As she states, her husband as her sole reader is complex: she and Hank are now one. The fact is that much writing, of any kind, does not exist in a *pure* mode or genre, regardless of intended audiences. Kate's ever-present awareness of audience enabled her to be explicit, to say directly what she needed to say—which is most important for purposes of healing. Ghosts, traumas, and bugaboos in our minds can be handled better only if they become visible, and writing makes them so.

Kate's Motivation for Writing about Trauma

Because Kate was not yet ready to talk directly about her journal at our first meeting, she gladly focused on the *meta-level* of her writing—why she did it and what she thought about it, even though this *language about her language* also elicited strong emotions. Here, she describes her earlier journal writing, then contrasts it with her current writing for healing.

> My approach to journal writing had been just savoring all day one beautiful thing. I kept a little log and wrote about one beautiful thing or memorable thing at the end of that day. I was really shifting to a more epigrammatic—a phrase or words or more often an emotion or event—going to the other extreme in terms of volume. But it was very productive; this savoring process has been very wonderful for me. But this (journal) is different, very conscious. They're written to Hank. They're very deliberate (wipes tear away).... Picking up a pen is my best tool for making meaning. Meaning-making is life long, but there are times when life is shattered, and you have to re-assemble little things and relationships. To look at a redbud and see the blossom, you've seen it year after year—but your relationship to it is shattered, is different. For this, I go back to very specific concrete things, names, events, things that may seem to be inconsequential.... The making of meaning is always a problem-solving activity, judgments. Our deepest humanity is always about being able to see, to notice, to reflect on those connections. This is what being human is all about. I did not want to go to grief counseling, because these are the processes that work for me. Therapy is for people who don't pose questions to themselves.

This turned out to be a very accurate description of what I found in Kate's journal: She asks many questions, some of which she turns over and over, viewing them from different perspectives, as she struggles to re-configure her relationships with, well, *everything*. Her loss was such a sudden rupture and rip in normalcy that none of the old rules applied. Her journal's tone reminds me of a cat who has survived a tornado, who ever-so-carefully steps out into a new world consisting of piles of splintered boards and chaos where once her home had stood. This was her central motivation—re-building meaning. Much of this process was conscious and deliberate, as she noted two years after losing her husband.

> First, my life was so shattered that the parts were all disconnected, and I felt unplugged. So, to begin the process of making meaning, I had to *will* to connect, to find relationships that are fundamental for meaning. So, second, I very consciously had to *CHOOSE* to make meaning. I had to do that consciously—and it started tiny. One idea. Then one relationship—mother/son. One friendship. Still, my relationship with all the larger orders of social and professional reality was fragile. I had to actively *choose* to reconnect and to extend the web of connections. . . . I suppose I've been "reconstructing reality," and I feel like I live in a somewhat different world. I wonder if real healing comes when past/present, old/new don't feel so separate. It's not that I just lost Hank, I lost "the world" I lived in with him. In a way, part of me and "that world" died, too. I've been rebuilding—from scratch, it feels—a new world. Maybe I was just radically innocent for way too long—and this "new world" is just post-depression loss of radical innocence.

Much of this conscious rebuilding in Kate's journal is *meditative* in that many entries first describe small, specific elements—a glimpse of her garage, her cat asleep on the bed—which she then connects to larger issues and values. Like Lucy in the earlier chapter, Kate's decades of experience with journal writing and her education and broad experience with language amount to confidence in knowing the processes that work for her. Note that she does not mention any kind of end product; she believes deeply that it's the *process* that matters, a stance that vastly differs from more novice writers. Kate believes in these processes so strongly that she easily dismissed grief counseling or therapy.

Kate's knowledge and high degree of self-awareness of her own writing and thinking processes prompted me to ask more specific questions about *how* she went about writing throughout this extremely difficult time. Her reply gave me a lot to think about.

> It's helpful to me to find a phrase—those are not trivial things. There's satisfaction in being able to capture an image, metaphor, opposition, juxtaposition. The reason it works stylistically is because it works emotionally. Sometimes you need to be a running river to find the right image or phrase, but I don't self-consciously search for such an image, because that self-consciousness can be crippling. But I'm aware of that, and I do come upon moments that help me coalesce meaning—when I can condense in words a feeling that helps me crystalize an understanding. The processes of exploring and then discovering such phrases are pattern-finding tools. You can't march out to find happiness. Happiness is a byproduct of marching out into life. Likewise, I can't march out to find one right phrase; finding it is a byproduct of exploration.

Here, Kate's first comment is rich in what it suggests about her as a veteran literacy and language expert who knows what is most important: matching often inchoate feelings and thoughts with the most precise and effective language. This is commonly expressed as, "finding just the right word," but it's clear that she explores first, and finding the *right* word may or may not happen. She seems to rely upon her emotions to communicate to her whether or not her language succeeds. If so, then the pairing of thought with language will *also* succeed stylistically—that is, her readers will get her meaning in short order. This highly-tuned sense of selectivity—for matching thought with language—appears to be a kind of basic *stance* for Kate when writing about trauma. I do not see it operating within her as a rigid condition or a rule, but rather, as a kind of instinct or *sixth sense*, likely a by-product of her education and deep experience with language.

When Kate observes that, "sometimes you need to be a running river to find the right image or phrase," she acknowledges that writers need to keep their words flowing and flowing until they float into just the right match-up between thought and language. Opening the valve of fluency—generating as many written words per minute as possible—is exactly what many of us need to do in order to reach—or to approximate—the point where we are satisfied that our language aligns with our perceptions of reality. As Kate summed up, "The self-conscious hunt is what's crippling."

Both of Kate's inclinations—letting the river flow while, in the shadows, *also* attending to pleasing mergers of thought and language—are true and perceptive. Overall, writers have little choice but to run hot and cold at the same time. Kate's approach here seems similar to an ingrained pattern within her thinking and writing, one that will be explored later—her ability to simultaneously hold two contradictory ideas in mind, without judging either. The overall effect, especially for writing-for-healing purposes, is that these delicate balancing acts enable writers to keep thinking. After all, if we *begin* with a judgment or conclusion, why go further? This was only one type of a rich variety of thinking strategies that Kate wove in and out of her journal, which I'll explore in the next section.

Thinking Processes in Kate's Writing about Trauma

Most people who have known and worked with Kate would identify her as a soft-spoken, thoughtful, cerebral person. This quality dominates her journal entries, which I have sorted into the following themes: (1) reifying, repeating, and reminding; (2) framing through names, images, and metaphors; (3) questioning; (4) connecting and interweaving; (5) connecting local with global issues; (6) balancing oppositions; and (7) solving problems. The bulk of this chapter, then, focuses on the variety and depth of Kate's thinking processes. I conclude with exploring some issues that are common to all of Kate's writing about trauma.

Reifying, Repeating, Reminding

In the journal entries made in the first days after Kate lost her husband in an accident, she appears, like anyone would in a similar situation, stunned into disbelief. James Woodward (1967) defines *reification* as, "the taking as real that which is only apparently real; the taking as objectively real that which is only subjectively real" and emphasizes that it is "ever present in mental functioning" for everyone (214). I believe it is a common and even natural response when we experience extreme stress. Kate is no exception. Each of the following excerpts appears at the end of much longer entries. Also, such entries appear throughout the journal.

- And yet . . . the Magnolias all around Merton Library . . . I wanted you to see them with your own eyes.
- Your white hat somehow in the field, the vineyard, has been put up on a post—to greet anyone who enters the vineyard. Okay, now, Hank—just come home.

- In the mail today was this card from Laura Chang. She wrote:

  > Dear Mrs. Jamison—Have you heard people calling Hank 'Teddy Bear'? That was how Hank was recommended to me a few years back when I needed a good attorney for a land deal. Thanks to him my land was saved from being taken advantage of. To me, Hank lives in people's hearts that he touched. Sincerely yours, Laura Chang. My teddy bear—come home.

- Andy [son] has so much unfinished business . . . he still needs a father, you. I, too, am stepping in your shoes . . . I may be a decent parent, but I'm not a father. Stay with us, Hank.
- I'm tired, aching. Want you home.

I believe that Kate is fully aware that her repeated request for Hank to "come home" and "stay with us" will never result in his suddenly striding into the living room. While these entries begin in a rational, controlled, and *contained* manner, they end on notes of deep pain clothed in *wishful* thinking. I view them as similar to what Joan Didion (2005) describes as "magical thinking" or, as Bronislaw Malinowski calls (1967), "an unwarranted extension of reality." Nonetheless, such thinking and writing represent an effective means of writing about trauma, though many readers would not think so at first glance. They would likely find such messages to be sad, useless cries in the dark, however plaintive. And they would be right.

However, there is more to this use of language. Kate's direct requests for her husband to come home serve as *reminders to herself—framed in positive ways*—that Hank indeed will not and cannot come home. In a shocked and stunned state, she feels the need to communicate the hard fact of his passing over and over again. Simple repetition helps us hold on when our world spins out of control. To repeat this message in a neutral or negative way, such as "You're dead and I'll never, ever see you again," is too harsh, too soon—way too soon. Asking her husband to return is a familiar command expressed in a very common (hence comfortable) syntactical pattern. As well, "home" is something she can see and feel; this word elicits positive emotions of the past. Kate's come-home requests are the gentlest reminders to herself that he is gone. They serve as concrete, tangible ways that allow Kate the time to more fully absorb her husband's non-existence. In a small way, they function to hold off or fend off a reality that is too harsh, too bizarre to grasp, until such time that she *can* better realize the truth. In these ways, this form of *magic* helps Kate to organize and integrate the sudden change in her life.

FRAMING THROUGH NAMES, IMAGES, AND METAPHORS

Here, *framing* means the explicit and implicit language and meanings we use to *couch* our messages in, as explored by Gardner (2011), Huckin (2002), and others. Like an actual picture frame, it can make a difference whether DaVinci's *Mona Lisa* appears in an unpainted frame of pine wood—or a wide, heavy frame, intricately carved and gilded with gold. Framing can also be evident in direct and indirect attitudes and values we convey before, during, and after our message. Of course, framing can appear in the words and phrases we select. For example, if we are writing about *taxes*, we may choose to frame this activity as *indirect charges*, as *infrastructure funds*, as *bleeding of the middle class,* or even as *membership fees*. Framing is the way we *present* a message, how we wrap it.

Framing can be direct, as in *naming* something, serving as a kind of *straight line* from the words to the issue at hand, in an attempt to be as clear as possible. Or, it can be indirect and suggestive, as in comparing one thing to another through the use of metaphor and simile, which usually provide readers and writers with more ambiguity and possibility in thinking about the relationships between the things compared.

Naming

Writers, who search for the most direct and precise term(s) to match their thought, are engaging in naming—the main way to frame an issue. Many skilled writers frame their points more or less automatically during the act of writing first drafts. Others may focus on framing during successive cycles of revision and editing. Throughout Kate's journal, I find *direct* and *indirect* framing. Direct framing occurs when she very explicitly *names* a particular phenomenon—from observations, to vague feelings, to attitudes, to behaviors, and to values. Such names usually have a single meaning. In some entries, Kate *named* her husband's specific characteristics. A single entry (April 16) lists and briefly describes twelve such qualities. Here are some examples from her journal.

- Hank the gourmet—pride in cooking for holiday dinners, we 5, eventually all good things.
- Hank the Depression Era Hausfrau—frugal, shopped w/list only & hunted best deals.

- Hank the Scholar—wanted to read a Hemingway short story? Read everything he wrote—1000s of pages. That was pre-Ben. Other reading themes: Northern territories, Canadian history, grapes. Lots of fiction too. Lots nonfiction. Lots.

- Hank the marathoner—literally, but also . . . built a house (not one but two), camped just about every camping trip when guys in scouts, Phi Beta Kappa, JD. Addict in good ways & bad.

- Hank the mystery man—rarely identified himself on phone—usually just stated "Hey"—& went on w/whatever subject. Listener beware!

- Hank the wordsmith—his humor & wordplay could catch you off guard—esp from someone often silent, gruff.

- Hank the herbal tea drinker—Yes, believe it or not. Never exclusively but a lot in recent years. Day he died I heard him claim to be an alcoholic—never before—when he was actually a practicing one.

Overall, in this context, naming helps Kate to *put a handle* on something, helps to demystify it, to manage it. Naming can establish the writer's sense of truth or reality, make an assertion, challenge a power relationship, or reinforce one (Lutz 1990, 14). While these descriptions include positive, negative, and neutral elements, their overall tone is whimsically affectionate. In a word, *balanced*—another key element of writing for healing, because it convinces everyone—especially the writer or speaker herself—that she is right to grieve—that the *entire* context definitely warrants her actions. Most important, though, is Kate's use of naming as a form of *bearing witness* or paying tribute to Hank—a foundational part of writing for healing. It's what happens at funerals. It's paying our respects. We are telling ourselves that there is now a gap, a void in life itself. Life, too, can be defined by what it is *not*.

Like many of us, Kate strives to name things that she is trying to understand. Even for experienced writers, it does not happen automatically or easily. It takes work. In one entry, cited later, Kate describes sorting through her husband's office and realizing that there are photos and mementos of their children and of other interests, but none of *her*. She names this as "not news" but a "felt reality." She then works her way toward this naming.

What I think I'm trying to say is this: Even though today's work was one more reminder of ways you did not recognize me much, it was also a reminder of all sorts of other ways in which you were *a good man* (italics mine). No secrets that I know of, not like I was *replaced* by anyone. You were just wrapped up in this kinda he-man world.

Such *working towards a name* typically involves elaborating, as well as qualifying statements to delimit the point. Such cycles of elaboration and qualification—moving forward and backward—allow expressive writers to more effectively match their words with their thoughts. Another device used in this passage is the statement, "What I'm trying to say is this," which functions as a *re-grouping*—a pause that may allow her to think of just the right term, as her thinking gathers momentum, rolling toward her precise target: saying exactly what she wants to say.

The ellipsis marks near the end of the following excerpt indicate omitted *re-grouping* language (for space reasons), which help Kate to name the issue at hand, *emotional matricide*. Kate's daughter-in-law had demanded that her husband, Andy (Kate's son), cut off all ties with his mother and brothers. Kate noted later that, "Desperate to save a failing marriage, he did as he was told." Therefore, on top of dealing with her immediate grief over her husband's loss, Kate was also groping to understand how her son could shut his family out of his life—enough reason to cause the most skilled of language-users to *re-group* in their thinking and language:

> I have many feelings about Andy, & concern certainly trumps them. But anger is one of the feelings—it's not at all how I'd characterize my feelings about Andy as a *person*, as a soul, but it is certainly how I feel about his *behavior*. I know I don't have the whole picture—& even if I were close, we're humanly incapable of omniscience. Still, I do know some things & I know that the behaviors are extreme. Usually extreme isolation, extreme moves to cut off communication signal not-so-positive states of mind or feeling: fear or anxiety or refusal to think, question. Ultimately, it's THAT which concerns me. . . . I accept Andy always—he can come "home," but yet I find his emotional matricide offensive, unjust, deeply wrong. . . .

Kate was able to withhold judgment of her son's behavior when he was married to an abusive and controlling wife because Kate never doubted that the real, loving son was "there" and would prevail. Indeed, he later divorced this woman, fully reintegrated with his family, and has happily remarried.

Framing through Images

Another form of naming is the use of imagery—using details to evoke sensory meanings and feelings, which help place the reader/writer there, in the moment. In one conversation, Kate stated, "There were years when I wrote poetry but not a lot, but at the moment it's not my medium of choice. I like poetic moments but I do not try to write poetry." After studying her journal, I found this to be an accurate assessment; consider this entry:

> Seeing the open garage door—door to your new temple—& your Puma chair. Place was empty. By the chair Ben's sketch pads. And your cigar. While I'm not happy about this, it's so poignant. It was a visual poem of Ben's grieving—or what I interpret as that.

In this excerpt, Kate assumes a *poet's stance*. That is, poets often begin with observing an everyday object and recognize its implied meanings and values, considering it as a kind of symbol, before crafting it into an artful patterning of language. Kate did not take the next step of writing this up as a poem, even though she begins by naming the garage with an image, "your new temple." Nonetheless, she records and notes the image, satisfied with it remaining a *visual poem*—in itself, an image. In numerous entries, as well as in our interviews, Kate assumes a poet's stance or point of view. This is revealed in what she selects to focus on, as well as her language choices and sensitivity to imagery. In one conversation, she talked about Cormac McCarthy's novel, *The Road*.

> I haven't finished it. It was too bleak. I couldn't finish it, even though McCarthy is a consummate craftsman. It is the most exquisite description of grief, a portrait of grief. This book was just too much the way I felt. It's page after page of just ashes!

Kate often employs images when she observes nature: In these passages, her own love of nature glows through, and Hank is always closely associated with the natural world: "We see traces of your handiwork everywhere . . . the Chambourcin had not only bud-burst but also leaf growth w/these infinitesimally small grape clusters, tiny perfect possibilities."

Another form of imagery in these pages is Kate's using them to project into the future, to what would have been.

> It's spring—it's a time of rebirth, renaissance. I think you would've come downstairs—thundered down the stairs—& banged around in the kitchen this morning w/ a slight glint in your eye, a lift in your chest. You would've stood in underpants, leaning on the counter, watching the birds on the railing as you ate your monster muffin & would've noticed, gladly, a leafing out of the oaks—last to leaf. The fullness in the yard—the splash of pink in the pots on the deck.

This projecting into the future through imagery seems to be another instance of *healing*, as she concludes this description of a spring morning, noting, "You seemed to be happier and becoming mellower."

Framing through Metaphors

Indirect framing occurs when Kate employs similes and metaphors, linking together two or more unrelated items, all in a condensed and compressed way. While such comparisons can often seem *direct* in their meaning, others can contain sufficient ambiguity or room for more than one interpretation to emerge. The following excerpts from Kate's journal contain such open-ended comparisons:

> The bud-burst everywhere has been late, but this cool morning sunrise was exquisite ... ordinarily my favorite time of year, this stage of pre-spring. *The beauty of the morning was the brick I've needed on my skull* ... no, you—gardener, viticulturist, naturalist you—won't be witnessing this spring ... I'm starting to "get it," starting to understand you're not really here.

This first metaphor example merges two very unlike things—the fresh beauty of a spring morning—and a brick on her skull. The emphasis achieved through this brevity and stark contrast seems to function as a harsh reminder to herself—a wake-up call (or a hard knock on the head!): "When my mind and spirit are bristling with grief." She seems to tell herself, "wade into the soothing beauty of nature." This powerful metaphor gives way to *naming* Hank, as discussed earlier, "I'm *discover-*

ing the subterranean web of memories & emotions—where one immediate memory or emotion *ripples through,* turning up others."

The second metaphor is effective in that Kate *discovers* something underground and unseen—how one memory or emotion triggers others. These subsequent *ripples* could be thought of as shock-waves from a mild earthquake. Or, the *subterranean* and *rippling through* could be equally appropriate for waves in deep water. This metaphor shows the ambiguity or multiple levels of meaning that such indirect framing can convey.

> So, when I wasn't out on the road (am) or trail (pm) enjoying this May day, I was in your office going through things. . . . Telling HER (or you) made me cry harder than I had all day. Margaret??? Why cry for Margaret? Because she's suffering too—as her 84 yr. old husband is weakening with a bad heart? Or because my emotions are exhausted & fickle? *This I can't explain, but something else I think I can:* All this picking up after you, going through all your damned messes, is a very effective way of processing, of feeling like *you with all your being are being pulled through me—through my mind, my heart, my tired body.* I'm witnessing, remembering, reliving & in some cases discovering you, but living and experiencing you.

This final metaphor, when Kate describes cleaning out Hank's office, is the most unique and powerful of the three, as well as of the entire journal. The passage begins with Kate's *re-grouping:* "This I can't explain, but something else I think I can: All this picking up after you. . . ." This *pause* for re-grouping allows her time to think, to gather steam as she rolls toward her metaphor. As Kate sorts through the papers, photos, and books, they *become* her husband, as Hank and all his stuff are *being pulled through* her mind, heart, and body. She, in effect, becomes a sieve or mesh filter through which every aspect of his life is wrenchingly strained.

Overall, imagery and metaphors are healing in different, complex ways. First, we should understand that such elements are *not* mere flourishes or ornaments of language, little baubles to pull out when we want to dress up a plain message. Instead, as Steven Pinker (2007) and others remind us, they are necessary tools of not just our imagination, but also of rational thought—and yes, of healing. Sometimes, imagery and metaphor can do the work of all three simultaneously.

So, how does such language help us to heal? First, metaphoric and imagistic language can help us heal because they *focus* our thinking and energy. When elaborating descriptive details about something, we often become increasingly specific. Consider the excerpt quoted earlier: "We see traces of your handiwork everywhere . . . the Chambourcin had not only bud-burst but also leaf growth w/these infinitesimally small grape clusters, tiny perfect possibilities." The most general term here is "handiwork everywhere."

Like a camera zooming in, Kate next moves to the specific type of grape plant, the Chambourcin, and then closer, to the bursting buds and growing leaves—and finally to the closest view of all—small, tiny, perfect clusters of grapes. In terms of healing, the more we can focus our attention, the better chance we have of understanding and internalizing something—and hence of effecting change, of healing. Metaphors, too, work to focus our attention on the very act of framing, as we pay little or no attention to facts or anything else beyond the frame we're building to hold the two items side-by-side. (While Kate employs techniques of naming, imagery, and metaphor—language which focuses and *identifies* things—she just as consistently *qualifies* and *parses* her meanings, clarifying and refining her prose.)

Second, images and metaphors help us heal because they are rooted in physical experiences. In these three examples, the metaphors are based on Kate's experiences with bricks, land beneath topsoil (or deep water), and a sieve. Among other things, basing one's comparisons on actual experiences makes them more convincing, because they are grounded in reality that we can touch, taste, smell, feel, and see. Third, because metaphors compare two or more unlike things, they open a door to help us think in a different way: The elegant grace of a spring morning becomes a brick on the skull. Such new or different ways of thinking can lead us to realizations or discoveries, which we are apt to more deeply remember and internalize. This is especially true for unusual comparisons, like this one.

Fourth, metaphors work to heal not just because of comparisons, but because of the *relationships* among the parts of the metaphor, especially the question of how well the parts of the metaphor fit together. Kate's third metaphor was written near the end of her journal, so the question becomes whether all she had been experiencing—all the people, events, memories, associations, sadness, confusion, and yes, the items in Hank's office—were being strained through her being? I would certainly say yes; this is a very appropriate, logical, and rational comparison. This metaphor is healings because it is also doing work for reasoning, as well as imagining.

Kate's uses of direct and indirect framing stand out because most of her writing *refrains* from making definitive assertions of any kind. She consistently and meticulously qualifies her statements, by adding details of what she *is* trying to articulate, as well as details about what she is *not* intending. As well, at the ends of such passages, she remains remarkably non-judgmental. As a reader, I found myself wanting Kate to take a stand far more often than she in fact does. However, these examples of direct and indirect framing reveal that she *does indeed* arrive at definitive *conclusions* throughout her writing, achieving some balance, although somewhat weighted toward the qualifying and the withholding of judgments.

There are two sides to this issue—to withhold judgment for extended periods versus making an assertion and putting it to (some) rest. Many writers err on one side or the other. Kate errs on the side of patient angels, as she works to deliberately disentangle her thoughts and feelings, to hold each thread up to the light, turn it around slowly, gently, so as not to tear it, studying it from different perspectives. In this sense, she is a model writer for purposes of healing. Many of us would not be able to maintain her standard. But we should try. Kate practices what general semanticists have long known—that if we judge, if we make our minds up about something, then why even bother to think further about it? Judgments stop thought. And writing about trauma depends upon thought. Kate told me that this habit might be somewhat innate, somewhat conscious, and *somewhat internalized* due to her background and education. When I asked Kate if maintaining such balance also carried any restraints or limitations, she stated, "Hamlet's dilemma—thinking can impede action (I think that's good. . . .)."

Questioning

Kate poses questions to her deceased husband, to herself, and occasionally, to both of them at the same time. Some entries are dominated by questions. Throughout her journal, questions functioned in different ways—to explore, to lead to *answers*, to express the impossible, and to mask *unsafe* thoughts.

Questions Used to Explore

Sometimes, Kate asks questions just for the sake of opening things up, for brainstorming issues to put on the table—maybe as a kind of *warm-up* activity, like stretching before jogging. The following brief paragraphs are from an early entry.

- Because much of our relationship was in our heads—in our awareness & understanding—it's hard to feel you're gone. You're still in my head. What's different?
- There's been so much commotion—scores of people to the house—40? 60? 80?—and hundreds at the service(500–600)—and phone calls & so on—so much of this that I haven't really faced stillness yet. It is different, but I haven't figured that out yet.

"What's different?" seems quickly placed on the table and then immediately abandoned for an entirely different topic. But we realize that *she* has not forgotten it at the end of the last paragraph. Throughout the grieving period of this entire journal, this two-word question is what she labors to understand. The quick and seemingly off-hand nature of this question—and her return to it—underscores Kate's nimbleness of mind, her lack of hesitation in asking it, even in the middle of things—and her confidence in returning to it. Overall, a less experienced or stunted writer would not interrupt herself for something she might consider to be *off topic*. Writing for healing requires that writers trust their tangents, that they be fearless about flitting here, there, and everywhere.

Questions Leading to Answers and Assertions

Asking questions—and then answering them—is a staple of writing for healing. Providing more than one *answer*, stated directly or implied, is even better:

Dear Hank,

You may be no Christ figure, but I've thought of you constantly in nearly those terms: In giving new life & rebirth in death. I don't mean any of the rebirth *justifies* the death—it doesn't. That's not, not, not what I'm saying. But I'm comforted in odd ways by your *active* presence, by the work or whatever made possible or triggered (not that it wasn't possible before) by your death. Not that it's a casual thing—don't want to overstate that.

> And, yet, somehow your life is unmasked more & continues to gather meaning & force even now. Am I crazy? It's one way you're alive with me.

The question at the end, "Am I crazy?" is answered in the next sentence. Kate notes that this is only "one way" that Hank is alive with her, holding the door open for *additional* answers.

Because Kate's journal is so full of questioning and drawing fine distinctions (i.e., *thinking*), few entries take a firm stand on any issue. Doubt and an open stance are hallmarks of her approach. However, in a couple of instances, questions seem to have allowed her to become more assertive.

> And I'm troubled—guilty to some degree—of feeling simultaneously grief for you—my face so wet that Lynn thought it had started raining again when she stopped Jasper [dog] and me—<u>and</u> a knowledge that there are chunks of the day when I feel liberated, free, happy. Like my three-year plus crippling depression just *snapped*. And, while I think *I* can make sense of these mixed feelings, I doubt others would easily understand them & I wonder . . . would you? Do you? I really don't know. There are <u>some</u> ways in which you were and still are inscrutable.

In the final sentence, Kate takes a strong stand, at least for her. Even though this conviction is couched in *mixed feelings*, and even though her firmness resides in *not knowing*, it nonetheless helps her draw a line in the sand. Kate later wrote me that Hank's inscrutability had struck some of her friends as being symptomatic of someone on the Asperger's spectrum, and one close friend had given her Christopher Slater-Walker's, *An Asperger Marriage* (2002). Hank had always been remote.

Here, Kate's habitual questioning—her great strength, allowing her to learn and explore—plays a role at the opposite end of the spectrum, as her questions seem to have backed her into a corner in which she *had* to admit a definite perspective.

Kate's questioning to explore and generate ideas is far more important than taking a stand and making assertions. However, Kate's writing demonstrates that assertions—especially those growing out of many questions—*also* provide writers a sense of control, a sense that they are in charge of their world—also crucial for purposes of healing.

Questions Used to Express the Impossible

The main function of rhetorical questions—those that can never be truly answered by anyone—is to express frustration, to give voice to the fact that the writer is trying hard to understand the unfathomable. The questions posed near the end of the previous excerpt cannot be answered. Nor can the question posed here.

> Although I continue to have moments varying from facial contractions to full blown crying, I mostly experience a dry, stony-eyed bewilderment. I don't like that stony-eyed bewilderment. If people we hardly knew can well up instantly with tears, why don't I? And yet, when the roles have been reversed, I know I do the same, just for example, when I was telling Laura White about Sharon's mother's death. So now—why won't those healing, washing tears come more easily? Is part of it the release of subterranean emotions, long constrained, that counters grieving? I suspect a little, and if so, I think you actually understand all that. But is part of it disbelief? My state of stunned stupidity?

Here, the first and second questions posed are essentially the same, with an example provided to illustrate and focus on the first version of the question. Next, the *answer* occurs as another question before being confirmed with, "I suspect a little. . . ." These give rise to an even larger question, "Is part of it disbelief?" In short, questions can generate more focused questions, as well as tentative *answers*. And these can lead to more complex questions.

Overall, such questions are often necessary and healthy when writing about trauma. There are several reasons for this. First, expressing this frustration satisfies the need for disclosure, for simply getting it out, reducing its weight in the mind and emotions. Second, during the process of writing, even though the writer may well know that such questions cannot be answered, the physical act of writing them anyway provides a brief respite or pause, which can allow us to gather our wits, so that we may focus on the next sentences, including those that may offer more insight into the issue at hand. Venting can aid fluency, which in turn can enhance thinking. Third, writing down such questions can place them into our subconscious, allowing them to resurface later with additional or new perspectives.

Questions Used to Mask "Unsafe" Thoughts

I do not think it's at all unusual for us to sense that our pets are somehow aware of the death of a loved one, or even if the spirit of the deceased somehow appears within a pet. Many years ago, my mother seemed convinced that her father was alive in the spirit of her pet basset hound. Charles, the dog, shared her father's stubbornness. Such associations occur in Kate's journal, a natural venue because it is so private. Most of us cannot publicly admit to such thinking. Consider the following examples.

April 10

Dear Hank,

Jasper thinks I've lost a few marbles, for I'm talking to you on most of our walks—sometimes crying, sometimes—like now—high as a kite. Jasper, by the way, has forgotten that he used to bark at you & have pissing contests with you—he's missing you. He mopes around lethargically & looks up, with close eye contact, mournfully. Kitty, too, is acting differently—to the tune of hiding in our bed under the covers—a bump in the middle of the bed. Even the telephone fell apart. It's broken. Animate & inanimate—we're not the same.

April 13

Dear Hank,

Have you come back to us in the form of the cat? The cat you swatted off the bed at every move—the cat you also tolerated when your allergies would have led most people to swat it out of the house??

I rarely used an alarm because you were our alarm. I still don't use an alarm (for me, I hardly sleep), but when I am on the edge of oversleeping, the cat gently paws my face, her nails retracted. Then she sits, paws folded under her chest, within a few feet of me wherever I go upstairs. She seems to be watching, protecting. Sure your spirit hasn't slipped inside her?

May 4

Dear Hank

. . . . But the boys. . . . Russ is churning with feelings, quietly, but he acknowledges, verbalizes it. Feels strange today. Ben hangs around *all* day. This is an altered reality, Hank. I wonder—have I gone a little crazy? If I have, I hope you'll send a deer my way before too long.

May 18

I told you earlier that I suspect you've come to visit in the form of the cat [smiley face drawn in parenthesis]. So today, the cat was not only under covers as she has occasionally done since you died, but on your side, tucked in exactly in your spot.

The first passage (April 10) is the first entry in this journal, just a handful of days since her husband's accident, caused by swerving his motor scooter to avoid hitting a deer in the road. During grief, associations become so strong, that it is easy to make this *transfer* of one person's qualities to that of a loved pet. We could also consider this another form of *reification* as explored earlier in this chapter. (Of course, none of this is to say that pets do not grieve for deceased owners or for the loss of another pet; many people believe that they do.) During this entire period, Kate associates her husband's qualities with those of Jasper, the dog, the cat, and even inanimate objects. When I asked Kate about her references to the cat—one of which included a smiley face she had drawn—she smiled and said, "I was a little facetious . . . and humor can give a different perspective. Hank hated the cat and the dog. And yet, there were times when I would come home and they would be like an old married couple, side by side."

A tinge of dark humor colors her request that Hank send a deer her way. Mild humor, stated or posed in questions, can mask or make safe those intense thoughts that we may *know*, under normal circumstances, are irrational—including the thought, however unlikely, that such an accident could end her own pain. Writing about such taboo notions gives them voice and shape, which helps writers assure themselves that they are indeed *not* crazy. When we write down such thoughts and make them visible, we *impose some distance between these emotional and irratio-*

nal thoughts and ourselves. In so doing, of course, we are re-constructing, re-assembling the self, which has been fragmented by trauma.

This section explored a few different functions of questioning oneself when writing about trauma. I'm sure there are far more. Kate's questions and her responses to them show that she is aware of her audience—her husband, herself, as well as other unknown future readers. At the same time, Kate's questions address her own issues. Overall, her background and training in language and literacy afford her the opportunity to believe that she *can*, somehow, through thinking and language, understand the sudden death of her husband. What is more, she seems confident she can accomplish this feat while *also* reconfiguring her sense of *normal life*.

CONNECTING AND INTERWEAVING

When we speak and write, regardless of the situation, our words *move* up and down: from the very specific and concrete (e.g., "Leda, our nine-year-old Australian Shepherd dog, turns over on her back, wanting to be petted"), to the general and abstract (e.g., "Human-animal interactions can be mutually beneficial"). These levels are like rungs on a ladder, from the ground, up, with plenty of steps in between the first rung and the last. One pattern in Kate's thinking is her *beginning* entries very specifically, then, moving up this ladder of abstraction, toward more generalized language and broader issues. Other times, she begins with the larger concept, then scales downward to specifics, weaving back and forth. Put another way—but not to mix a metaphor too badly—Kate's writing is often similar to dropping a stone into a pool, which creates concentric rings of larger, more encompassing ideas, flowing outward from this center:

> KATE: I like grounding grief in MY world of experience. Last night I re-read what I'd written a year ago. There was lots of stuff I'd forgotten and I'm glad to have that history—the stuff that happened as well as what I was thinking about it. *I had to do it in a big-time way—process both my concrete experiences and their larger philosophical implications.* That's the most valuable way for me to do that. That's what life is about, witnessing and then integrating it into your life. I might launch it with an image or memory but it's more of a weaving back and forth, digging and reaching, letting myself branch out.

RF: So you typically begin with something specific and concrete, and then move to reflection?

KATE: Yes, but it's far more intertwined.

Kate's journal is saturated with connections of all types. One entry begins by noting that she had just finished baking a birthday cake for her son. This in turn leads to a previous birthday cake that Hank had baked for the same son, who never came home to share it. This evolved into a discussion of the son's girlfriend, whom Kate feels is unnecessarily controlling her son, keeping him distant from his own family. The letter ends with a discussion of anger—at what her husband felt then, as well as how he *might* have responded to the current situation. Kate consistently makes connections without boundaries, linking people, ideas, places, books, movies, objects, and events across time and space.

A few weeks after the loss of her husband, Kate made the following entry, part of which appears below:

Dear Hank,

The roller coaster day—like previous ones—comes to an end.... I don't wholesale cry much but a dozen—maybe two dozen—times a day, I'll break out of my workaday mentality & remember something specific about you, which causes me to wince & contort my face, have watery eyes, but not to really cry. I see Russ in your brown casual work pants—like you. Tonight—until almost midnight—he was stretched out on a hospital bed in ER—wearing a Ben and Jerry blue T-shirt & your own brown cuffed pants. He'd cut his hand and Ben [Russ's brother] took him to ER—he got stitches & will be okay—but it was so ominous being there, in ER, in some of the same rooms you'd been in or near. He was so like you—he *is* part of you—he is literally, biologically, & psychologically part of your legacy. I look at Russ's shoulders, his jaw line, the break of his toes—he's got lots of you in him. He's one way that you live on. He's not you—he's Russ—but there we are—the web of interrelated parts of life. That sense of the interrelatedness of all things is part of what helps me with what was good & lost & what was very imperfect. We're growing and learning through all of this.

Only a few weeks after Kate had been in a hospital's emergency room, tending her fatally injured husband, she was suddenly thrust back to the same place, with her injured son. In this situation it would be impossible for anyone *not* to connect father to son, one fear to another. I feel confident that, at that time, this connection was all too obvious to Kate. How could it not be? However, most important of all, *she wrote it down anyway. She directly stated "the interrelatedness of life," rendering it concrete and visible on the page.* She next noted its purpose and function. Even if a particular thought is starkly obvious, as this one was for Kate, it is important to write it down, to make it real, to remember it, to think on it later, if even unconsciously. Concepts and phrases like "the interrelatedness of life" are fine and good. We can certainly understand why and how this notion might comfort those who have lost a loved one. But such concepts remain maddeningly abstract and unanchored to everyday life. Kate makes the concept come alive by connecting it to her son's trip to the emergency room—and this cannot be fully realized unless it is made visible on the page.

Another of Kate's connections warrants a closer look. The following excerpt moves up and down the ladder of abstraction, easily ebbing and flowing, back and forth across the large and small:

> So, when I wasn't out on the road (am) or trail (pm) enjoying this May day, I was in your office going through things. While I was there I felt very matter of fact—cheerful even—or sometimes pissed at your messes—but not particularly sad while I worked. Exceptions: when Debbie wanted to confess she'd never told you how much she admired you & she wished she had. She'd worked for lots of bosses & you were different—something Pam and Rose both said at different times. You were clear and fair about work stuff & you never expected to have coffee made or things like that. And that, of course, triggered tears, tears in other places, other moments—talking with Meghan Morehouse over lunch, talking with Donna & later Katie Bauman. . . .
>
> This I can't explain, but something else I think I can: All this picking up after you, through all your damned messes, is a very effective way of processing, of feeling like you with all your being are being pulled through me—through my mind, my heart, my tired body. I'm witnessing, remembering, reliving & some cases discovering—you, but living & experiencing you. I'm in your office & I feel in some ways my absence. There's lots of stuff about boys, camping, cigars, scouts; there's *nothing*

about me. This is not news, but it's again a felt reality. But also felt is the goodness, the habits, the peculiarities, the limitations (cigar peels, ointments, Tums, etc.), the general responsibility & connectedness-to-county people, the quality of your service . . . I felt all that being pulled through me.

What I think I'm trying to say is this: Even though today's work was one more reminder of ways you did not recognize me much, it was also a reminder of all sorts of other ways in which you were a good man. No secrets that I know of, not like I was *replaced* by anyone. You were just wrapped up in this kinda he-man world & in that world you were funny, you farted (you had a can of air freshener), you had loads of pictures & reminders of your children, you had various camp things, you had lots of contacts & notes work related (&/-), some w/friendly overtones. And the absence of me in mementos doesn't mean I was *entirely* absent . . . I, too, have more kid stuff in my office, but that isn't b/c I didn't think about you at work—or in the bulk of my life—was not reflected accurately by my mementos in my office. Yet, it's true to some degree that we were absent from each other's lives more than we might have been, & yet . . . we had mutual trust, I think, in each other's basic goodness. Part of what I'm trying to describe is that working through your office today just affirmed so much of what I've always felt—have known. I felt lots of dimensions of your personality & liked it, admired it mostly. Also felt the keen focus of the he-man world & work issues.

Here and in many other entries, Kate's connections help make the small and seemingly insignificant, important. Actively weaving in and out of large and small so frequently is, in one sense, simple repetition, which further drives home the point that small is large and vice versa. Doing so can make large and small merge into much the same thing, unifying them, making them more whole, more healing. Let's take a closer look at how a single sentence connects the large and small:

> This I can't explain, but something else I think I can: All this picking up after you, through all your damned messes, is a very effective way of processing, of feeling like you with all your being are being pulled through me—through my mind, my heart, my tired body.

This sentence *moves* from the large ("something" she can and cannot explain), to the small ("picking up after you"), to the slightly larger ("your damned messes"), to even a bit larger ("effective way of *processing*")—and then to the largest, most abstract element of the whole piece: "all your being . . . being pulled through me." Finally, the sentence ends by subtly descending the ladder to "my mind, my heart, my tired body." Therefore, the most general notion here—"all your being . . . being pulled through me"—is expressed as a kind of metaphor—a language device that takes this vague feeling *back down* the ladder in the other direction—a sophisticated use of language. Also, this sentence has a long and complex structure. That is, Kate's skill with syntax is automatic. She has at her fingertips a variety of complex forms in which to *pour* her meaning. Overall, when skilled writers add details to their independent or *base* clauses, they often move toward greater specificity. The more specific a writer is, the more firmly anchored in reality she is. When a trauma casts us into an unreal or surreal world, grounding ourselves in reality is, well . . . healing.

Second, in this entry, the minutiae of life—the cigar peel, the roll of *Tums* antacid tablets—reside right next to the large metaphysical notion of her deceased husband "being pulled through" her. Especially within such a brief passage, it is hard to imagine a greater *range* between the concrete and the abstract. It is hard to explain why or how someone's thinking can deftly scale up and down the ladder of abstraction, linking the large with the small—and midpoints in between. Some of Kate's ability, of course, is genetic, but her experience and education in language also play a significant role. One must have both confidence and flexibility of mind and language to freely *range about*, connecting large and small.

I have long considered this skill to be the primary criterion for *thinking in writing*. General semanticists (e.g., Korzybski 1995 and Hayakawa 1991) would consider this ability to be necessary for mental and emotional stability. Consider the speaker or writer who *cannot* communicate in ways that scamper up and down the ladder of abstraction—those who are stuck on either end of the ladder, unable to move up or down. On the most general or upper end of the ladder, we see the literary theorist or the sociologist who speaks in the broadest, vaguest of terms: "Facilitators may wish to acknowledge echoes of programmatic effectiveness in a multitude of instances after the fundamental processes have evidenced success." Entire documents can read like this, with nothing to grasp onto, nothing to see, touch, taste, or smell. On the opposite end of the ladder, this neighbor entangles herself and her listener in a quagmire of details:

> When I went into the garage I found the cat's water bowl turned over and the water soaking my box of newspapers I'd put there to take to the recycling center—the one that's past Broadway—no—maybe it's over by West Boulevard, where they had the street torn up last week, when I was trying to take my lawnmower to be fixed, the one with the broken cable, the one that turns on the self-propelling wheel, the one that I just had fixed last week . . . and found the cat on my way out, who had been trapped in there, and. . . .

This neighbor has no hope of finding a larger category to make his message briefer, no hope of finding a straighter line to his point. He could have saved everyone's time, confusion, and anguish by simply saying, "It's been a busy day, I almost forgot the cat." Being frozen or stuck on any rung of the ladder means you do not have much of a chance to make connections—and connection-making is crucial for writing as healing, as we suture pieces back together into a new whole.

CONNECTING LOCAL WITH GLOBAL CONCERNS

I asked Kate about a trend I had discovered in interviewing other people about their writing about trauma: "Do you ever think about *larger* social or environmental issues, such as climate change or poverty?"

> Yes, I would say so. No matter what I'm writing about—everything we do is motivated by deeply held values and beliefs—all shaped and constrained by larger issues. I try to open students' minds to issues . . . students who had never thought about water (engineering students), but then empower them—*you* are the future and have the resources. This is an example for work. But my own struggling with grief is so compounded—I don't tell my kids this—but I struggle to have hope that there *is* a positive world for them. I hope we don't bequeath them something so toxic that. . . . I told myself, "Kate: you have to have hope, you can't teach kids without having hope. . . . Overarching all of this is this deep concern for the world. The child in McCarthy's

book has a father who goes on to give everything he can to his son. That's the hope McCarthy is after.

When I first asked writers if they connected their own trauma to larger societal dilemmas, I expected them to say "No" or "Seldom." After all, I reasoned, they had their own intense battles to take care of first. Of course, a few did not, but the majority did indeed make this connection, at least in a *background* kind of way, as Kate did. The social problems likely fade into and out of their consciousness as they are writing. This link merits more investigation than I have been able to do here.

However, as described elsewhere in this chapter, Kate engages in the same basic movement of connecting smaller issues to larger issues *within* her private writing, so to explicitly link her local concerns with global ones would not be terribly different. I suspect that the main healing benefit is one of perspective—zooming in on your own problems and then zooming out on more global concerns, maybe allowing one perspective to inform the other. In a best-case scenario, a kind of dialogue would evolve between local and global issues. Finally, direct and even subtle connections between our own private issues and society's larger dilemmas may be a step toward the writer's engaging in the *helping the self through helping others* paradigm.

Balancing Oppositions

> And I'm troubled—guilty, to some degree—of feeling simultaneously grief for you—my face so wet that Linda Schneider thought it had started raining again when she stopped Jasper [dog] and me—*and* a knowledge that there are chunks of the day when I feel liberated, free, happy. (Kate's journal entry, April 19)

One of the most striking features of Kate's journal is her consistently focusing on two opposite ideas or things at the same time. This *balancing of oppositions* can be life/death, good/bad, confusion/clarity, her viewpoint/her husband's viewpoint, and so forth. You could also refer to this characteristic as Kate's exercising multiple perspectives, in that she never mentions the positive without reflexively citing the negative and vice versa. These simultaneous oppositions typically refer to herself, though she also describes a few oppositions within her sons' lives. In terms of the writing's structure, this balancing can occur between one journal entry and a much later entry. Balances can also appear within a single phrase or sentence, between two consecutive sentences, and within and between paragraphs and sections.

In the following example, Kate describes a family dinner:

> Dear Hank,
>
> Last night we had Sunday night dinner—the boys, Linda and Grandma—& to be sure, the dinner was not up to your standards. The potatoes were rock hard—but the ham and rest were good. It was good hearing everyone—seeing the conversation move naturally, noisily, being whole, being family. Not whole and whole both—you weren't there & yet you were.
>
> And then we watched the video of the service. It was, as the real one, exquisite & slightly troubling both. The beginning & . . . the tributes of Bob, Elaine, Mindy, Rob, & Terry & our three handsome boys—then Pat—were all so good. Again, early on I was moved to almost tears. . . . I wrote something that rambled here so much I ripped it out, but the ramble worked as good enough brainstorming for an email I subsequently wrote [to the] boys. I tried to explain to them that I thought the service was masterful but—because it *did* reflect some realities—was also troubling. For me, maybe not others, it reflected some of the "separate spheres" that were part of our lives. I tried to explain that those "separate spheres" were sometimes hurtful for me, but I didn't think they were a result of patriarchal or sexist assumptions on your part—I didn't think you could help it & I explained why—anyway, I thought the service was wonderful, even if sad. If we had shortcomings, I feel we'd accepted them, understood them—mostly.

In this entry, simultaneous oppositions dominate to the point that they seem painful for Kate, being pulled this way and that. Like much writing for purposes of healing, I suspect this entry was indeed painful to write. But as many researchers also agree (Pennebaker 1990; DeSalvo 1999), writers usually feel better later. Such oppositions help us to heal in two main ways. First, as discussed in the earlier chapter on Lucy, writing can help us figure out how we are alike other people and how we are unique—*simultaneous differentiation and integration*, a primary way we think. In this passage, Kate notes how she and her husband differed from each other—their *separate spheres*. However, at the same time that she differentiates, she also integrates herself with Hank, noting how they both accepted and understood these issues.

Second, as Kate made clear in our first interview, she kept this journal for purposes of *witnessing* her inner stream of thought—the memories, concepts, ideas, perceptions, values, sensations, and images that constitute our consciousness (e.g., James 1974; Moffett 1992). Kate has long practiced yoga and meditation. She understands the value of witnessing, focusing, and suspending our inner stream. Throughout her journal, Kate rarely judges any one side of an issue over another. Instead, she gives voice to each side and moves on. Clearly, this can be considered *witnessing*: simply acknowledging reality, in order to better *accept* reality, all to help her effectively deal with it. Such holding back, in effect, can allow time for emotional and rational processing to do their work in smoothing out the rupture or split—in re-assembling pieces into a new or different whole. When I consider Kate's entire journal, I find clear evidence that she indeed *resolves* the major oppositions or *problems* she raises, as the next section tries to clarify.

Solving Problems

In our first interview, Kate noted that she did not need a mental health professional to talk to her about her grief; she knew how to do that for herself, in the pages of her journal. And she did. As this chapter tries to unearth, Kate engages in numerous language and thinking strategies, cognitively and emotionally driven, that clearly lead her to *solve* problems. However, two caveats must be emphasized.

The first caveat is that we do not (cannot) construct knowledge purely on our own; much of it is socially constructed—conceived and revised over and over again through our interactions with others and through our tidal waves of engagements with other people, including the ways in which people represent reality. Kate describes how her own thinking and writing are socially constructed:

> I think my knowledge (and my journal) is socially constructed—mediated by and saturated by the social—but not that we humans aren't also witnessing directly things that are *not* socially constructed. I think of almost all truths as 'triangulated' with person A and person B observing points 1 and 2. In physics, there is more consistency in what's observed about point 1. In

my journal, what's being triangulated is more socially-complex (in my view). But it was more important to me to be as honest as possible—*not* to distort, exaggerate, etc.

The second caveat is that the serious issues and problems that people write their way through can never be *solved* completely. They can be organized, reduced, deflated, demystified, made less intimidating and scary, made more tolerable, made easier to live with—but never wiped totally clean from our psyche.

Given these complexities and caveats—or *because* of them—Kate's journal demonstrates clear movement toward resolutions and mending of issues that fragmented her internal life during this period. These *solutions* include the following: (1) working through—acknowledging and articulating—the initial shock of her sudden loss and her new reality; (2) freely engaging in what Didion (2005) calls "magical thinking," while simultaneously recognizing it as not real; (3) resolving minor, everyday irritants that may or may not be related to larger traumatic issues; (4) bridging some of the gap between oppositions, such as those focused on her relationship with her husband and children; and (5) resolving issues indirectly through acknowledging positive elements and striving for a positive tone in her writing.

Working through Initial Shock

One of the most basic and immediately useful forms of writing about trauma is explaining things to ourselves—just the facts, along with whatever else we can muster into words at this fragile time. During intense and sudden grief, it seems common for people to tell what happened over and over again. This simple repetition works to convince us of this rupture in our normal life. This is the core of Kate's journal: vigorously exercising her nimble, flexible mind, as she relentlessly sorts out events large and small, people, conversations, observations, and feelings. The main strength of her writing in this regard, as noted earlier, is her consistent practice of admitting to every opposition or contradiction, while suspending judgment.

Freely Engaging in Magical Thinking—While Not Believing It

I think it is normal to think (usually privately) that a newly-deceased loved one will, somehow, come back—or that he or she never left—or even that we can continue to communicate with each other. We think and say and do things that we *know* are not anchored to reality. Didion's

The Year of Magical Thinking (2005) is a close description (and meditation on) such behavior. Following are some examples of magical thinking from Kate's journal:

- Each entry begins as a letter with, "Dear Hank."
- One entry states, "Your [Hank's] picture is on my dashboard and I talked to you much of the way there, some of the way back."
- Many times throughout Kate's journal, after expressing how she does not understand her loss and sudden new reality, she asks Hank to return, as in this entry: "I'm tired, aching, want you home."
- Kate expresses not only how their dog suspects that "something is wrong," but also states, "I've told you earlier that I suspect you've come to visit in the form of the cat (smiley face)."
- Kate later describes how the cat now lays in Hank's place on the bed.

Didion observes that, especially in her time of sudden loss, the ordinariness of her life at the time of the event "prevented me from truly believing it had happened." I believe it requires courage or confidence to allow ourselves to even give voice to such thoughts, privately or publicly. Given the intense trauma of the moment, I think it is wise to give ourselves permission to think, believe, and say such things—even though we know, in our heart of hearts, that they are not real. Such *fabrications* can be fairly simple and direct, as I take these quoted here to be, or they can take the form of an elaborate mind-game. For example, my old friend, Tom Trusky, was known for his elaborate practical jokes and his talent for creating illusions and perceptions that were entirely his creation. He was skilled at creating fake stationery and other documents, communicating well-selected, even private information to unsuspecting recipients, as he uncannily imitated the voices and styles of the "authors" of these messages.

When Tom died suddenly of a heart attack, I harbored the suspicion that he had faked his own death, so that he could collect insurance money from his named heir, who would then channel it to him on the opposite coast, where he would be living, smugly grinning, with his significant other, who had recently re-located there. I had fleeting thoughts of visiting New Jersey and spotting him across the street. Following the news of his death, such illusions constantly flickered across my mind. I didn't speak of this to anyone. In the front of my mind, I knew this was impossible—and yet, I entertained the notion, almost trying to wish it into existence. All this time of wishful or magical thinking, I was joining *with* Tom in savoring his ultimate trick, gaining pleasure in his ability to pull off his crowning, complex ruse. Again, we were cohorts in a masterful trick. Like Kate and her husband, we became, in a sense, one, in parallel action, albeit imaginary.

Such magical thinking, at least for some people, may be a *pre-condition* or necessary first step before we can proceed to other more rational forms of healing. I believe such magical thinking has a healing function because the survivor becomes a *participant with the deceased in some activity*. And activity and participation essentially mean *life*. As participants, we are more fully engaged in the illusion and hence more convinced of it, like becoming absorbed in a book or a film. In Kate's examples quoted here, she is talking with Hank as they are both traveling in the car. As well, she is interacting with Hank as she interacts daily with her cat and dog. In my case, I was doing what I had done in the past—serving as an accomplice with Tom in an elaborate joke, as we would take turns as creator or co-conspirator. Other than actually believing in our magical thinking, the worst thing we can do is to *prohibit ourselves from ever doing it in the first place.*

Two years after Kate lost her husband, while she was reviewing a draft of this chapter, I asked her if she still writes letters to Hank, to which she replied,

> I do *not* still address Hank directly in my journal, but I *am* still writing to heal and grow. I feel like I've grown a lot, but am still processing things related to the trauma of losing him and the world we shared, still rebuilding and processing emotion about him and everything much more freely. I cried and cried when I read this. . . .

Also two years after Kate's loss, and because her journal so assiduously addresses and honors Hank, I asked her, "Did you ever think that Hank could read or hear or sense your words, in *any* kind of way?" She stated, "No—I don't/didn't think he could hear me."

Writing can help us heal from another variation of magical thinking. During intense grief or trauma, seemingly lurking behind every move we make is a *reminder*—some small details that immediately open up a floodgate of associations with our loved one: Every person or object evokes intense associations, because of our raw, acute awareness of the new void in our life. These intense associations should be acknowledged but then soon controlled. For example, in one entry, Kate noticed a broken rose stem, moving her to tears, because of the memory of Hank it evoked. Any insignificant detail can set off tears and deep feelings of loss. Writing can become the best counter-balance to these sudden and emotional encounters, because the act of writing removes us to a quieter, more rational context, as we tap into our inner stream *without* being surrounded by such reminders.

Resolving Small Irritants

Sprinkled throughout Kate's journal were a handful of small, unrelated issues that she included in her letters to Hank. Examples included how to manage the many friends and relatives who were there to help her, an encounter with a rude individual at a gym, and dealing with an acquaintance who wanted to use her husband's name for a *cigar benefit*, when neither smoking nor advertising were deemed worthy pursuits by Kate. While these are largely unrelated, minor issues, I mention them because I believe that they, too, play a small role in Kate's healing. Their relatively trivial nature helps her to regain an everyday perspective and helps to anchor her to the humdrum life that had been shifting beneath her feet. Maybe more importantly, these small occurrences are the stuff of many evening conversations between spouses at the end of the day. Including them in her journal is likely a natural habit that is too early in her grieving period to break. Continuing them may provide some shred of continuity in a life that had been instantly ruptured beyond recognition.

Bridging Oppositions

As described earlier, Kate's journal consistently articulates oppositions—two sides (and sometimes more) to every issue she raises. When Kate sorted through her husband's office, she noted the absence of photographs or mementos of her. Several other entries throughout her journal echo this theme. In the following entry, she begins to mend this issue:

> Dear Hank,
>
> We're both practical people . . . we go on, we're task-minded, we get some things done. We're both practical but we're sensitive & feeling in places & pockets & moments & in some ways, everywhere and always we both knew to package our sadness &

put it away & just go on. So that made us productive but left us sometimes groping to express ourselves meaningfully, authentically. And on my morning Hank-cries with Jasper, sometimes there is no coherence, no coherence at all, the tears just come & I babble.... There is no point, no message that is immediately obvious. But I also feel a sense of you that is not gone at all ... and some of this sense is bound up in memory & legacy & honoring you. And I find blurry the lines between presence & absence, loss & lease, past & present.

I feel simultaneously more deeply appreciative of you & all we shared together & more keenly aware of ways I was <u>not</u> in your conscious life ... and yet the latter doesn't stop me from mourning what was good & deep & tightly bound. We were human, saturated with humanness, & I mourn losing you, all of you, including your human imperfections. You had some; so do I. I hope before too long you can turn me, tempt me, to have Hank-laughs, to walk & remember things that most of all make me smile & especially laugh. For now—it's Hank-cries & spring & I want to make sure your garden and vineyard live on in your way.–Love, K.

Kate begins resolving this disconnect by identifying herself with Hank—by putting them together, side by side, in their consistent practicality, their "packaging sadness," putting it aside, and going forward. In a sense, Kate's solution resides within the problem itself, as she in effect says, "If I feel resentful over my absence in your life, then I'll do what you always did—what *we together* always did—put it aside and move on. In expressing herself, she also tries to satisfy (or solve) another issue—how their moving on habits limited their communication. She resolves their apartness by stating that they were, after all, merely human—and that it does not diminish that which was "good & deep & tightly bound."

Another entry in which Kate focuses on this issue of her husband being "distant" and "remote" occurs near the end of her journal in an almost off-handed way, as Kate recounts spending time with Janet, her husband's sister:

Later: The day continued to be beautiful to the last ray of sunset—but full of mourning. Janet and I are talking a lot & one or the other of us breaking down now and then. Janet found it difficult seeing the spot on Granger Road, finding unexpectedly your scooter parked in the garage.

In the vineyard, Janet wondered if I thought you had a chronic anxiety disorder—and we both wondered if whatever . . . other things . . . gist of discussion was thinking you shouldn't be *judged* for some of your remoteness. Now later, I'm too tired to make sense—but missed you all day long.—Love, K.

At least for me, this brief note represents the most solid evidence of resolving the theme expressed in different ways throughout Kate's journal—Hank's remoteness. It's important in several ways. First, it initially comes from Hank's sister, one who had known him long and well. Second, like most good conversations, it was a mutually agreed upon conclusion, making it a bit more persuasive to Kate herself. Third, and most importantly, it *names* the issue that has nagged at Kate throughout this time—"chronic anxiety disorder." She uses this term, "anxiety," two days later, noting that both nature and nurture may have *given* Hank some anxiety, which he "then dealt with not so efficiently." This name, *chronic anxiety disorder*, helps her healing by reframing the problem as something, which anyone, including Hank, may not be able to control, and hence, should not shoulder all of the blame for the resultant behavior. This conclusion, then, may lighten Kate's load, by reducing her disappointment in Hank's behavior, as well as by lessening her likely unease at admitting this disappointment during a time of grief. Another possible healing function of this conclusion is Kate's acknowledging that Hank gave her all of the love and companionship he was able to give.

An equal or greater issue that Kate struggles with throughout her journal is her worry about her three sons. She sometimes summarizes how they are dealing with the loss of their father: One son wears his father's tweed jacket; one wears canvas pants like his father's; another uses his father's coffee mug; one drinks alcohol a bit too much. These are relatively small waves in her voyage. However, Kate is wracked with worry about one married son, Russ, who has increasingly distanced himself from his family (e.g., he did not attend his father's graveside service).

In many entries, Kate struggles to understand why and how this son is divorcing himself from his own family, all the while not judging or evaluating his behavior whatsoever—a strong characteristic of her writing for healing. For instance, she states, "I'm worried sick about Russ and yet *he's* the one who needs to make peace with himself." As a reader, I sometimes thought she was too cautious, too even-handed. After many entries of holding back and suspending the lightest shade of judgment, Kate seems to solve the issue in a few different ways. First, she finally makes an unmistakably clear judgment, writing, "It's very weird, H. It seems like he's sold us down the river. . . . It seems like he's abdicated *all* love, respect, appreciation, and understanding of what he had." This unmistakable judgment ("he sold us down the river") is a real turning point in Kate's heretofore suspension of judgment. I view this naming as a very positive change in her writing and thinking, as at least an initial and definite resolution, allowing her to proceed from this point.

Similarly, she labels this same son as "Russ 1" and "Russ 2." The first is the son they know and raised, while the second is the newer, disaffected son. In both instances, Kate has arrived at a conclusion and *names* it; in effect, she imposes some distance between her perceived failure as a parent and Russ's responsibility for himself. She confirms this resolution soon after these entries when she confidently declares, "I open my arms and welcome truth to prevail" and "H, our three sons are all going to wake up today and somehow go on with their lives." Here, this resolution in no way fixes the relationship with her son. It does, however, seem to move Kate's own perceptions and stance toward her son's behavior to a more realistic and positive level. Many parents eventually have to realize that their children behave in ways they may never understand—behaviors shaped by a complex tangle of forces beyond their control. Kate seems to have arrived at this realization, one which is both sobering and liberating.

Issues Influencing Kate's Writing about Trauma

As a sensitive, intelligent, accomplished, caring individual, Kate uses writing as a form of healing in many interesting ways. I have tried to describe them in the most direct, realistic way I can in this chapter, in my attempt to be true to her and her work. Her clear, seemingly effortless prose helps us to see the numerous cognitive strategies she slides in and out of with ease. In most ways, her writing for healing is very unique. This is no surprise, as far too many variables are in play when anyone writes through their trauma. Nonetheless, in this section I would like to summarize some of Kate's approaches through some different lenses, similar to those used to explore Lucy's writing in the previous chapter. These common issues are process and fluency; "the other thing;" simultaneous differentiation and integration; and tapping into the inner stream.

Process, Fluency, and Flow

In an early interview, I asked Kate if there was a specific point or any kind of critical juncture when she realized that her writing was helping her, and she replied, "I have great faith in the process itself—regardless!" As a veteran language expert, Kate is well familiar with all kinds of reading and writing processes and products—and how processes lead to the best products. My point is this: Not every entry you make in such a journal will seem *good* or *productive* or *useful* or whatever; overall, such writing is a leap of faith—you have to do it consistently—as work—and trust in the process itself. People who do not traffic in words every day can easily stop writing because they do not understand the importance of process and hence have little trust in it.

As explained in the previous chapter focused on Lucy, fluency in writing is directly connected to our thinking. In an interview, Kate stated, "I'm letting myself unleash, letting myself explore. . . . In this journal, I gave myself permission to experiment, to run and stumble." Clearly a fluent writer, Kate gets thoughts down on paper quickly and easily. She told me that writing her journal by hand was slow—but this slower pace allowed more ideas to surface in her mind. Another indication of her fluency appears in one entry, at the end of a busy day: It is unusually brief, as she notes how physically tired she is—a fact that is even more visible on the page, as her handwriting droops and a few words are incompletely written. Even when she seems to be nodding off to sleep, she writes smoothly and coherently. Also, addressing each journal entry as a letter to Hank helps convince her that she is writing to an intimate, deeply trusted reader. This is true, even though she admits that she can never totally dispel the notion of some other audience over her shoulder. As noted earlier, her journal confirms this.

Another related—but more basic—reason undergirds Lucy's and Kate's fluency in thinking and writing. Simply put, they find exploratory, thoughtful, expressive writing to be enjoyable in and of itself—and to better understand what *enjoyment* means in this healing context, psychologist Mihaly Csikszentmihalyi (1990) articulates the differences between "enjoyment" and "pleasure":

> Experiences that give pleasure can also give enjoyment, but the two sensations are also quite different. For instance, everybody takes pleasure in eating. To enjoy food, however, is more difficult. A gourmet enjoys eating, as does anyone who pays enough

attention to a meal so as to discriminate the various sensations provided by it. As this example suggests, we can experience pleasure without any investment of psychic energy, whereas *enjoyment happens only as a result of unusual investments of attention* [italics mine]. A person can feel pleasure without any effort . . . . But it is impossible to enjoy a tennis game, a book, or a conversation unless attention is fully concentrated on the activity. It is for this reason that pleasure is so evanescent, and that the self does not grow as a consequence of pleasurable experiences. Complexity requires investing psychic energy in goals that are new, that are relatively challenging. (46–47)

As Csikszentmihalyi shows, this psychic energy invested in challenges helps lead us to *flow* experiences, where we lose track of time and disregard our physical surroundings. This is what often happens to writers in the act of writing, because they find it enjoyable—so enjoyable that it may become their life's work, as it has with the people explored in this book. It is enjoyable for them *because it leads to their developing a more integrated and complex self.* They see it as worthwhile and permanent, unlike the far more ephemeral *pleasures* that quickly dissipate. This enjoyment in creating—and re-creating—ourselves into more complex beings is the active ingredient in motivating literate behaviors and in constructing meaning, regardless of the form it takes. Of course, this is *not* to say that those who write for purposes of healing are having a peachy time doing so, but they *trust in the process* sufficiently to see them through. Both Lucy and Kate stated directly that such in-flow and deeply absorbing writings usually result in such feelings of enjoyment.

The Other Thing

As in the earlier chapter on Lucy, Kate has an abundance of *other things* in her life that serve as counter-points or points of comparison. Different kinds of work and escape sometimes deflected her trauma, but more importantly, they often helped to shape her thinking and writing. For Kate, these activities included working in her vineyard, listening to Krishna music, reading fiction and nonfiction, attending movies and plays, drawing, and sculpting. The main difference in how Lucy and Kate used *other things* is that Kate's other things operated more subtly in the background of her writing, while Lucy's were often immediate and present in her writing, such as her fund-raising events and her children's basketball games.

In an early interview, Kate noted that, "I found music incredibly, incredibly powerful. Probably *the* most powerful. I respond to music more emotionally and powerfully." Also, she described "lots and lots" of secondary source material flowing through her professional and personal life, stating, "I'm reading more about Buddhism and meditation practices. Here in the journal I don't directly reference these sources; it's subtle and indirect. I absolutely will seek source information as much as I can that's relevant."

Also, Kate spoke of her reading of Cormac McCarthy's *The Road* (2006), citing its bleak imagery as reflective of her own internal landscape. She especially noted the importance of "literature that deals with the complexity of being human; not that that would trump working with a counselor, but English teachers deal with character development." She identified Didion's *The Year of Magical Thinking* as her "most recent big thing."

SIMULTANEOUS DIFFERENTIATION AND INTEGRATION

Like Lucy in the previous chapter, Kate's journal also reveals her writing as demonstrating *simultaneous differentiation and integration*—how she is similar to other people and how she is different from them—in effect reaffirming who she is in a world that is currently chaotic. This is visible in a single line from our interview, when Kate stated, in reference to Hank: "How can I be alive and you're not?" She is at once integrated *with* her husband—in the past—as well as differentiated *from* him—in the present time. Her sense of past has not yet caught up with the present. This is one basic way that trauma splits or fragments us.

To see this more clearly, I will compare early journal entries with much later ones. For example, in our first interview, Kate stated that McCarthy's descriptions of a land laid to waste in ashes accurately reflected her own internal feelings when she began her journal after her husband's death. While this is a form of *integration* in identifying herself with a hell-scape, by the end of her journal, she often celebrates the glories of a blooming spring. In effect, she has integrated her previous internal hell-scape into a green spring-scape.

Similarly, a constant refrain throughout the first three-quarters of her journal is summed up with, "I don't understand!" Kate stated, "My whole journal is a question and an attempt to understand." Not that any human being *can* understand death and sudden death—but it's crucial that she state it anyway. In this theme, Kate is certainly differentiating herself from other people. In the final third of her journal, this theme appears much less often. More importantly, she now focuses more on the "oneness" of nature and "the web of life" to be found in people and the natural world.

TAPPING INTO THE INNER STREAM

More consciously and frequently than Lucy, Kate taps into her inner stream, engaging in witnessing, focusing, and suspending thought. She is well-familiar with meditation practices and is aware of the similarities between meditation and writing: "I see the goals of meditation and writing as holding some very parallel processes—zooming in and zooming out. Looking at and letting go of . . . there are a number of ways these are very parallel." During our first interview, Kate used the term, "witnessing," with no prompting whatsoever from me. In fact, when she said it, I had no inkling that I would explore any of these language experts' writing within the meditation-based framework of witnessing, focusing, and suspending one's inner stream of consciousness.

Witnessing and Focusing the Inner Stream

Many of the excerpts from Kate's journal can be considered as witnessing or giving voice to her husband's rich and varied accomplishments, habits, experiences, beliefs, and values. One clear example included earlier was Kate's *naming* and describing Hank's various roles, such as "Hank the scholar" and "Hank the gourmet cook." About such witnessing, Kate stated that,

> The writing did not intensify the sadness, but . . . it helps me intensify goodness. First, it gives me space and time to witness those feelings and to let them bubble up from my sub-consciousness. I'm just giving space to witness—to just greet that sadness and shake hands with it. I'm letting it be present, then reflecting on it. Grief is really about realigning relationships—not with people but with the world, the universe, because everything changes: How can I be alive but you're not?"

Here, unlike Lucy, Kate seems to witness and focus at the same time. Naming her husband as "Hank the gourmet cook," for example, can only be accomplished by aiming her attention at specific areas. At the same time, she is merely witnessing this fact—as Kate says, "letting it be present."

Suspending the Inner Stream

This means turning off or at least reducing the volume of that little voice inside of us. Again, this seems to operate in a more complex way with Kate. In a later interview, I asked her about this important stage, and she replied,

> That's a very deliberate move in meditation—to do that first, to clear the plate, to turn off the backtalk. So yes, I agree. But doing that is another story. At the moment of writing I am so focused on what's at the end of the pen, and I can toggle back and forth—but I don't know that I'm turning off backtalk, but I am focusing—and this shift in focus can turn it [her idea] around, so that I can look at it from different sides. As a writer you can be in it but you can stand back and walk around it and look at it. *Even within first person you can shift back to third person thinking mode.* That may be partly where the power in writing is, that range in perspective, but you can also stop on a dime, hold it, put it in other contexts.

Kate states that she "toggles back and forth" between focusing and suspending her thinking. This observation demonstrates the flexibility inherent in writing. We can focus, yes, but at any time, we can pause and *hold our thought still*, so that we can view it from different perspectives. As we view it from different perspectives, we are led back into focusing. In short, the brief time or space between focusing and pausing in order to re-focus can be thought of as *suspending* thought. Any change of focus, from one element to another, can be considered a *brief rest* from the first topic, an efficient suspension of thought.

Healing Through Inquiry into the World around Us

Overall, throughout her journal, Kate assumes the identity of one who believes deeply in inquiry—of puzzling around in her head, of searching, analyzing, and connecting. Whether intended or not, this stance and language can be thought of as a kind of advocacy for her late husband to assume the same perspective, however impossible that may be. It's possible (if not natural) that they did not always share this approach during their lives together. She writes to (re)connect herself to him—and in doing so, to enact a larger mutual understanding, in short, to reconnect that which had become disconnected, to shore up the perceived fragments into a whole. To heal.

Abundant references to nature also undergird this journal. The final, one-line paragraph of one entry states, "The mourning dove coos." In many entries, she seems compelled to reflect the sterling freshness and grace of the natural world. Nature seems to be the basis or background or *yardstick* with which Kate measures the large, unfathomable questions and issues that weigh her down. Another basic metric that Kate returns to again and again is her capturing and celebrating small glimpses of everyday reality, which subtly direct her toward larger meanings.

I suspect that she has somehow instilled this trait in her own children. In her journal I found a note written in someone else's hand. It seems that one of Kate's sons had found her journal and read some of it. On the final page, written in pencil, is his note: *"Do you remember the past x-mas when Andy gave Dad a new wheel barrow?"* I somehow doubt if Kate's son had read much of his mother's journal, but his slight note, about this small flicker of memory, signals to me the full blaze that writing can become.

6 COMMON THREADS

INTRODUCTION

Claire, the young teacher you encountered in the previous chapters, could not engage in writing about the single trauma that was most eating away at her: the sexual abuse that she and her two sisters suffered at the hands of their brother. She overcame her reluctance, wrote through the trauma, and for the next ten years, enjoyed her career as a successful educator. After those ten years, we re-connected. Here is an excerpt from Claire's recent note to me:

> Just so you know, I don't think I'll EVER forget you or your class. I still talk about what I experienced in your class to this day, to other educators, and to my family and friends. I actually have one friend who is experiencing a very traumatic divorce. She came home one day from work, and the whole house was empty, including the cabinets, the linen closets and the refrigerator. He also drained her bank account and left her with nothing. We would often talk about what was happening, but that never seemed like enough (for whatever "enough" means). It never seemed like talking gave her any solace or comfort. So I introduced writing to her. She said she didn't like to write because she's "not good at it." (Personal Communication, September 9, 2013)

Unable to convince her friend that sustained writing was worth a try, she had enough experience and belief in writing to strongly recommend it. She has worked for the past ten years to "spread the word." But her experiences using expressive writing in her classrooms were not always themselves without trauma.

Working on this long project and book has allowed me to arrive at two simple but fundamental beliefs. First, Claire's friend does not have to be a "language expert." She only has to write and keep writing, and then, if possible, work with a writing professional. To be entangled in a web of severe trauma and never write just because you're "not good at it" is profoundly tragic. My second revelation from this book is that language experts who know and understand the powers of composing must nurture this practice in their own colleagues, students, and others, however they can. Some of them, like Claire, will help to carry the ball forward. Small changes can lead to qualitative changes.

Each writer in this study is starkly unique. The complete individuality that drives composing through trauma is the most powerful argument for advocating its integration into many areas of our daily lives—into our education, our work, our creativity, our culture. However, this unrelenting focus on the individual is also its chief limitation. For many people and institutions, from schools, to businesses, to governments, the valuing of people's individuality is time-consuming, expensive, messy, ambiguous, and threatening—sometimes even scary. This is the central conundrum of this book. But we don't have any choice except to take the side of the angels, to insist that we compose our way through traumas, as individuals and as a culture.

Much of this book focuses on reporting the varied, often complex thinking processes of a wide variety of writers who struggle to understand their unique traumas. In attempting to convey their experiences, I've included their written texts, their written and spoken reflections on this work, and their spoken and written language collected from personal interviews and correspondence. I have tried to identify and describe their thinking and writing—a complex web of different personalities, purposes, audiences, texts, processes, and contexts. In the case studies of Lucy and Kate, I focused first on characteristics that were unique to each, such as Lucy's public writing and Kate's reliance on the personal letter genre. I then described elements shared by both writers, ranging from fluency, to simultaneous differentiation and integration, to connecting local issues with global issues. While these are my choices and categories for clarifying what people do when they compose about trauma, many *other* metrics are also useful for gauging thinking and written discourse.

One easily applied rubric, for example, is Lee Odell's "Assessing Thinking: Glimpsing a Mind at Work" (1999), which describes and defines six features of writing that identify thinking processes: 1) dissonance; 2) selecting; 3) encoding/representing; 4) drawing on prior knowledge; 5) seeing relationships; and 6) considering different perspectives. The author offers a series of questions to guide analysis for each category. For instance, with "dissonance," he asks if writers point out things that puzzle them, and if they notice ways in which people's actions seem inconsistent with their words. (See Appendix C, "Assessing Thinking," for a table adapted from Odell's framework.)

In sum, the vigorous thinking and writing that occurs when people focus on trauma can be analyzed and validated through many approaches; certainly, there are far more than those described in this book. After all, the primary writers explored herein are mature, unique individuals. The multiple ways in which traumas affected them, along with their myriad written, spoken, and visual ways of responding to these challenges, increase the level of complexity and uniqueness of each case. Despite these abundant idiosyncrasies, this chapter describes some important commonalities in these writers' thinking and composing processes, while others include issues of audience, genre, and rhetoric.

WRITERS FELT OVERWHELMED, BUT SOON GAINED MORE CONTROL

When some of these writers first wrote about significant trauma, they felt overwhelmed. When sharing their writings was part of the process, the readers were frequently overwhelmed too.

When other people were part of the process, such writing was sometimes overwhelming for their readers. Many of these writers reported "how hard it was to write," and a few people experienced physical nausea and nervousness. Invariably, though, they were glad they had begun the process because the more they wrote, the better they felt about it; the more they wrote over time, the more "distanced" they became from their topic, which allowed them to more actively explore their thoughts and options for *how* they might regard their trauma in the future.

The main reason these writers felt overwhelmed is that such writing asks them to stand smack in the middle of a frenetic traffic intersection, where powerful forces madly crisscross each other, cars zooming by from all directions, in deafening chaos. Such composing demands that words collide with images; past collides with present and future; public and "knowable" facts merge with private thoughts; emotion melds with reason. As would be true for a real cop at a congested and chaotic intersection, it takes sustained practice and patience, over time, to slow things down, to impose some pattern and order.

COMPOSING ABOUT TRAUMA REQUIRED UNIQUE MOTIVATION

By its very nature, writing about trauma has to be internally motivated, more so than what occurs in other types of writing. Lucy and Kate are not writing in order to earn a grade, to submit to a publisher, or to gain any kind of reward. Their motivation instead comes from an authentic, deep-down desire for understanding, for making meaning from chaos. If we think of the other extreme, external motivation, we find student writers who harbor precious little motivation for writing about issues to which they see no connection. While internal motivation solves the problem of student writers who often feel precious little desire to write reports and research papers, other problems arise. For instance, it's not always easy to tap into internal motivation, because it can be buried beneath several layers of social and cultural conditioning. Many people have internalized from teachers and others that they dare not use the word, "I," much less write about such personal topics as being raped.

OTHER PEOPLE AND ACTIVITIES SUPPORTED WRITERS

Feelings associated with trauma are fragile and place us face-to-face with our own vulnerability. It only makes sense that the most human of feelings requires the support of other humans. This human link provides the needed grounding, contact, and feedback. In short, other humans provide reality for the unreal situations writers find themselves in. Family members and close friends were indispensable for enabling these writers to gain measures of comfort and control through composing in word and image. Lucy, for instance, found strength in her husband, children, colleagues at work, and especially one close friend. She also found hope in her students, but always in ways that were professional in nature and focused on *their* learning.

The most common (and powerful) theme in these writers' interactions with people is that of "helping themselves through helping others." Lucy relentlessly worked to raise thousands of dollars for "The Lucy Fund," to support research in metastatic breast cancer. Kate has become a Peace Corps volunteer. Another writer studied but not included in this book founded a non-profit organization to promote children's literacy.

The writers in this study often engaged in other creative activities, which were not highlighted here, but certainly seemed to have a positive effect. These activities included growing grapes, writing poetry, reading, researching, traveling, studying music, painting, and creating non-profit organizations. At the least, these activities served as a counterpoint to or relief from or diversion from writing. Creating in any way has always been considered a healthy activity. For many years, art, music, and poetry therapy have continued to gain acceptance in the US and in many other cultures. For example, there are now approximately seventy-two music therapy programs (approved by the American Music Therapy Association), at the bachelor's through PhD levels, across the United States.

Discouraged Writers Found Ways to Continue

Most of the writers in this study were experienced educators who embraced the liberal arts tradition. They were trained to constantly question not just facts but nearly everything else—from broad values, to detailed procedures. As committed to writing and expressive language as these people were, each of them had moments of uncertainty, questioning whether their writing was actually helping them. Such doubt is a natural phenomenon or "stage" for most writers, regardless of their topics, purposes, and readers. Experienced writers deeply know that any writing is a proverbial crap shoot—or at least starts out this way. And, of course, they also know that some writing is sabotaged or no longer relevant or sufficiently motivating to continue, so they will abandon it—but never completely discard it, because they know that it may "fit" another context, at a later time.

Another complication is that the feelings we experience when composing through trauma can be quicksilver and seem a little "magical" to us. One writer included in this book owned a long history of child abuse and flashbacks that interfered with her daily life. When she began writing about her personal experiences, including but not limited to traumas, these flashbacks suddenly disappeared. Such instant changes are not typical. More often, writers gradually gain control over the varying degrees of beastliness that had controlled them. Many shades of gray color this issue, and these veteran language experts have internalized this reality. They know that feeling confident about their writing on Tuesday may not be true on Wednesday. They know that they may experience these same extremes within a single day or even an afternoon. They expect some up and down rides, but always know the turbulence won't last.

My concern is for people who do *not* yet realize that this question, "Is composing helping me or not?," is cemented as a two-valued, yes-no question. They believe that if composing is not helping on Monday afternoon, that it will never-ever help. This is thinking that's frozen in time. In such cases, writers must be patient, wait, and dig deeper. As a matter of fact, writing itself may be the best or only way to resolve this issue, this "trauma-within-a-trauma."

WRITERS FACED UNIQUE FORMS OF WRITER'S BLOCK

As discussed earlier, it's relatively common for people who write about trauma to feel uncomfortable, sometimes even ill, when initially writing such topics. Most writers improve relatively quickly, and continue doing so over time. More often, these initial feelings of discomfort seemed to be subtle ones, to the point that it took writers some time to recognize their existence. Such feelings gradually "swelled" into a positive realization that writing clarified the dimensions of their trauma and shifted them into an overall, considerably more positive frame of mind. In all, it seems to me that few feelings have such a dualistic nature.

As well, these writers were well acquainted with the common variety of writer's block: becoming easily distracted; simply not feeling up to it, trying, but producing little, like they were pulling the proverbial teeth. We may have too many ideas swirling about in our heads about what we want to say, or we may want to cover too much ground—and become stymied, not knowing where to start. Other times, we may have no trouble putting words together and often have a "global" idea of where we're headed, but we may get stuck at a "middling" level, such as not knowing where to take a specific paragraph. At such times, the writers in this study did things that they knew from experience usually worked for them: they switched to writing something for a different purpose, audience, or genre; they took a walk; they did household chores; they gardened, read, watched television, or listened to music.

Once in a while, though, writers experienced a qualitatively different form of writer's block, in that it was a combination of some or all of the blocks described in the previous paragraph, in addition to—at the same time—feeling helpless to stop the stream of words and images rushing into their consciousness. One writer, who had lost her teenaged daughter in a car accident, described this intermingling of different forms of blocking:

> If the flow of images is too upsetting (such as picturing my child's last few seconds in that car), I do have to consciously stop that line of thinking. I have developed "safe" places in my mind and do make myself turn my thinking to one of those safe places.
>
> I think I'm more frustrated with myself when I have images and words that need to be written about and I choose not to do it. Why? Am I lazy? Am I avoiding? Do I think it's not important enough since I don't think I'm a good writer? Do I use time as an excuse? Sometimes I do. If I choose not to get out of bed and write thoughts that seem to be begging for paper, often I can't retrieve that particular slant and then again feel a bit of frustration, or perhaps, even a loss. (Personal Communication, July 6, 2009)

While I was curious about exactly what these "safe" mental places were, I did not ask. It felt too intrusive. The writer's "consciously stopping that line of thinking," seems to be an example of "suspending" her inner stream of thought, discussed elsewhere in this book. It's also interesting that the less intense forms of blocking seem more troublesome for this writer. I suspect that the intense and more mundane forms of blocking are somehow connected, but that question will have to wait.

Faith in Writing Sustained Success

The writers in this book believed that sustained writing will work its way to a resolution or balance of some kind. One writer clarified her notion of writer's block and her faith in the process itself:

> Sometimes, late at night, there's a stream of words and images that I can't stop. My solution is to get up and write them down. Then I can sleep. Other than this, I have trouble even relating to the question. I always want to write, and where there's a stream of words and images, my primary impulse is to write it down. Times when I cannot write? Yes, there must be some, but generally, if I truly cannot write (I'm making a presentation, for

example), I'm so focused on something else that I don't think about writing. I often interrupt what I'm doing if that flow of language begins in my head. If I'm driving, I pull over. If I'm riding a bicycle, I stop.—Oh, I remember once when there was a powerful stream of language in my head and I could not stop. I was on a 100-mile canoe trip, the weather was bad, the current was strong, and both my paddling partner and I were having to work as hard as we could to keep the canoe moving in the right direction. I was nearly in tears, wanting to write, and finally I called to Holly, "I have to write!" It was a nuisance, but we maneuvered the canoe out of the channel, tied up to a mangrove, and I wrote. If it's an incessant voice that I don't want to hear, writing is what frees me of it. When I write it down, it's no longer inside me. I've made a life of externalizing internal speech. (Anonymous, Personal Communication, 2011)

This writer is a seasoned language expert—a university professor and well-published author who focuses on writing about the natural world, through poetry and literary nonfiction. It seems natural that writers would solve the problem of writer's block by writing.

This writer, along with Lucy, Kate, and others like them, have long-since internalized the notion that composing occurs in rough stages, as a highly recursive or cyclical process in which their words and thoughts constantly shuttle back and forth, each changing the other. There are three primary reasons that these writers (consciously or unconsciously) know that composing through trauma is effective. One reason for their faith is that they know directly or strongly intuit that writing and thinking are tightly braided together, that visible words lead to more or different thinking, which in turn leads to more or different words, as the cycle continues. The first reason for their faith is that trauma has prompted these writers to abandon most of their preoccupations with plodding earthly concerns, which allows them increased energy and time to devote to thinking and writing. When everyday life's trivial concerns have been shaken off, larger, human issues surge into sharp relief.

The second reason for this faith in written and spoken informal language is that people knew that it would not be formally evaluated. If this were the case, they would "censor" themselves and avoid saying things that their reader may not accept. Striving too diligently to please one's audience, then, can hinder pleasing one's self, even displacing what the writer needs to say to herself. When writers detect varying degrees of distrust in their readers, they not only censor themselves, but they also write considerably fewer total words, as well as fewer words per minute (see for example, Elbow 1998). This *lack of fluency* often means that writers do not allow themselves sufficient time and language to arrive at their intended meaning. That is, visible language generates more language and more thinking, in turn extending the thinking-writing cycle. Writers need to generate enough ideas in their writing for them to discover exactly what it is they want to say, what they most want or need to write about. As well, fluency must be practiced and learned, where writers are allowed to compose whatever they want, as fast as they can, for, say, ten minutes, as in most classroom exercises.

The third reason that writers maintained faith in the writing process itself is that they enjoyed the times when thought and language flowed in parallel streams, so as to be nearly indistinguishable. It's not just the sheer rush and burn of fluency that writers feel, but also the sense that they are engaging in serious intellectual activity, such as reconciling oppositions, solving problems, asking and answering their own questions, and connecting and interweaving concepts.

WRITERS PURSUED OPPOSITIONS

In several different genres, the writers in this book engaged head-on with trauma. Almost regardless of the form used, oppositions or conflicts (naturally) surfaced. But once in a while, even though writers directly stated that they were writing about trauma, they *avoided* doing so. Most often, such writing takes the form of circling around and around the issue at hand, dealing out a series of vague, general, and abstract phrases. With some writers, this approach turns out to be a natural stage they must go through before they lessen their sometimes subconscious defenses and start facing issues more directly.

Kate, in Chapter Five, best exemplifies the dogged pursuit of oppositions. Such writers grapple with words and ideas, tugging and pulling between many types of *oppositions*, including 1) the whole idea, tone, or attitude they wish to convey vs. the individual parts (e.g., words, phrases, and sentences); 2) the past time period in which the traumatic experience occurred vs. the current time period; 3) the need to focus on negative experiences vs. the impulse *not* to sound completely negative; and 4) the experiences they wish to *show* in their writing (i.e., sensory images and details objectively conveyed) vs. the more general statements of the experience's overall effect.

Writers Manipulated Images

Writers manipulated mental and actual images that helped them to think more deeply and in broader terms. In "Healing Images: Historical Perspective," Anees Sheikh (2003) summarizes historical and recent research (clinical and experimental) that explores the uses of imagery to treat numerous physical and mental issues, including obesity, insomnia, phobias and anxieties, depression, cancer, and chronic pain. He further notes that this research often verifies what has been recorded in many ancient cultures throughout history (3). Sheikh credits Carl Jung for defining mental imagery as a dynamic process: "Jung remarked that when we 'concentrate on a mental picture, it begins to stir, the image becomes enriched by details, it moves and develops . . .' (Jung, 1976, p. 172)" (Sheikh 2003, 17). The active, flexible nature of mental imagery is especially potent and "combustible" when it interacts with language.

In my own work, actual representations in art and photographs significantly helped writers to understand their trauma (see Chapter 4, *Seven Writers Composing in Word and Image*). I encourage people to draw and paint their own images for use in various writing assignments focused on trauma. Short of this, manipulating personal photographs or "stock images" from the Internet was especially effective in helping writers actually "see" and consequently unpack their traumas with language. Writers changed their image's foreground, background, facial expressions, color, positions of people, and other pictorial elements. Manipulating actual images to depict "what is," and especially, "what *should* be," helped writers gain more ownership of—and hence control over—the image and associated trauma. Such visual and verbal interactions were especially useful.

Many years ago, I became so convinced of the value of using images to teach writing that I began requiring students to actively manipulate pieces of art or personal photographs in ways that paralleled and extended or "fed" their written text. (Since then, considerable research evidence has accumulated to support the benefits of combining word and image; see Chapters 1 and 4). Everything they wrote in language had to be accompanied by a visual text as well, and their writing had to thoroughly integrate and reference their visual text. I encouraged writers to develop these in tandem with each other, though some writers found it easier to complete the visual or the text first. Though not included in this book, other forms of media, such as video, music, and graphics have also proven to be fertile fields for interactions with spoken and written language.

Many writers used images to help them consider alternative scenarios to feeling victimized by trauma. A few, such as Khanh and Minji in Chapter 4, created original drawings and paintings in tandem with their writing about trauma. Most others, though, chose to use computers to manipulate personal photographs. This category includes the use of imagistic thinking and language. Generating and manipulating *all* forms of imagery, internally and externally, seemed to help writers understand that 1) their trauma can have more than one reason or explanation; 2) they are not the only one experiencing the trauma; and 3) they can retrieve the past as well as project into their future, to hypothesize scenarios which may reduce their trauma's grip on them. For example, Lucy (see Chapter 3, Lucy) imagined a specific future scene with her family, gathered at their farm, as her own children, now grown, lovingly tended to their own small children. In effect, Lucy tried to place herself there, as she lived with the knowledge of her terminal illness.

Writers Read Widely to Enlarge Their Context

Reading widely is crucial to understanding that "we are not alone" in whatever trauma we're facing. Discovering larger contexts helped not just the writers themselves, but also helped them assist others in their small response groups. Most of the writers described in this book were active readers. If the writers were students in my classes, they read and discussed numerous publications focused on research linking writing to wellness. They were also required to read examples of professional writers who had transformed their pain into fiction, nonfiction, and poetry. (Such texts are cited throughout this book.) Those writers not in my classes vigorously searched out all manner of readings they deemed relevant to their trauma. With no exceptions, they reported solid gains from such reading and talking about their reading.

Students in my courses seemed to benefit from the imagery found in readings from professional writers who focus on trauma in their fiction and literary nonfiction. For example, Maya Angelou's *I Know Why the Caged Bird Sings* details her grandmother taking young Maya to see Dentist Lincoln when she had a severe toothache. This chapter's imagery is both real and imagined, as Angelou creates a powerful alternative scenario of how her grandmother stood up to the bigoted dentist. As well, George Michelson Foy's essay, "Burning Olivier: The Brief Life and Private Burial of an Infant Son," articulates the author's experiences in an unflinching narrative, laced with potent imagery. In short, robust imagery within the complete context of written discourse vividly illustrates the intense powers that language can exert on trauma. Thoughtful and well-crafted literary fiction and nonfiction (and of course, poetry) can most persuasively communicate the "lived" experience of trauma.

Reading fiction also helps us to be more empathetic with other people. Especially for readers who are writing about trauma, it's important that they identify with the main characters and that they are "emotionally transported" to the characters' place, time, feelings, and experiences (e.g., P. Matthijs Bal and Martjin Veltkamp, 2013; David Cormer Kidd and Emanuele Castano, 2013). Among other effects, reading fiction helps writers about trauma understand (in both intellectual and emotional ways) that they are not alone in their suffering. Fiction can powerfully teach us about these issues because we have to vicariously (but actively) *participate* in the making of meaning afforded by the text. Reading to understand trauma is the reciprocal side of writing to make sense of trauma.

Writers also benefitted from using *informational* nonfiction, which contains more straightforward and "objective" accounts of its subjects. Lucy and Kate, the oldest and most experienced writers included in this book, instinctively sought out credible information from secondary sources related to their trauma. Lucy, for example, investigated metastatic breast cancer from many perspectives—its past, present, and future research agendas, its sources of funding, and journal articles and web sites reporting clinical studies. She also read about the concept of death from literary and philosophical perspectives.

However, the younger writers in this study were less inclined to automatically seek external and more objective sources of information, which is why I began to require students to conduct outside research for some of their writing projects. The chief benefit of their integrating objective information into their writing is that it can starkly clarify that "they were not alone" in their particular trauma. The person who harbored unresolved feelings about her adoption researched the laws and number of adoptions that prevailed in the same location and time as her own adoption. She also investigated prevailing attitudes and values of the time, from the viewpoints of childless parents, adoption agencies, and others. The student who felt guilt over a drug arrest in his small town discovered that, in the broader context of different areas of the country, which bear different laws, attitudes, and values, his worries stemming from his small town did not seem so tragic after all. Widening, opening up, the private and restricted context proved to be invaluable in fostering writers' sense of wellness.

THREE THINKING PROCESSES SHAPED WRITERS' SUCCESS

In addition to the thinking processes commonly employed to describe thinking (e.g., classifying, analyzing), three other terms better capture the cognitive processes of these writers. These distinct yet overlapping processes seemed to contribute the most to these writers' success: 1) simultaneous differentiation and integration; 2) witnessing, focusing, and suspending the inner stream of thought; and 3) ignoring boundaries. All of these habitual thinking strategies are clearly visible in actual writing samples. When we try to make sense of a new, sudden reality, such as a serious trauma, we work hard to re-adjust or re-orient our new state to our previous "normal" selves. It seems logical, then, that we would constantly search out how and why these two states of mind are different and alike. This simultaneous differentiation is occurring not just within us, but also between us and other people and contexts.

The second common thinking process—witnessing, focusing, and suspending the inner stream of thought—allowed writers to sit back and absorb, as objectively as they could—what was happening to them. What they may witness from actual experience or from their own flow of thought, could then become an object for interrogation or reflection—an object or idea to focus upon. The suspension of the inner stream of thought is difficult to notice in writing, if not impossible, but we do see this at work in how writers "switched off" troubling or scary images that entered their consciousness.

The third major thinking strategy or habit is that writers often ignored "boundaries"—of time, space, topic, and relationship with others. Writers focused on the past, present, and projected into the future, and did not feel restrained from doing so, even within a single piece of discourse. This is mainly a function of private, close-to-the-self writing, even though we see this freedom in more public writing about trauma, as well. I should note that this "ignoring of boundaries" is a rhetorical "stance" that writers chose and did not deviate from in the middle of their writing. They were certain of what they wanted and what they were doing.

Finally, these major thinking processes are each abetted by the basic cognitive strategy of *ranging* up and down the "Ladder of Abstraction" (Hayakawa and Hayakawa 1990) and *connecting* general and abstract ideas to specific and concrete examples and illustrations.

INTERNALIZED PRINCIPLES OF RHETORIC GUIDED WRITERS' BASIC DECISIONS

Throughout this study, these writers never consciously or directly communicated anything about their work in standard rhetorical terms, such as, "Now I'm going to admit and then dispel my reader's opposing argument." However, writers did indeed draw upon their background knowledge of rhetoric, especially in making basic decisions. Lucy's knowledge of the standard rhetorical triangle of writer, reader, and purpose, steered one of her bedrock decisions. When she wrote for her close friend and not for the public audience of the *Caring Bridge* website, her message changed shape, focusing more on herself, as writer, skewing the triangle's relationships in her direction.

Other basic rhetorical principles allowed writers to succeed. Their knowledge of basic literary genres allowed them to "shift gears" easily, from one genre to another, because they did not consider any one genre as a mold or pattern that could not be broken. Lucy and Kate approached their writing, as Kate noted, knowing that "form and meaning are intertwined." Writers shifted smoothly among several genres and symbol systems, including narrative, poetry, exposition, art, and personal letters.

Lucy could not have reformulated her prose into free verse without knowing the elements of each—and that one could be cast as another. Writers without this knowledge and "trust" in the plasticity of genre could not have transformed their prose in this way. When Anne was creating her monster and angel images (see Chapter 4), her knowledge of the "concrete poem" genre (in which language is arranged on the page to *look* like the person or object that is key to the poem's meaning) allowed her to integrate one symbol system (language) within another (art).

Kate relied upon the letter genre, but was not stifled by it. She had maintained a personal journal her entire life. As well, she had taught this genre and had read the journals of other professional writers and students. She knew that this or any other genre could "fit inside of another." Letters can occur within the journal genre, just as poetry can. Knowledge of these genres allowed writers to somewhat easily shift gears *without* distracting them from their ideas, which would likely happen if they had little or no experience with these other forms.

Such rhetorical roots run deep in this book. The word, "catharsis," in Aristotle's ancient treatise, *Poetics*, was used to describe the workings and effects of art and drama, especially tragedy. The work of Josef Breuer and Sigmund Freud (1974) in the early twentieth-century led us to our current, broad understanding of catharsis as a theory of emotional release, a kind of purging or cleansing that may lead us to a more balanced, calmer state of mind. Much of this book, then, is situated within the principles and practices of the ancient (but ever-evolving) realm of rhetoric.

Kenneth Burke (1969, 43; cited in Enos 2010), James Kinneavy (1980), and others laid solid foundations for our current notions of rhetoric. Today's scholars continue to shape rhetorical theory in important and useful ways. I regret, though, that a sturdier bridge has yet to form between the work of scholars in composition and rhetoric and those in such fields as psychology, counseling, medical anthropology, and others focused on the treatment of trauma. Such work, though, has begun. A clear review of the history of rhetoric and its relationship to writing pedagogy appears in Erika Lindemann's *A Rhetoric for Writing Teachers* (2001). Some excellent recent contributions to the complex intersections between rhetoric and trauma can be found in the work of Shane Borrowman (2006), Jennifer Trainor (2008), Kimberly Emmons (2010), Michelle Payne (2000), Wilma Bucci (2002), Rebecca Nowacek (2011), and Carol Berkenkotter (1995). Other avenues relevant to the study of trauma that are rooted in rhetoric is that of scholars who explore emotional and bodily connections to text, such as, Sondra Perl (2004); Kristie Fleckenstein (2003; 2009); Laura Micciche (2007); and Thomas Selzer and Sharon Crowley (1999). These scholars demonstrate that rhetoric is alive and well.

Writers Accepted All Knowledge as Partial

Early twentieth-century rhetorician and literary critic Kenneth Burke maintained that none of us can *ever* know everything about any topic or subject. In his vision of the rhetorical parlor/cocktail party, he believed each of us can only listen in, then briefly join the conversation before we leave the party. Today, considering our ever-advancing technology—not just in generating new knowledge, but in making far more of it available to more people than ever before—this is even more true. The writers herein had long since internalized this notion that knowledge will always be incomplete, due to their education backgrounds, their teaching experience, and their own writing and learning.

Nearly anyone who keeps a diary or journal and writes mainly in expressive language, for whatever reasons, has to believe in self-sponsored inquiry. Their implied premise or stance is that they *don't* know everything about their subjects, so they write to determine what they do know, as well as what they do not know. Kate (Chapter 5) may be the writer who best demonstrates this belief. She consistently asks herself questions, a sure sign that she realizes her knowledge is partial. When she speculates upon "answers" to her own questions, she again highly qualifies her responses. As well, Kate consistently qualifies her assertions, meticulously delimiting them with phrases such as, "some of the time" and "often" and "seldom." She hardly ever makes blanket assertions or generalizations.

Another reason I believe Kate demonstrates that all knowledge is partial and contingent or ephemeral is her awareness of the natural world and its primary characteristic of change. When she writes, "My approach to journal writing had been just savoring all day one beautiful thing," its wisdom resides not only in the beauty of nature, but in the felt knowledge that this "one beautiful thing" may not be there tomorrow. Later, she writes,

> It's spring—it's a time of rebirth, renaissance. I think you would've come downstairs—thundered down the stairs—& banged around in the kitchen this morning w/ a slight glint in your eye, a lift in your chest. You would've stood in underpants, leaning on the counter, watching the birds on the railing as you ate your monster muffin & would've noticed, gladly, a leafing-out of the oaks—last to leaf.

I have to believe that Kate's fervent belief in nature and change helped her to project into the future, taking a momentary "breather" from the oppressive present. This projecting, this rhetorical principle, enables Kate to imagine not just what she's lost, but also to find solace in her and her husband's mutual bond—to nature, as well as to each other.

Writers Reflected on Everyday Life

Most of these writers included observations of everyday life in their journals, which grounded them in reality. Kate, for example, describes walking her dog in the early morning, pruning grape vines, and talking with her neighbor in her driveway. Lucy describes the family dog and fixing dinner with her children. The simple act of recording everyday details seems to lead writers into reflecting on them. Observing and commenting on the mundane is an ancient rhetorical practice, going back to the times of the classical scholar, Desiderius Erasmus (1466–1536) and the "commonplace book." According to "Reading: Harvard Views of Readers, Readership, and Reading History," the commonplace book "has its origins in antiquity in the idea of *loci communes*, or "common places," under which ideas or arguments could be located in order to be used in different situations."

I did not ask writers if they were *consciously* aware of well-known authors during their composing about trauma. (It only came up once, when Kate compared her world view to that created by Cormac McCarthy in *The Road*.) Nonetheless, because of my past experience with Lucy and Kate, I am certain that a few key authors exerted some influence on their writing, however indirectly or subtly. One such writer is Michel de Montaigne (1533–1592), the French Renaissance scholar often regarded as the father of the personal essay as a literary genre. Lucy and Kate would have both been aware of Montaigne, whose three volumes of *Essais* reflect upon his everyday life occurrences. Bakewell's (2010) description of Montaigne's writing mirrors the work of the writers in this book: "He contradicted himself, preferred specifics to generalities, embraced uncertainty, and followed his thoughts wherever they led."

Lucy and Kate were much more familiar with the work of E. B. White (1977, 41–55 and 178–187), the twentieth century's master of the personal essay. After years of writing for the *New Yorker*, White moved to a farm in Brooklin, Maine, where he focused on writing serious essays, such as "The Ring of Time" and "Coon Tree," which described everyday events (from watching a circus performer's practice session, as she rides a horse around a ring, to the raccoon that lives in a tree in his front yard). These "small" events gradually unfold into sober meditations on larger human and social issues, such as the nature of time and nuclear proliferation.

Including everyday experience in their explorations of trauma anchored writers in reality—its familiarity, safety, and normalcy—all things they desperately need during times of chaos. The simple observation and recording of an everyday event seems to calm and "center" writers enough, so that they can begin "edging out" into more abstract thinking about their trauma, asking and answering their own questions, connecting the everyday to the unknown elements of their "new reality" imposed by trauma. These common observations prompt or enable links to others, forming a chain that leads to an abstract issue about trauma. In one instance, Kate notices the open garage door, prompting her to refer to it as her late husband's "temple"—a packed metaphor. She then focuses on his Puma chair and her son's sketch pads on the floor near it, where she then notices her husband's cigar, leading her to the issue of her son's grieving process.

COMPOSING ABOUT TRAUMA LED WRITERS TO HELP OTHERS

Writers who seriously tackle trauma are largely invisible to others. Nearly all of the language experts I've interviewed over the years do not in any way identify themselves or publicize their habits. They view it as a highly private activity. Also, writing about trauma remains a taboo.

However, these mature, responsible professionals do not want to be perceived as narcissistic, or even as "New Agey" or "kooky." They are well-grounded people, anything but narcissistic or trendy. Nonetheless, revealing to casual acquaintances that they write about traumatic experience is like explaining a recent hitch-hiking trip to the Burning Man Festival. At least since the 1960s, American popular culture has represented many practices that do not conform to traditional and conventional expectations of the scientific method as being "in deep space," unanchored to everyday life. To a lesser extent, the same claim can be made about academic culture. The people I worked with for this book are anything *but* self-centered "space cadets" just because they addressed their own trauma. (Even I was surprised to discover that these writers often linked their private traumas to global concerns, ranging from poverty, to violence, to the destruction of our natural environment.)

These writers were also inhibited by another social trend, but from the opposite direction—our society's worship of the "business model." The corporatizing of many institutions, especially education, often deems "bottom-line results," expressed only in monetary values, as the only thing that matters; that the mending of a fragmented selfhood is a waste of time because it can't be quantified. Caught between these two extremes, we can hardly blame writers for their reticence. Overall, these are not optimal conditions for legitimizing the serious pursuit of writing our way through trauma.

The larger point here is that behind every utterance, spoken, written, or contemplated, an action or deed often awaits. It was typical for writers to "help themselves through helping others." This movement occurred fairly quickly and naturally after a sudden traumatic experience. How each writer shapes her own contribution must "fit" with her own situation and values. Lucy labored vigorously to raise funds for metastatic breast cancer research, spearheading "Parties for Life," marathons, and other events. About a year after her husband's sudden death, Kate left her job as a professor and joined the Peace Corps. Another writer (not included in this book) founded a non-profit organization that provided freewriting and art supplies to students, in memory of her teenaged daughter, killed in a car accident, who cherished creating language and images. This organization also raised funds for these "book bags" by selling cards her daughter illustrated. Another writer turned her energies toward writing about nature, giving workshops for aspiring poetry and nonfiction writers who harbored a deep appreciation for the natural world. These writers' turning toward others speaks not just to the frailty of the human condition, but also to its resilience—reason enough for hope.

The common threads described here, along with the earlier chapters detailing writers interacting with trauma in words and images, inevitably lead us to ask, "So, what can we do about it?" We now turn to a few major recommendations.

7 Recommendations

Introduction

Of the four recommendations in this chapter, the first one recapitulates insights from previous discussions. The remaining three are newly presented. I begin with what I hope is an obvious conclusion: because writing about trauma addresses basic human needs, we should establish such writing, in word and image, as a basic human right. This will necessarily include viewing such composing as a legitimate academic pursuit—one fueled by practical and desperate needs, not just in education, but in other institutions and systems. Most people will not be accustomed to thinking of composing about trauma as a basic human right. But in an information society, it makes sense. As I've maintained throughout these pages, this will open up many doors to understanding and learning about ourselves and our world.

Second, I urge that we support the innovative work that contributes to the theory and practice of composing through trauma. Third, our usual way of thinking and talking about trauma and death, ways that are often reinforced by cultural practices, must begin to change. Trauma—and especially death—must be nudged from the shadows of fear and allowed to become part of our living written texts. Finally, the paradigm shift involved in modifying how we commonly think about death necessarily means that we consider composing about trauma as a kind of prayer.

Establish Composing about Trauma as a Basic Human Right

Composing about trauma should be accepted as a basic human right because it addresses basic, immediate human needs. Many informed people and professional organizations agree that we live in an age of significant, rapid change, mainly driven by economics, technology, and media (see, for example, David Shenk [1997], Neil Postman [1993], and Robert Putnam [2000]). While it's hard to see when we live here, it's obvious to me that America is hyper-anxious, technologized, bureaucratized, and fragmented. As early as 1881, America was diagnosed by neurologist George M. Beard as leading all other "civilized" nations in nervousness, anxiety, and depression. Elaine Showalter's (2013) review of recent books on depression reveals that things have not changed.

> "It has not escaped many observers that today we are drenched in anxiety," says the medical historian Edward Shorter. ". . . Depression has become a mass illness." Shorter cites statistical evidence: "Within a given year, one in 10 Americans today will have a mood disorder, the great majority of them major depression." The psychiatrist Jeffrey P. Kahn sees an even worse trend . . . with "the commonplace anxiety and depressive disorders" affecting at least 20 percent of Americans. That's some 60 million people. (2)

While we can debate the whole issue of stress and anxiety, the quicksilver roiling and shifting of American culture, the social adjustments and re-alignments required, have to be hardest on young people. Educational and health establishments, such as the World Health Organization, the United Nations (e.g., see the UN's Millennium Development Goals), and the Center for Disease Control, as well as professional organizations, such as the American Academy for Pediatrics, document a growing list of social ills negatively affecting young people. These include, but are not limited to, the following issues: suicide; violence (physical, psychological, and virtual); poverty; gaps between the rich and poor; racism; broken homes; substance abuse; learning disorders; illiteracy; homelessness; hunger; self-mutilation, anger; and other mental health issues such as gangs, body image, gender identification, bullying, AIDS/HIV infection, unwanted teen pregnancy, and sexually-transmitted diseases (STDs).

These issues are common topics for writers working their way toward a less fragmented selfhood. The variety and severity of these ubiquitous problems demand that we employ composing through trauma, not just in schools, but in other institutions that connect to these issues. As Richard E. Miller (2005) observes, "Personal experience [is] the preeminent site where institutions and individuals intersect and meaning gets made" (31).

Establishing composing through trauma as a basic human right will finally address the eternal lament of, "We must address students' individual needs." This cry, from politicians, educators, administrators, and policy-makers, is often expressed as a need for "individualized instruction," as "teach the student, first," and the ever-popular, "I teach *students*—not math or English." Such altruistic mantras have floated forever in the educational ether, while, at the same time, these "leaders" champion lowering budgets, increasing class sizes, abolishing tenure, and reducing teachers' salaries and pensions.

I feel certain, though, that none of the methods available to individualize instruction can equal the simple act of allowing students to compose about, to work through, the obstacles in their lives, their traumas, large and small. Through their descriptions, qualifications, definitions, comparisons, and metaphors, individual students come into stark relief. How they define their traumas and how they address them will place them into sharp, indelible focus in their teacher's minds and hearts. Such writing does not have to be graded, does not have to be made public or shared, and does not even have to be read and commented upon (students can select those entries or "posts" they want to share with their teachers and others). When teachers protest, "I am *not* a psychiatrist or psychologist," I heartily agree with them. Nobody is asking them to be. However, teachers should not automatically exclude some focus on the learner's *using* writing about trauma for purposes of healing, thinking, and communicating. We can recognize that learning and growing are human activities, best fostered as one human being to another.

A few brave teachers, though, understand the powers of such composing and use it to address their students' needs. As the following section clarifies, they face huge challenges. Claire, quoted throughout this book, is one such hero. Here, she describes her high school class in which students wrote about their traumas.

> My class became an emotional mess, and the students loved every minute of it. Weekly, students would have what we called "crying sessions." Both male and female students were opening up about everything, from abuse, to the death of a pet. Some would even cry, and could not articulate why they were crying! I wouldn't say my room was depressing, but . . . well, emotional. Everyone always wanted to discuss and write about their thoughts and feelings, so much so that I was losing the academic elements, or at least that's how I saw it.

These students seemed to be starving to articulate their traumas. This is hardly unusual in today's America, with our heavy load of disrupted family life, substance abuse, real violence, media mayhem, non-stop contentiousness, cultural shifts, and the disintegration of institutions that used to help us be a more cohesive society. All of this and more contributes to a twenty-first century where we labor under so much stress that we have deep needs to make sense of it all, to turn our anxieties into something more positive, or at least more tolerable. This is the first "conclusion" here. Opening this pressure valve, even a little bit, allows for all other types of learning to flow more easily.

Also, Claire's fear of losing the emphasis on pure academics is a primary concern for any teacher. For whatever reasons, she was unable to see through the charged atmosphere of her classroom to identify and exploit all of the academic possibilities in composing about trauma—from revision, to primary and secondary research activities, to students transforming their prose into a variety of genres for many different purposes and audiences. As I hope this book has detailed, "academic thinking" flourishes in composing about trauma, offering teachers what may be new strategies.

Experiencing resistance and fear from school administrators, Claire voices another important issue about her students composing about trauma.

> The event that caused me to stop having my students write about their lives in such a personal way happened during my third year of teaching. I had a student who wrote about attempting suicide, but she wrote at the very top of the entry "Do Not Read." Previously, I told the students that they could use their notebooks to vent, and if they had an entry that they didn't want me to read, I would respect their wishes. And it took a while to develop that amount of trust from them, but eventually they started believing me....
>
> Well, through a series of events, the student ended up in the counselor's office and she mentioned to the counselor that she had written about suicide in her writer's notebook earlier. Naturally, I was reprimanded for not reporting the entry to the "proper authorities." My desire to use writing as a therapeutic tool was irrelevant to all of my superiors, and proved to be a liability. I was told that I was held responsible for every piece of writing in the writer's notebooks because it was a tool for my

class. So even if the child took the notebook home on their own and wrote about harming themselves or someone else, I was held accountable.

It scared me, so I stopped having kids write about their lives, or at least the parts that needed healing. Instead, they wrote about their first day of school, vacations, boyfriends/girlfriends, school, and current events. And if somehow one of these topics generated the slightest whimper, I'd shift gears and draw their attention away from the brooding emotions. Cold-hearted, I know. But it's safe. I actually went the past five years not even doing a writer's notebook. However, I am using one this year because I'm in a different district and its part of the curriculum. To be honest, I became nervous the minute I saw the neatly stacked boxes of composition notebooks inside of the resource room. All I could see were more crying sessions and potential lawsuits (I'm in a district where lawsuits against teachers are extremely popular). So I'm sticking to the curriculum, and I'm using them strictly for academic purposes—constructed responses on theme, context clues, grammar, vocabulary, and rough drafts of expository writing.

But, there's always a "but . . ." *But*, I strongly believe in using writing as a tool for healing. I believe in the process, no matter how nebulous the process may be. I believe in it so much that, as soon as I get the money, I'm going to return to school for a degree in counseling. . . . So, I'm going back to school, hopefully within two years! I think I would thoroughly enjoy counseling because then I'd be able to spend my entire time helping people heal. And all I'll need is a little training, a couch, and a composition notebook.

Claire was punished for her good and noble deed of experimenting with courageous classroom writing. Had she known that her student had written about suicide, Claire would certainly have acted. The narrow response of Claire's counselor and principal is understandable given their immediate responsibilities and lack of awareness of how symbols can positively interact with forging whole human beings. But this is not the major tragedy here. The worst part is that Claire now plans to leave teaching, but she will become an informed counselor who knows the power of expressive written language. Nevertheless, as I hope I have shown, it is not necessary to be a mental health professional to help students. Teachers and sound writing pedagogy can engage students' hearts and minds.

In establishing composing about trauma as a basic right, Claire's case underscores an important point: we have to recognize this field as a legitimate, academic pursuit. Here is a litany of standard and heralded characteristics of academic thinking: selecting, inquiring, analyzing, focusing, synthesizing, hypothesizing, researching, naming, describing, observing, connecting, evaluating, visualizing, defining, comparing, contrasting, using metaphor, organizing, specifying, generalizing, developing fluency, recasting one genre into another, and communicating with real audiences for real purposes. As I hope this study has demonstrated, each of these elements often occur when we compose through trauma. They apply across ages and levels of education.

But there are other practical reasons to use expressive writing, primarily simple human needs. According to the *New York Times* (The Editorial Board, December 17, 2013), Finland, the country long-heralded as having the world's best school system, provides "daily hot meals; health and dental services; psychological counseling; and an array of services for families and children in need. None of these services are means tested." America would seem to have a greater need than Finland or other high-achieving countries because other developed countries embrace far less violence and the many forms it can take, from automatic assault weapons, to representations of violence in media. (For untold viewers, the mere inclusion of violence legitimizes and even glorifies it. Too, violence that occurs before, after, or simultaneously with scenes depicting sex helps viewers associate them and regard them as a single "natural" phenomenon.)

I recently visited an inner-city school in a district often recognized as one of America's worst. Classes had ended for Christmas break, but I spent a brief time with two students, as all three of us were waiting—me for the principal, the two children for their mother. The inquisitive little girl was a second-grader named "Millionz," and her polite brother was a first-grader named, "Cash Money." (I had no time to reflect upon their unique names, other than to note that they revealed their society's values; we were too busy playing with my camera and drawing pictures of Mickey Mouse.)

I met the principal for the first time, a youngish, African-American woman, who glowed with warmth, concern, and energy. Even though my visit had nothing to do with teaching, learning, or writing, and even though I did not ask, within a few minutes, I learned how demanding her daily job was—a spontaneous and instant outpouring. One reason for her outburst, I'm sure, was the time of our meeting, on the last day before vacation. She was exhausted. So, I listened as her daily burdens came flooding out: her students bring loads of problems with them to school each day—broken homes with no structure to their daily lives; substance abuse; lack of affection from adults; poor health and nutrition—an endless supply of psychological and emotional problems. I learned that a psychiatric treatment organization had partnered with the school, and that two daily classes were comprised only of students with psychological and emotional issues. The principal stated that every day she had to "talk down" children who were intensely acting out such problems.

In the principal's cascading descriptions of her students' psychological and emotional needs and how the school had tried to address them, she never once mentioned the school's writing program or how it might be used to help her students. When I finally mentioned my interests in composing and trauma, her response was that her teachers (of first through sixth-graders) were often afraid of writing—of any kind—and that they considered themselves poor writers, and so avoided it in their teaching. While this school may be on the extreme end of this scale, I believe it represents an all-too-common situation: kids who desperately need ways to handle their psychological and emotional issues, so that they can better learn, are, at the same time, denied access to personal writing and composing about trauma. Such composing would develop their thinking and academic performance, and would, at the same time, develop their self-understanding, allowing some light and order into their internal chaos.

Finally, establishing composing through trauma as a basic right addressing basic needs requires that education policy makers stop turning their noses up at any hint of "the personal." Policy makers should no longer deny its pivotal role in thinking, defining selfhood, and developing maturity. Despite some states' resistance to the "Common Core Standards" (for the wrong reasons), they have been adopted in nearly every state, controlling all levels of education. The most serious objection from my perspective is that these standards nearly eliminate discourse that is "personal" in nature, which is the lifeblood of composing, not only about trauma. Louise Rosenblatt (1995) states that purely rational thinking "lacks the conflicting impulses or emotional perplexities out of which thinking usually grows in real life. Reason should arise in a matrix of feeling" (216). Through imposing the Common Core Standards, corporate America has ordained for us that reason, somehow, can no longer "arise in a matrix of feeling."

After four decades in education, I remain convinced of only one truth: teachers of any level, grade, or discipline, are not motivated by the pursuit of personal wealth. How could they be? Teaching, no matter the context, is a demanding, complex profession. It attracts my favorite kind of people: humane, selfless, idealistic, bright, hard-working, dedicated. Despite this (or because of it?) K-12 teachers woke up one morning a few years ago and found that the "Common Core Standards" had taken over American education. Most of us agree there should be some "common" standards across America. It makes sense. Most of us agree that these new standards are a notch better than what we had before.

However, the creation of the Common Core Standards involved almost no real teachers in its initial development. Instead, the standards were largely the work of politicians and corporate businesses (such as the Pearson Publishing conglomerate and Achieve, Inc.). Dianne Ravitch (2013) and others have "followed the money" and made this case better than I can here, but these new "laws" that teachers must follow have essentially banned writing related to an individual's selfhood, especially the use of personal experience as "evidence" in students' writing. I am definitely not advocating that students stop learning from secondary source information, such as original documents and encyclopedias. What I do believe in, though, is validating and honoring students' *first* form of evidence, their *first* source of information: their own lives.

Restricting students' use of personal experience is wrong on so many levels that teachers hardly know where to start in resisting it. Students are, in effect, barred from learning about who they are and who they may wish to become; they are banned from thinking in language, from using language to shape their own identity, or to explore options. In effect, they are prohibited from imagining and dreaming with words. The fact is that students who desperately feel the need to write about their traumas often do so, regardless of what the official assignment requests. In this era of CCS, if these K-College students (and their teachers) dare write about their personal conflicts, they are made to feel like they are committing high treason, like they should begin packing for a new assignment at a labor camp.

We should not forget, of course, that the Common Core Standards were preceded by the "No Child Left Behind" legislation. Before that, it was "America 2000." (And before that, it was "Johnny Can't Read"—or write or do math or comprehend current news events.) The mega-programs of CCS and NCLB were created for purposes of national *assessment*, but are packaged and sold under the label of "reform." Twenty years ago, James Moffett (1998) asked a more basic question about such programs—one that we need to keep asking.

> But why should education be mobilized anyway around the question of national assessment? Why should we even assume that assessment of any sort is a major way to reform schools? Why not mobilize for things that experience *does* indicate, like personalizing learning, integrating the curriculum, renovating teacher training, or organizing community networks? Why not, in other words, focus on the learning environment and learning processes themselves? Why on *assessment?* (134)

The most basic answer to Moffett's question is that teachers do not *begin* their work, do not begin conceptualizing their work, with assessment. They begin with people, with learning and teaching. Beginning the reform process with "assessment" is the holy mantra of the American business model. This leads to another answer: We've focused on assessment since the 1980's because the now entrenched corporate model in education and corporate dollars put it there.

In the Reagan era, we were also told that American students were ignorant of what was going on in the world. As a result, almost overnight it seemed, a commercial television venture, "Channel One," sprouted in many school districts throughout the land, broadcasting soft news programs. Like all American TV, the eight-minute news program only served as an excuse to beam glitzy commercials for M&M candy and the latest Nintendo game to captive students. Such "programs" amount to little more than the creation of false needs that can then be filled by products. So, to venture a fuller response to Moffett's question, only profiteers seem to focus on assessment and accountability. Teachers are too busy actually teaching. They know that learning is complex and developmental and that "growth models" dictated by those used to selling cars and laptops don't work in teaching people. We are therefore left with impossible "standards" that real teachers and students cannot achieve fast enough, if at all. The result is that private, for-profit businesses will consume public education. This, I think, is why the most powerful forces in America focus on *assessment*: they see a big, fat "market demographic" for peddling their products and services. Teachers, on the whole, are too trusting and non-judgmental to see this. All their lives, accumulating personal wealth was never in their heads or hearts.

The corporate moguls who orchestrated the sudden take-over of American education continue to predict that these standards will result in a massive drop in students' test scores. If schools fail, then the giant door of profit swings wide open for selling all the snake-oil remedies imaginable—tests, products, technology, training, ad infinitum. Pavlov's corporate dog-of-profit has pounced.

The devaluing of personal or expressive discourse denies anything connected to students' identity formation. If teachers and administrators go strictly by the rules, then students will have no opportunity to get to know themselves, a key to education for centuries. As well, expressive language is the "matrix" from which other forms of discourse evolve, discourse for other audiences and purposes. If students cannot explain something to themselves or to trusted others by using informal and personal language, they have much difficulty explaining it to more distanced and less trusted readers. Outlawing the personal dimension in teaching and learning is diametrically opposed to our best thinkers about thinking, such as John Dewey, Louise Rosenblatt, James Britton, Stephen Pinker, and Howard Gardner. Composing about trauma is the perfect pedagogy through which students can learn to control emotion and begin to impose more rational thought. Again, Rosenblatt clarifies the roles of emotion and reason in a way that is uncannily relevant to composing through trauma.

> John Dewey and other pragmatist philosophers remind us that in actual life constructive thinking usually starts when there is some conflict or discomfort or when habitual behavior is impeded and a choice of new paths of behavior must be made. Such thinking, therefore, grows out of some sort of tension and is colored by it. The tension contributes the impetus to seek a solution, but intelligent behavior results from thought brought to bear on the problem. Moreover, the validity of the thought will usually depend on whether emotion has been controlled and has not obscured the actual situation. Impulse is needed to arouse thought, incite reflection and enliven belief. But only thought notes obstructions, invents tools, conceives aims, directs technique, and thus converts impulse into an art which lives in objects (Dewey, *Human Nature* 170–71). (Rosenblatt 1995, 216)

These thoughts were echoed by Erika Lindemann (2001), who reflects on students in our current media-drenched environment: "Because other media threaten to recreate us as plastic people, Disney delusions, or Madison Avenue stereotypes, we want students to write honestly, with a kind of tough sensitivity, about subjects that matter to them" (7). What could matter more to students than the problems and issues encountered while they're growing up?

Every day, in every community, students walk into the classroom with serious psychological and emotional needs that must be addressed before (or in tandem with) focusing on their academic work. In the absence of productive and legitimate ways to fill this void, such as exploring it through writing and imagery, they often turn to representations produced by popular culture's electronic media—not just film, advertising, and television, but also "social media," such as Facebook and Twitter. Media representations are all around them, attractive, and instantly accessible. As well, future generations of young people will continue to regard media as "closer" to reality than previous generations. Other students who are "hurting" but are not sure why or what to do about it, may try to purchase solutions, given the constant bombardment of ads they experience day in and day out. When consumption fails, they may start acting out their anger, loneliness, and despair, as we have seen in an endless series of mass killings.

Notions of education, technology, society, media, and culture seem too over-sized, too inflated, and too complex for mere mortals to comprehend (as much as we try to do so). They are nonetheless deeply entrenched mega-systems. I've argued elsewhere (Fox 2001) that these mega-systems constantly influence each other, as one rises to dominate, before giving way to another system's expansion. These massive spheres of influence mutate and often drown out the central concern of this book—the human voice and the raw spirituality it seeks to nurture. Plainly, things are out of whack. Neurosurgeon, Eben Alexander (2012), puts it this way:

> The physical side of the universe is as a speck of dust compared to the invisible and spiritual part. In my past view, spiritual wasn't a word that I would have employed during a scientific conversation. Now I believe it is a word that we cannot afford to leave out. (82)

Composing about trauma, of course, is a symbolic act, as are the other media messages that engulf us. Symbolic acts, for purposes of work and entertainment, constitute the air we breathe, usually willingly, if not voraciously. They will become more common at the same time that they become increasingly and tantalizingly attractive to us. In most ways, resistance is futile. We cannot remove ourselves from the times in which we live. One central question is, "Do we satisfy ourselves with mainly consuming symbolic acts for external purposes? Or, do we invest in generating our own symbolic acts to create meaning for purposes of health and growth?

Support Inquiry and Research Related to Composing about Trauma

Composing through trauma is a multidisciplinary field, connecting to such disciplines as psychology, writing, rhetoric, visual and media literacy, medical anthropology, medical humanities, health education, prison reform, and many more. It should not be surprising, then, that the promising pockets of research and application sprout up in many places, seemingly independent of each other. This diversity has its benefits but the lack of a unified or coherent base for such work also means it is under-funded (if funded at all). Such composing is also poorly understood by the general public, creating a cycle that stunts its development. Despite these circumstances, many projects deserve recognition, only a few of which I can note here.

One recent study reported in the *American Journal of Psychiatry* (Heim et al. 2013) found that sexual and emotional abuse experienced during childhood left specific scars on the brain. The researchers found that thinning of the cortical fields occurred in different locations, depending upon whether the victim suffered sexual abuse or emotional abuse. The authors concluded that such "neural plasticity," when occurring during childhood development, "may shield a child from the sensory processing of the specific abusive experience by altering cortical representation fields . . ." (616). However, this scarring may also be the foundation for behavioral problems later on in life, such as sexual dysfunction. This information, if verified by future research, could provide a psychological basis that writers could use to more fully comprehend their own trauma. As the writers in this book demonstrate, research into secondary sources not only adds to the writer's supply of "evidence," but helps distance the writer from the trauma.

Other research on the brain focuses on the neuropsychology of spiritual experience. Princeton University's Center of Theological Inquiry includes an international team of scholars of theology and the sciences called, "Inquiry on Religious Experience and Moral Identity." One participant, Dr. Brick Johnstone, believes that the "euphoria of spiritual experience is triggered by brain biology. . . . It relates to the release of biogenic amine neurotransmitters such as dopamine and serotonin" (Barna 2013). Johnstone and others define "spirituality" very broadly, as something that is not governed by any particular religious affiliation. Everyone, including atheists, can experience spirituality. Johnstone's goal is to find ways to train the brain to generate positive emotions: "There are ways to get along better with others," he stated, "and they are brain-based" (3). Understanding how the brain generates positive mental sates such as empathy and forgiveness may allow us more precision in how and when we use language and imagery to address trauma.

Another new approach to help people deal with trauma comes from the United States Army, which is focusing on the high number of suicides committed by active-duty military and veterans. The numbers recently reported in *USA Today* (Zoroya, October 7, 2013) are deeply disturbing: from 2001–2013, three thousand service men and women took their own lives; in 2012, the Army alone reported an average of six suicides per week; and the Department of Veterans Affairs estimates that twenty-two veterans kill themselves each day (1). The Army and the National Institute of Mental Health are applying a set of risk factors (e.g., psychiatric illness, deployment history, substance abuse) to a "computer assessment" of soldiers, all to identify people who should receive special care. Once soldiers or civilians have been identified as high-risk, I hope they receive help to systematically use writing and imagery. I recently met with a veteran who told me, "If I didn't write letters every day, I never would have made it through Iraq."

A new and equally promising research approach is the use of computer databases to study the language of people who have been filmed as they talk about their trauma. This can be very useful for researchers who cannot afford costly travel for personal interviews (not to mention the difficulties of obtaining human subjects approval). For example, Marco De Martino (2012) researched gender differences in illness narratives available on two web sites: www.healthtalkonline.org and www.youthhealthtalk.org, databases of patients describing their own experiences. He transcribed 1,859 interviews with cancer patients. Using a key word comparison method, De Martino found that men's key words contained more technical terms than women's, noting that such language may enable men to establish a sense of control, in this case, over their own illnesses. Among De Martino's conclusions are that 1) men generally do not wish to voice their emotions directly, instead preferring to "deflect" them by using humor, irony, and technical jargon; and 2) women engage more fully with the experience of illness by expressing their uncertainties and negative feelings (slide 32).

In addition to using technology to identify and research people in need of trauma care, the University of Zurich recently studied "cybertherapy"—how effectively online therapy works (Bittel 2013). Participants who were compared to those receiving face-to-face therapy indicated their online experience was more "personal" than those in the traditional setting (8). Also increasing are online "Confession" web sites. Some are religious sites, but not all, such as Dailyconfession.com, grouphug.us, post-secret.com, and ivescrewedup.com. Their popularity indicates that such sites serve a purpose. However, the positive effects of these sites have to be weighed against what is often lost when humans distance themselves from communicating face-to-face. Professor James Quick, of the University of Texas at Arlington, concisely sums up the pros and cons of such sites:

- We often . . . like to carry on appearances that we're all fine and dandy, and we don't always want people to know the depths of our souls. So anonymity lets us flush that stuff out there and walk away. (McClatchy Newspapers, *Columbia Daily Tribune*, February 23, 2010, 10)

In another study, online therapy proved beneficial when patients counseled each other. Bret Shaw, Fiyona McTavish, and Robert Hawkins (2006), examined how women with breast cancer used imagistic writing (e.g., description, similes and metaphors) to help themselves and their readers in an online support group to cope with noxious treatments and pain. The researchers studied their "text-based visualizations." After analyzing 6,000 messages posted by 145 women, the researchers arrived at four basic categories: 1) visualizations about treatment, 2) visualizations projected to others, 3) visualizations to comfort or heal, and 4) visualizations of a religiously spiritual nature. One interesting observation was that a common image of cancer treatments was the "battle" metaphor which posits chemo treatments, for example, as weapons for waging war against cancer. The authors observe that this type of image can allow the writer to accept the chemicals' side effects as "more tolerable" (8). Similarly, some patients' imagistic language suggested that their loss of hair was a positive sign that the chemo was working, even though there is no clinical evidence that hair loss indicates a reduction in cancer.

Like many of the writers explored in this book, our understanding of illness or trauma is the main influence that determines how we cope with such experience. Shaw, McTavish, and Hawkins (2006) suggest that instead of cancer patients just writing to each other online (including written images), that sending actual, graphic images, too, could further increase patients' coping abilities. This is precisely what the writers in Chapter 4 accomplished, but in a face-to-face situation. I can't help but wonder about using both face-to-face and computer-mediated approaches, especially when both venues employ actual, pictorial imagery as well as imagistic language.

Other promising applications of using language and imagery to address trauma occur in hospitals, schools, and prisons. Expressive writing therapy is now used in major medical organizations, such as Duke University in North Carolina, the City of Hope Cancer Center and The John Wayne Cancer Institute in California, and Piedmont Hospital in Georgia. Writing is used in the treatment of physically and psychologically abused women, AIDS/HIV patients, soldiers experiencing PTSD or Post-Traumatic Stress Disorder, and suicidal people (Anderson and MacCurdy 2000). In 2009, due to a growing awareness of the mental trauma faced by hospital workers ("second victims") who grieve the suffering and loss of their patients, the University of Missouri Health System established a peer support program called the "forYOU Team" (*Mizzou Weekly*, September 5, 2013).

While public education seems to be light-years away from embracing composing about trauma in any informed and systematic way, a few signs of hope flicker in the distance. Four days after the mass shooting of elementary school students and teachers in Newtown, Connecticut, the National Council Teachers of English posted eighteen sources for teachers to use in helping their students to read, write, and reflect on this barbaric crime ("Responding to Tragedy in Schools: Supporting Teachers and Students," December 18, 2012 http://www.ncte.org/responding).

While it's imperative for students to compose about negative emotional experiences, everyone needs to write about positive emotions (e.g., Burton and King 2004). One study explored how young college students used the *intentional activity* of writing letters of gratitude to improve their sense of well-being (Toepfer and Walker 2009). The researchers hypothesized that writing three letters of gratitude, over time, would "enhance important qualities of well-being in the author: happiness, life satisfaction, and gratitude" (1). The results indicate that "writing three letters of gratitude positively impacted the two sub-domains of well-being: happiness and gratitude" (191).

While enhancing well-being is important for most people, for prison inmates (and society at large) a far greater need is rehabilitation and reducing the number of repeat-offenders who return to prison. According to Liam Allen (2011), in the United Kingdom, "in 2009, 59% of prisoners who served sentences of fewer than 12 months were reconvicted within a year. The future for young offenders was 72%."

This Writers in Prison Network (WIPN), which began in 1992, funds writers-in-residence in sixteen prisons throughout the UK. In addition to learning creative and autobiographical writing, inmates develop their skills at oral storytelling, staging plays, publishing magazines, making videos, producing radio shows, and recording rap music. This program's multi-genre approach is innovative and practical at the same time. Allen reports that "little research has been done to measure the impact of the arts in prison. Writers in Prison Network co-director, Clive Hopwood, is confident its work 'helps contribute towards people not reoffending, or reoffending to a lesser degree.'" Allen shares an ex-prisoner's view of his experience in this program:

> Before, I didn't know how to express my emotions, it used to come out in bad ways, but now I'm a hell of a lot calmer. . . . It usually used to come out in violence, it did boil over inside and get worse and worse, and then it would explode.

Allen further shares that this prisoner now, "actually feels the anger flowing through my pen and on to the paper."

Composing about trauma has not yet developed into a coherent field of inquiry. These examples of research and application are scattered among many disciplines, to the point that it's nearly impossible for anyone to know of activities that are related to his or her own work. Nonetheless, the people driving the promising projects described here understand one simple fact: that America is fissured and fractured on two levels. The first level of fragmentation occurs in race, ethnicity, gender, age, socio-economic status, and political affiliation. The second level of fragmentation resides in violence, illness, abuse, and emotional upheaval. Both levels splinter the wholeness, the unity, of our external and internal lives, fragmenting exactly that which makes us human. Only education—especially reading and composing—can help us gather up the shattered pieces and re-assemble them again into a greater whole than we had before.

EDGE DEATH OUT OF THE SHADOWS OF FEAR

What is death? A scary mask. Take it off—see, it doesn't bite.
—Epictetus, c. 110 (quoted in Lapham 2013)

Americans, I believe, especially fear death. We are too submerged in work, materialism, and instant gratification to think about it. I doubt if at least a generalized fear of extinction will ever dissipate, but we should at least slowly ease it out of its shroud of unspeakable horror. Michel de Montaigne (1533–1592), a philosopher and "father" of the personal essay, asked a simple, logical question about death that we continue to avoid.

> You have seen enough men who were better off dying, thereby avoiding great miseries. Have you found any man that was worse off? How simpleminded it is to condemn a thing that you have not experienced yourself or through anyone else. (Quoted in Lapham 2013, 47)

At age seventy-eight, Lewis Lapham described the world around him, as his body tells him he will not live forever.

> Within the surrounding biosphere of news and entertainment media it is the fear of death—24/7 in every shade of hospital white and doomsday black—that sells the pharmaceutical, political, financial, film, and food product promising to make good the wish to live forever . . . remember that the leading cause of death is birth. (13)

The insistent fear of death is good for business in America. We live in a profit-driven, cultural labyrinth that covets the 18–35 year-old demographic with the most "disposable" income, accomplishing two objectives simultaneously. First, it pumps the screaming algorithm that youth means spending money, even if you don't have it: Let's travel, party, eat out, drink, get high, drive fast and furious, ignore debt, downplay hard work, and multiply ourselves on Facebook. Live large like Brad and Angelina. Second, when the decades stack up and "disposable" income dries up, then the second live-forever wave washes upon the shore; buy a gym membership, age-less skin cream, a few facelifts and tummy-tucks, supplements, a hair transplant, vitamins, an exotic cruise, Spanx.

Technology and products can indeed help our lives, but this assistance comes with a huge expense that goes unnoticed. The entangled web of media technology and profiteering removes us, layer by layer, distancing us from "first-level" or everyday reality, in effect removing us farther from nature—the only real model for life that we've ever had. Each layer of artifice imposed between humans and nature appears evermore authentic and hence enticing. When we are so far from nature, is it any wonder that we fear death? Is it any wonder that we remain unaware of using language and imagery to demystify trauma?

Sherwin B. Nuland's *How We Die: Reflections of Life's Final Chapter* (1993) articulates the clinical and biological elements of death because he believes we need to demystify it.

> Only by a frank discussion of the very details of dying can we best deal with those aspects that frighten us the most. It is by knowing the truth and being prepared for it that we rid ourselves of that fear of the terra incognita of death that leads to self-deception and disillusions. (xvii)

When we are immersed in a culture that worships youth and health, and that, at the same time, scares the bejesus out of us about facing death, then we can understand how writers such as Lucy and Kate are dyed-in-the-wool heroes.

Consider Composing about Trauma as a Form of Prayer

Composing through trauma should be given its rightful place—as one kind of prayer—albeit sometimes secular—among *many* kinds. What I do *not* intend is any doubt or denigration toward people who devoutly believe in an omnipotent God or who practice any religion, formally or informally. I have nothing but respect for those who practice and actually live and apply their religion, whatever it may be, wherever they may live.

In this section, then, I speculate on how composing through trauma and informal prayer may share certain characteristics. I'll focus on the most common and informal of prayers, those that petition a higher being for something that we desperately need and want, such as to spare the life of a loved one. Anna Ulanov and Barry Ulanov's (1982) description of prayer is essentially similar to the expressive language used by the writers described in this book:

> Everybody prays. People pray whether or not they call it prayer. We pray every time we ask for help, understanding, or strength, in or out of religion. Then, who or what we are speak out of us whether we know it or not. . . . The language of primary-process thinking is not verbal. It comes in pictures and emotion-laden wishes and is private to ourselves, not really communicable, even though we all share it. This language of images and values feeds our outer language of words. . . . The first speech is the language of instinct, emotion, and images. . . . If prayer is, as we believe, primary speech and the most direct line of communication we have to our interior reality, then every denial of that reality, every judgment or retreat from it that shuts off access to it is a serious diminishing of ourselves. It is in fact, a kind of refusal to be. (1–6)

While we can debate the degree of similarity between composing through trauma and prayer, I believe that both of them are broadly instinctual and spiritual—something we do when we believe we're up against oblivion. Also, of course, both may be learned. Both are expressions of hope, a belief that we will somehow be okay, whether through our own thinking and language or through our interactions with other people, or from a supreme being's intervention. Such hope may lead to confidence, which may lead to possibilities.

Hope necessarily resides in the future. Ulanov and Ulanov maintain that in prayer we admit the future to ourselves, which gives us the *basis* for anticipation and hope—a kind of grafting of the present onto the future (11). This is the same reason that people compose about trauma—to establish hope that has some solidity and sense of "permanence" to it, because it is rooted in the physical process of writing, involving many senses, as well as establishing a written record. Our desire to have an actual, tangible basis for hope is the reason that I often require writers to create and manipulate actual images, which are even more concrete, and hence closer to reality, than the more abstract words on a page.

The urge for both composing and praying wells up from our deep knowledge that we are simply human, in moments of profoundly realizing our limitations and frailty. As such, both composing and prayer have to be regarded as the most honest and sincere of symbols. This alone should warrant our respect. As well, both may be viewed as a stated or implied rejection of our limitations, which should warrant our respect for the durability of the human spirit. Regardless, in prayer and composing through trauma, we are left with sincerity and spirituality, the most valued qualities of what it means to be human.

While some people regard composing through trauma as narcissistic, I believe that just the opposite is the case—that both composing and prayer are far from self-absorbing activities. Both are dialogic by their nature, as they state or strongly imply an "other." Those who pray, as well as the writers in this book, are addressing "others." As Ulanov and Ulanov (1982) state, a kind of dialogue occurs: "The otherness of prayer is shown to us in many ways, large and small. The small ways happen first. In the process of confessing who we are, we find ourselves addressed by the otherness within ourselves and the otherness within our world" (9).

When we compose through trauma, we also confess who we are, whether we aim our discourse at ourselves or others. On a basic level, Lucy writes to her friends on the Caring Bridge web site, and Kate writes letters to her late husband, and students address their peers and instructor. On another level, those who pray and compose about trauma also speak to the "otherness" within themselves and within the boundaries of their own lives. It's difficult, if not impossible, for us to confess without also becoming aware of how others may compare.

There are more similarities. Composing about trauma and the act of prayer may be better understood if I present them sequentially, as very rough links in a kind of "chain."

Prayer and composing about trauma are very private transactions, held close to the self. It's widely accepted that Jesus and Thomas Jefferson believed in the privacy of prayer. (Prayer that is not done in private, but in public, must necessarily be regarded as more of a "performance.") The closed nature of both activities allows us to listen to our interior selves, because we shut out the intruding voices and competing noises of our clanging culture. It is a time and place for stillness and honesty. Privacy and silence encourage not only reflection, but fluency as well: when interruptions cease, one thought can more easily flow into another. As Peter Elbow (1998) and others have argued, when we shut out external stimuli, we can focus better, enabling the right words to flow more easily.

Prayer and composing about trauma merge our thinking and speaking to ourselves, with listening to ourselves. At the same time we are speaking (or thinking or writing), we must necessarily listen to our interior selves. These are obvious reciprocal processes, but because of the serious context, we do both with greater intensity. In composing about trauma, our speaking and listening can fuse and result in what Csikszentmihalyi (1990) describes as a "flow" experience. In prayer, this merging may consist of our own earthly thinking/speaking and God's presence, which may be manifested in speaking and listening through us. (Modern civilization includes a lot of collateral damage. One tragedy is that too many people are afraid to be, or don't know how to be, alone with their own thoughts.)

Prayer and composing about trauma often depend upon images saturated in emotion. If we are silent and private for purposes of praying and composing about trauma, then we may generate more thought and language—and by so doing, may allow more emotion-laden imagery to surface. As we've seen in this book, the written and actual images used by writers are often fraught with emotion. The same must often be true with prayer (and composing about trauma), in that emotion-laden imagery can motivate and generate thinking and language, focus them, sustain them, and shape them. In turn, thinking and language can have the same effects on imagery. The interaction of emotion-soaked imagery and the free use of language is highly "combustible" in elaborating thought.

Prayer and composing about trauma lead to a clearer, stronger "voice," and broader, deeper thinking. The more we are silent and private, the more thought and language can "rise to the surface"; the more thought we generate, the more emotion-laden imagery can well-up. The result is that we then become more confident to use language to interact with imagery and imagery to interact with language. The more confident we become, the clearer and stronger our own "voice" or persona becomes.

Prayer and composing about trauma help "move" us outward to the social world of other people and ideas. As we move our internal concerns into the world beyond ourselves, interacting with the appropriate other people about our fears and traumas, it's been my experience that the response will be positive, or at least sympathetic, to our stronger (and hence unique) voices. The usual response is one of care and concern, as people recognize (consciously and unconsciously) the honesty and sincerity of our clearer and stronger voice. In fact, it often invites these other people to respond in the same way. The result is that we are on a more informed, useful, and faster track to reckoning with our issues. The personal cycles (above) continue, as they merge with the personal/social cycle, each enriching the other, as the cycles of thinking and perceiving continue.

Prayer and composing about trauma can lead us to express our felt changes through some external construction or art form. The final link in this "chain" is far less common than what I've sketched in the first three points, but here it is: when all of the above occur through engaging in composing about trauma or consistent prayer, some people may experience a kind of "transformation" in their overall perception of life; they may feel profoundly moved through a shift of consciousness. We can never precisely define what such a transformation is, but it tends to enlarge our worldview, making us more understanding, tolerant, sympathetic, empathetic, and sensitive to people, events, and ideas than we had been before. James Moffett's (1998) description of spirituality captures this view of transformation.

> Spirituality is connectedness. The more spiritual a person, the more he or she identifies with the rest of humanity and nature and sheds feelings of boundaries. The more we identify with others, the better we treat them. . . . People of higher consciousness feel their innerness, their essential being, as a solid reality independent of validation by others. (71)

When composing through trauma leads us to "mending" or making whole our former fragmented selves, and we engage the same ideas in social interaction, the natural next step is creation—the making of anything (e.g., writing a poem, establishing an organization). Such transformations, of course, can lead to all manner of creations, from spending more time with loved ones, to mowing the lawn of an elderly neighbor. Given the right circumstances, some transformational experiences are expressed through forms of art. Examples are not hard to conjure, from Michelangelo, to Vincent Van Gogh; from Johann Sebastian Bach, to George Frederick Handel; from Gerard Manley Hopkins, to Paul Gauguin, to William Blake, to Pablo Picasso.

These ideas are not meant to serve as six golden steps to mega-bliss. Most of us don't possess Michelangelo's sense of form or Van Gogh's vision of the night sky. These are only possibilities, however hopeful. Great artists and geniuses and other rarified phenomena is not the stuff of this book. While Lucy, Kate, and the other people whose cases are explored in these pages are educated and bright, they are down-to-earth, regular people, who faced straight upward, into the unknown, and worked their way toward a measure of meaning. In pursuing and constructing the possible meanings within each trauma, these humans not only absorbed light, but reflected it back on us all.

CODA

Throughout the past twelve years, this book has germinated and budded, risen and fallen, in more forms than I can recall. A final disclaimer, with apologies to Edna St. Vincent Millay: words, images, and symbols "are not all: they are not food nor drink, nor a roof against the rain. . . ." (2007). This book is not for everyone. Using symbols to understand the self, to impose some order on chaos, are symbolic actions that will elude many of us. One reason is that words and images are not reality, but mere *representations* of reality. As we plunge further into technologically mediated life, we deal with representations of representations of representations, ad nauseum.

The only upside of this predicament is that many people do indeed accept symbols as reality—one reason for this book. Nonetheless, this book's major limitation may be that it's just another puff of wind blowing us away from nature—from unspoiled grass, trees, sun, and sky. Nature has long been our best model for everything—life, death, art. By the end of Millay's poem, though, I don't think she'd trade her love for anything. The same holds true for me. Despite the limitations of using words and images during times of trauma, I don't think I would trade them for anything, neither food nor drink. Nor would the writers I worked with.

True to nature's cycle, the people in this book have moved on. Kate gave up her tenured university position to join the Peace Corps, where she is thriving in a blooming new life in Asia. To read her blogs about her daily life is not just to appreciate her sharp, sensitive skill in writing; it's also like having a front row seat, watching springtime. In the summer of 2012, four years after her initial diagnosis of Metastatic Breast Cancer, Lucy died. Her son Nick, now a sophomore in college, has taken over "The Lucy Fund," which she founded and raised thousands of dollars for. Yesterday, Nick posted an update on the *Caring Bridge* web site, and he has, somehow, inherited his mother's true voice. Lucy will always be the hero of this book.

Despite the gifts of courage and inspiration I received from Lucy, Kate, and the other writers herein, I also experienced some doubts along the way. Most of them surfaced gradually and have added depth and richness to my experience. I hope this brief recounting will inform future interrogators of writing and trauma.

A consistent dread (a lesser monster) was that my writing would become hopelessly academic and pedantic. When you live your life awash in stilted, vague verbiage, it's hard to avoid. For eons I've told my students that the easiest prose to write is that which is the hardest to read: polysyllabic and puffed-up generalities, all wrapped up in tangled syntax. Conversely, the hardest prose to write is the easiest to read. I always hunger for (but fail at) what Orwell wanted: "prose like a windowpane"—smooth, transparent, lucid. Avoiding gobbledygook is harder to do than most people believe. Anyone who traffics in language has a moral obligation to clarity. I apologize here for any slips into sludge that have managed to slide past me.

A related apprehension was that my writing would sometimes slide over the edge and be too sentimental, if not dreary. When you are writing about people you admire, it can sometimes be hard not to "overwrite." Added to this is my immersion in the topic itself, not to mention my chronic devotion to it. If either of these scenarios came to pass—being too academic or too sentimental—then I feared something greater: losing the profound and fragile humanity embodied in these people and their spirit. I have too much respect for them and their work to risk such a loss. I hope I have not.

Parts of this book are plainly hard to read, due to the writers' intensity of feelings and their naked honesty. These parts were hard for me to write. One fear was that readers would think I was trying to shock them, trying to amp-up the intensity and number of "jolts-per-minute," as they say in the land of entertainment and advertising. I am sensitive to this view because of my long history of opposing what I've called "Sensationspeak." To be accused of something that I've spent much of my life fighting was an unsettling thought.

Nor did I want, throughout this project, to be considered an exploiter of other people's trauma, that I was, in effect, pimping their illnesses or misfortunes. I believe that this would never enter the minds of people who know me, but most readers will not have known me. I suppose that you can only take my word for it, that this remains the farthest thing from my intent.

While I've long considered myself a "strong" person in most regards, I felt that sooner or later, this whole trauma business would snow-ball and "get to me." And it did. When I was working at home by myself, there were a few times when I sat down and cried. This led to another realization—that the people described in this book are far braver than I would be under similar circumstances. When I was a child and experienced my first death, my grandfather, I never forgot his hand-plow, sitting in the middle of his garden, a furrow only half-completed. I don't know if this book marks the end of that row, but I can only hope that its seeds will emerge—light green, bending to the sun's arc across the sky.

Notes

1. Actual, physical imagery, such as a photo, can indeed serve as an effective "other thing" when writing for healing, functioning in a similar intermediary way as that of a painting or sculpture, removing us a bit from the direct heat of the trauma under consideration. See Chapters 2 and 4 for more detail on "the other thing." Also see Fox (2011).

2. For detailed discussions of transcendental meditation's positive effects on the human psyche, please see the Transcendental Meditation Program web site, which includes information on 600 scientific studies, at www.tm.org/research-on-meditation.

Works Cited

Alexander, Eben. *Proof of Heaven: A Neurosurgeon's Journey into the Afterlife*. New York: Simon and Schuster, 2012. Print.

Allen, Guy. "Language, Power, and Consciousness: A Writing Experiment at the University of Toronto." *Writing & Healing: Towards an Informed Practice*. Eds. Charles Anderson and Marian MacCurdy. Urbana: NCTE, 2000. 249–91. Print.

Allen, Liam. "Can Writing Stop Prisoners Reoffending?" *British Broadcasting Company*. March 2012. Web. 2 July 2015. http://www.bbc.co.uk/news/entertainment-arts-12879042.

Anderson, Charles, and Marian MacCurdy. *Writing & Healing: Towards an Informed Practice*. Urbana: NCTE, 2000. Print.

Anderson, Charles, Karen Holt, and Patty McGady. "Suture, Stigma, and the Pages that Heal." *Writing & Healing: Towards an Informed Practice*. Eds. Charles Anderson and Marian MacCurdy. Urbana: NCTE, 2000. 58-82. Print.

Arnheim, Rudolph. *New Essays on the Psychology of Art*. Berkeley: U of California P, 1986. Print.

Bakewell, Sarah. "Montaigne, Philosopher of Life, Part I: How to Live." *The Guardian*. 10 May 12010. Web. http://www.theguardian.com/commentisfree/belief/2010/may/10/montaigne-philosophy.

Bal, P. Matthijs, and Martjin Veltkamp. "How Does Fiction Reading Influence Empathy? An Experimental Investigation on the Role of Emotional Transportation," January 30, 2013. doi: 10.1371/journal.pone.0055341.

Barna, Mark. "Health Psychologist Chosen for Theology-Science Fellowship." *Mizzou Weekly* 35.1 (2013). Web. 26 July 2015. http://mizzouweekly.missouri.edu/archive/2013/35–1/johnstone/index.php.

Berkenkotter, Carol, and Thomas N. Huckin. *Genre Knowledge in Disciplinary Communication: Cognition/Culture/Power*. Mahwah: Erlbaum, 1995. Print.

Berman, Jeffrey. *Risky Writing: Self-Disclosure and Self-Transformation in the Classroom*. Amherst: U of Massachusetts P, 2001. Print.

Bittel, Jason. "Therapy by Internet May be More Effective than You'd Think." *Future Tense*. 1 August 2013. Web. 2 July 2015. http://www.slate.com/blogs/future_tense/2013/08/01/therapy_by_internet_may_be_more_effective_than_you_d_think.html.

Brand, Alice, and Richard Graves. *Presence of Mind: Writing and the Domain beyond the Cognitive*. Portsmouth: Boynton/Cook, 1994. Print.

Borrowman, Shane. *Trauma and the Teaching of Writing*. Albany: SUNY P. 2006. Print.

Breuer, Josef, and Sigmund Freud. *Studies in Hysteria*. New York: Penguin Classics, 2004. Print.

—. *Studies on Hysteria*. New York: Pelican Books LTD, 1974. Print.

Britton, James, Anthony Burgess, Nancy Martin, Alex McLeod, and Harold Rosen. *The Development of Writing Abilities (11–18)*. London: Macmillan Education for the Schools Council, 1975. Print.

Brodie, Fawn. *Thomas Jefferson: An Intimate History*. New York: W. W. Norton, 1974. Print.

Bucci, Wilma. "The Power of the Narrative: A Multiple Code Account." *Emotion, Disclosure, and Health*. Ed. James Pennebaker. Washington, DC: American Psychological Association, 2002. 93–125. Print.

Burke, Kenneth. *A Rhetoric of Motives*. 1950. Berkeley: U of California P, 1969. Print.

Burton, Chad M., and Laura A. King. "The Health Benefits of Writing about Intensely Positive Experiences." *Journal of Research in Personality* 38 (2004): 150–63. Print.

Charon, Rita. *Narrative Medicine: Honoring the Stories of Illness*. New York: Oxford UP, 2006. Print.

"Commonplace Books." *Reading: Harvard Views of Readers, Readership, and Reading History*. 2015. Web. 25 July 2015. http://ocp.hul.harvard.edu/reading/commonplace.html.

Csikszentmihalyi, Mihaly. *Flow: The Psychology of Optimal Experience*. New York: Harper and Row, 1990. Print.

De Moor, Carl, Janet Sterner, Martica Hall, Carl Warneke, Zunera Gilani, Robert Amato, and Lorenzo Cohen. "A Pilot Study of the effects of Expressive Writing on Psychological and Behavioral Adjustments in Patients Enrolled in a Phase II Trial of Vaccine Therapy for Metastatic Renal Cell Carcinoma." *Health Psychology* 21.6 (21 Nov. 2002): 615–19. Print.

De Martino, Marco. "Illness Narratives: A Corpus-Based Analysis of Gender and Identity in Patients' Accounts." *International Interdisciplinary Conference on the Taboo*. University of Bologna. Forli, Italy, 2012. Conference Presentation.

DeSalvo, Louise. *Writing as a Way of Healing: How Telling Our Stories Transforms Our Lives*. Boston: Beacon Press. 1999. Print.

Didion, Joan. *The Year of Magical Thinking*. New York: Alfred A. Knopf, 2005. Print.

Dierking, Rebecca. "'Writing Down is a Way of Letting Go': Individuals Using Writing to Return to 'Remembered Wellness.'" PhD diss. University of Missouri. 2012. Print.

Eco, Umberto. *The Theory of Semiotics*. Bloomington: Indiana UP, 1978. Print.

Elbow, Peter. "Collage: Your Cheatin' Art." *Writing on the Edge* 9.1 (1998): 26-40. Print.

—. *Writing with Power*. New York: Oxford UP, 1998. Print.

—. *Writing without Teachers*. New York: Oxford UP, 1998. Print.

Elbow, Peter, and Pat Belanoff. *A Community of Writers: A Workshop Course in Writing*. New York: McGraw-Hill, 1999. Print.

Emig, Janet. *The Composing Processes of Twelfth-Graders*. Urbana: National Council Teachers of English, 1971. Print.

Emmons, Kimberly. *Black Dogs and Blue Words: Depression and Gender in the Age of Self Care*. New Brunswick: Rutgers UP, 2010. Print.

Enos, Teresa. *Encyclopedia of Rhetoric and Composition: Communication from Ancient Times to the Information Age*. New York: Routledge, 2010. Print.

Fleckenstein, Kristie. *Embodied Literacies: Imageword and a Poetics of Teaching. Studies in Writing and Rhetoric*. Carbondale: Southern Illinois UP, 2003. Print.

—. *Vision, Rhetoric, and Social Action in the Composition Classroom*. Carbondale: Southern Illinois UP, 2009. Print.

Flower, Linda, and John Hayes. "Taking Thought: The Role of Conscious Processing in the Making of Meaning." *Thinking, Reasoning, and Writing*. Ed. Elaine P. Maimon, Barbara F. Nodine, and Finbarr W. O'Conner. New York: Longman, 1989. 185212. Print.

Fox, Roy F. *Images in Language, Media, & Mind*. Urbana: National Council Teachers of English, 1994. Print.

—and Amy Lannin. "Belly Up to the Pond: Teaching Teachers Creative Nonfiction in an Online Class." *The Writing Instructor.* (Sept. 2007): n.p. Web. 10 July 2015. http://www.writinginstructor.com/foxlannin

—. *Harvesting Minds: How TV Commercials Control Kids.* Westport: Praeger, 1996. Print.

—. *MediaSpeak: Three American Voices.* Westport: Praeger, 2001. Print.

—. *Updrafts: Case Studies in Teacher Renewal.* Urbana: National Council Teachers of English, 2000. Print.

—. "Images, Words, and 'Healing': An Experimental Course." *The International Journal of the Image* 1.4 (Dec. 2011): 83–98. Print.

—and Myung Hye-Huh Kim. "Visual Thinking in the Composing Processes of English Language Learners." Unpublished manuscript, last modified, 2011. Microsoft Word file.

Foy, George Michelson. "Burning Olivier: The Brief Life and Private Burial of an Infant Son." *Harper's Magazine.* July 1999. Web. 10 July 2015.

Gardner, Howard. *Frames of Mind: The Theory of Multiple Intelligences.* New York: Basic Books, 2011. Print.

Gee, James Paul. *An Introduction to Discourse Analysis.* New York: Routledge, 2010. Print.

Gilmore, Leigh. *The Limits of Autobiography: Trauma and Testimony.* Ithaca: Cornell UP, 2001. Print.

Hayakawa, S. I., and Alan R. Hayakawa. *Language in Thought and Action.* 5th ed. San Diego: Harcourt, Inc., 1990. Print.

Heim, Christine M., Helen S. Mayberg, Tanja Mietzko, Charles B. Nemeroff, and Jens C. Pruessner. "Decreased Cortical Representation of Genital Somatosensory Field after Childhood Sexual Abuse." *American Journal of Psychiatry.* 170.6 (June 2013): 616–23. Print.

Huckin, Thomas. "Critical Discourse Analysis and the Discourse of Condescension." *Discourse Studies in Composition.* Ed. Ellen Barton and Gail Stygall. Hampton, 2002. Print.

Husain, Arshad. *Hope for Children: Lessons from Bosnia.* Tuzla: Behram-Begova Medresa Tuzla, 2001. Print.

James, William. "The Stream of Consciousness." *The Nature of Human Consciousness.* Ed. Robert Ornstein. New York: Viking, 1974. 153–66. Print.

Johnson, Wendell. *People in Quandaries: The Semantics of Personal Adjustment.* New York: Harper and Brothers, 1946. Print.

John-Steiner, Vera. *Notebooks of the Mind: Explorations of Thinking.* New York: Oxford UP, 1997. Print.

Kabat-Zinn, Jon. *Mindfulness for Beginners: Reclaiming the Present Moment—and Your Life.* Boulder: Sounds True, 2011. Print.

Karpiak, Irene. "After Life Review: Autobiography as 'Art of the Future.'" *Studies in Continuing Education* 32.1 (2010): 47–60. Print.

Kidd, David Cormer and Emanuele Castano. "Reading Literary Fiction Improves Theory of Mind. *Science* 342.6156 (October 3, 2013): 377–80. Print. doi: 10.1126/science.1239918

Kim, Myung Hye-Huh. "Putting Images into Second Language: Do They Survive in Written Drafts?" *English Language and Literature* 36.6 (2010): 1255–79. Print.

Kinneavy, James. *A Theory of Discourse: The Aims of Discourse.* New York: Norton, 1980. Print

Korzybski, Alfred. *Science and Sanity: An Introduction to Non-Aristotelian Systems and General Semantics.* 5th ed. New York: Institute of General Semantics, 1995. Print.

Kosslyn, Stephen, William Thompson, and Giorgio Ganis. *The Case for Mental Imagery.* New York: Oxford UP, 2006. Print.

Lakoff, George and Mark Johnson. *Metaphors We Live By.* Chicago: U of Chicago P, 2003. Print.

Lauer, Janice M. *Invention in Rhetoric and Composition.* Anderson, SC: Parlor Press, 2004. Print.

Lepore, Stephen, and Joshua M. Smyth, eds. *The Writing Cure: How Expressive Writing Promotes Health and Emotional Well-Being.* Washington, DC: The American Psychological Association, 2002. Print.

Lindemann, Erika. *A Rhetoric for Writing Teachers.* New York: Oxford UP, 2001. Print.

Lucas, Janet. "Getting Personal: Responding to Student Self-Disclosure." *Teaching English in the Two-Year College* 44.3 (May 2007): 367–79. Print.

Lutz, William. *Doublespeak.* New York: HarperCollins Publishers, 1990. Print.

Macrorie, Ken. *Writing to Be Read.* Portsmouth: Heinemann, 1986. Print.

Malinowski, Bronislaw. "The General Theory of Magic Language." In *The Language of Wisdom and Folly.* Ed. Irving J. Lee, 242. San Francisco: Institute for General Semantics, 1967. Print.

McCullough, David. *Truman.* New York: Simon and Schuster, 1993. Print.

McLuhan, Marshal. *Understanding Media: The Extensions of Man.* New York: New American Library, 1964. Print.

Micciche, Laura. *Doing Emotion: Rhetoric, Writing, Teaching.* Portsmouth: Heinemann, 2007. Print.

Millay, Edna St. Vincent. In *Living Literature: An Introduction to Fiction, Poetry, and Drama.* Ed. John Brereton. New York: Pearson and Longman, 2007. Print.

Miller, Richard E. "Fault Lines in the Contact Zone." *College English* 56.4 (April 1994): 389–408. Print.

—. *Writing at the End of the World.* Pittsburgh: Pittsburgh UP, 2005. Print.

Moffett, James. *Coming on Center: English Education in Evolution.* Portsmouth: Boynton/Cook, 1992. Print.

—. *The Universal Schoolhouse: Spiritual Awakening through Education.* Portland: Calendar Islands Publishers, 1998. Print.

Murray, Donald M. *Learning by Teaching.* Portsmouth: Heinemann, 1982. Print.

—. *A Writer Teaches Writing Revised.* Independence: Cengage Learning, 2003. Print.

National Council Teachers of English. "Responding to Tragedy in Schools: Supporting Teachers and Students," 2012. Web. 10 July 2015. http://www.ncte.org/responding.

Neisser, Ulric. *Cognition and Reality: Principles and Implications of Cognitive Psychology.* San Francisco: W. H. Freeman, 1976. Print.

Nowacek, Rebecca. *Agents of Integration: Understanding Transfer as a Rhetorical Act.* Carbondale: Southern Illinois UP, 2011. Print.

Nuland, Sherwin B. *How We Die: Reflections on Life's Final Chapter.* New York: Vintage Books, 1993. Print.

Odell, Lee. "Assessing Thinking: Glimpsing a Mind at Work." *Evaluating Writing: The Role of Teachers' Knowledge of Text, Learning, and Culture.* Eds. Charles R. Cooper and Lee Odell. Urbana: National Council of Teacher of English, 1999. 7-22. Print

Ornstein, Robert E., and Claudio Naranjo. *On the Psychology of Meditation.* New York: Penguin Books, 1977. Print.

Paivio, Allan. *Mental Representations: A Dual Coding Approach.* New York: Oxford UPress, 2001. Print.

Payne, Michelle. "A Strange Unaccountable Something: historicizing Sexual Abuse Essays." *Writing and Healing: Toward an Informed Practice.* Ed. Charles M. Anderson and Marian M. MacCurdy. Urbana: National Council Teachers of English, 2000. 115-57. Print.

Pennebaker, James W., ed. *Emotion, Disclosure, and Health.* Washington: American Psychological Association, 2002. Print.

—. *Opening Up: The Healing Power of Expressing Emotions.* New York: The Guilford Press, 1990. Print.

—. *Writing to Heal.* Oakland: New Harbinger Publications, Inc., 2004. Print.

Perl, Sondra. *Felt Sense: Writing and the Body.* Portsmouth: Heinemann, 2004. Print.

—ed. *Landmark Essays on Writing Process* Volume 7. Davis: Hermagoras, 1994. Print.

Petrie, Keith J., Roger Booth, and James Pennebaker. "The Immunological Effects of Thought Suppression." *Journal of Personality and Social Psychology* 75 (1998): 1264–72. Print.

Piaget, Jean. *Play, Dreams and Imitation in Childhood.* New York: W.W. Norton & Company, 1962. Print.

Pink, Daniel H. *A Whole New Mind: Why Right-Brainers Will Rule the Future.* New York: The Berkley Publishing Group, 2005. Print.

Pinker, Steven. *The Stuff of Thought: Language as a Window into Human Nature.* New York: Viking Adult, 2007. Print.

Postman, Neil. *Amusing Ourselves to Death: Public Discourse in the Age of Show Business.* New York: Viking, 2005. Print.

—. *Technopoly, the Surrender of Culture to Technology.* New York: Vintage. 1993. Print.

Pratt, Mary Louise. "Arts of the Contact Zone." *Professing in the Contact Zone: Bringing Theory and Practice Together.* Ed. Janice M Wolf. Urbana: National Council Teachers of English, 2002. 118. Print.

Putnam, Robert D. *Bowling Alone: The Collapse and Revival of American Community.* New York: Simon & Schuster, 2000. Print.

Ravitch, Dianne. "Bridging Differences." 2013. Web. 10 July 2015.. http://blogs.edweek.org/edweek/Bridging-Differences/2013.

Rilke, Rainer Maria. *Letters to a Young Poet.* Trans. Stephen Mitchell. New York: Vintage, 1986. Print.

Rosenblatt, Louise. *Literature as Exploration.* 5th ed. New York: The Modern Language Association of America, 1995. Print.

Salomon, Gavriel. *Interaction of Media, Cognition, and Learning.* Mahwah: Erlbaum, 1994. Print.

Selzer, Thomas and Sharon Crowley. *Rhetorical Bodies.* Madison: U of Wisconsin P, 1999. Print.

Shaw, Bret, Fiyona McTavish, and Robert Hawkins. "Emotional Benefits of Visualizations in Coping with Noxious Treatments and Somatic Pain: An Ethnography of a Computer Support Group of Women with Breast Cancer." Paper presented at the Annual Meeting of the International Communication Association, Dresden International Congress Centre, Dresden, Germany, 2006. Lecture.

Schmandt-Besserat, Denise. *How Writing Came About.* Austin: U of Texas P. 2006. Print.

Scholes, Robert E. *Textual Power.* Urbana: National Council of Teachers of English, 1985. Print.

Sheikh, Anees A., Robert G. Kunzendorf and Katharina S. Sheikh. "Healing Images: Historical Perspective." In *Healing Images: The Role of Imagination in Health.* Ed. Anees A. Sheikh. Amityville: Baywood Publishing Co., Inc., 2003. Print.

Shenk, David. *Data Smog: Surviving the Information Glut.* San Francisco: HarperEdge, 1997. Print.

Shenk, Joshua W. "The Suicide Poem." *The New Yorker.* June 14, 2004. Web. 10 July 2015. http://www.newyorker.com/archive/2004/06/14/040614ta_talk_shenk.

Showalter, Elaine. "Our Age of Anxiety." *The Chronicle of Higher Education.* 8 April 2013. Web. 10 July 2015. http://chronicle.com/article/Our-Age-of-Anxiety/138255.

Siegel, Daniel J. *The Mindful Brain: Reflection and Attunement in the Cultivation of Well-Being.* New York: Norton, 2007. Print.

Singer, Jessica and George H.S. Singer. "Writing as Physical and Emotional Healing: Findings from Research." *Handbook of Research on Writing: History, Society, School, Individual, Text.* Ed. Charles Bazerman. New York: Erlbaum, 2008. Print.

Smyth, Joshua M, Arthur A. Stone, Adam Hurwitz, and Alan Kraell. "Effects of Writing about Stressful Experiences on Symptom Reduction in Patients with Asthma or Rheumatoid Arthritis: A Randomized Trial." *JAMA: Journal of the American Medical Association* 281.14 (14 April 1999): 1304–09. Web. 10 July 2015.

Stanovick, Lucy. Unpublished manuscript, last modified, 2012. Microsoft Word file.

Stokes, Suzanne. "Visual Literacy in Teaching and Learning: A Literature Perspective." *Electronic Journal for the Integration of Technology in Education* 1.1 (2001).

Toepfer, Steven M. and Kathleen Walker. "Letters of Gratitude: Further Evidence for Author Benefits." *Journal of Writing Research* 1.3 (2009): 181–98.

Trainor, Jennifer. *Rethinking Racism: Emotion, Persuasion, and Literacy Education in an All-White High School.* Carbondale: Southern Illinois UP, 2008. Print.

Ulanov, Ann, and Barry Ulanov. *Primary Speech: A Psychology of Prayer.* Atlanta, GA: John Knox Press, 1982. Print.

Vygotsky, Lev. *Thought and Language.* Cambridge: MIT Press, 1986.

White, E.B. *Essays of E.B. White.* New York: HarperCollins, 1977. Print.

Willis, Judy. "Writing and the Brain: Neuroscience Shows the Pathways to Learning." *National Writing Project,* May 3, 2011: http://www.nwp.org/cs/public/print/resource/3555.

Woodward, James. "Reification." *The Language of Wisdom and Folly.* Ed. Irving Lee. San Francisco: Institute for General Semantics, 1967. 214-220. Print.

Appendix A: The Course Syllabus

Teaching Therapeutic Language, Literature, & Media

Give sorrow words.

—William Shakespeare

Meaning is not 'already there,' waiting for you—complete, defined, clear. Rather, you must create it for yourself, from part-to-whole, from whole-to-part. (Anonymous)

Required Books

Writing as a Way of Healing: How Telling Our Stories Transforms Our Lives. DeSalvo, 1999.
Writing and Healing: Toward an Informed Practice. Anderson & McCurdy (eds.), 2000.
Finding a Voice: The Practice of Changing Lives through Literature, Trounstine and Waxler, 2008.

Required Articles & Chapters

"Introduction" to *Writing and Healing: Toward an Informed Practice.* Anderson & McCurdy (eds.), 2000.
"Suture, Stigma, and the Pages that Heal." Anderson, Holt, McGady. In *Writing and Healing: Toward an Informed Practice.* Anderson & McCurdy (eds.), 2000.
"All Writing is Autobiography." Donald M. Murray.
"From Secrecy to Psychopathology." Wegner & Lane.
"The Other Side of Darkness: The Comedy in Chaos." In Pain and Possibility . . . Rico, 1991.
"A Personal View . . . : Four Cases of Student Depression." In Student Depression: A Silent Crisis in Our Schools and Communities. Lebrun, 2007.
"The Power of the Narrative: A Multiple Code Account." Wilma Bucci. In Anderson & McCurdy (eds.), 2000.
"The Place of Poetry Therapy in Psychology: Historical and Theoretical Foundations." Mazza. 2003.
"Metaphor and Therapy." In *Healing with Stories: Your Casebook Collection for Using Therapeutic Metaphors.* Burns (ed.), 2007.

"What Is Changing Lives Through Literature?"; "Can We Change Lives?"; "Where Does Literacy Fit In, and What Does Gender Have to Do with It?" and "CLTL Teaching Strategies" in *Finding a Voice* . . .

"A Strange Unaccountable Something: Historicizing Sexual Abuse Essays." Michelle Payne, in *Writing and Healing: Toward an Informed Practice*. Anderson & McCurdy (eds.), 2000.

Selections from *Words and What They Do To You* (Catherine Minteer) and from *Language in Thought and Action* (Hayakawa and Hayakawa).

"The Parallel Chart." In *Narrative Medicine: Honoring the Stories of Illness*. Rita Charon, 2006.

"Pain Management." From *Etcetera: A Journal of General Semantics*. Charles Russell.

"Burning Olivier." From *Harper's Magazine*. M. Foy.

"Dog Day Literacy." From *English Education*. R. Fox.

"Your Cheatin' Art." From *Everyone Can Write*. Peter Elbow.

COURSE DESCRIPTION

What do we mean when we speak of "composing as a way of healing" and the "therapeutic uses of language and other symbols"? New fields of inquiry are emerging, but with inconsistent names (e.g., "Resilience"; "Emotional Literacy"; "Spiritual Studies"). How should we use words, images, music, and other symbols in such ways—whether it be temporary academic or personal problems, psychological trauma, or disease? How is "writing to heal" similar to "writing to learn" and "writing to communicate"? What roles do other literacy activities and symbol systems—especially reading and viewing—play in using therapeutic language?

How can writing processes and strategies that are described primarily from a cognitive perspective—one that values linearity, sequence, cause-effect, logic, and propositional thinking—and those that are rooted in "other ways of knowing"—ways which value physical sensations, emotion, images, silence, intuition, spirituality, chaos, and the unconscious—be integrated or reconciled to assist people who engage in writing about trauma? How do the therapeutic uses of symbol systems align with professional standards for English and Language Arts professionals? This graduate seminar will explore these thorny (but endlessly fascinating) issues.

Please note that Dr. Glenn Good, MU Professor of Counseling Psychology, will serve as a course consultant for your instructor or GRAs. If you feel a need for counseling, please consult us first, if possible. As well, contact information for MU Student Counseling Services is http://counseling.missouri.edu; Phone: 573.882.6601; 119 Parker Hall, MU Campus; M-F 8 am—5 pm.

Major Course Principles

This course will provide students with the opportunity to engage in the following activities: Use evidence-based and standards-based teaching to *also* enhance students' wellness.

- Use a variety of writing prompts and literature to elicit and develop oral and written language to explore major life events.
- Revise writing as a means of increasing one's control over major life events.
- Employ specific elements of general semantics to explore major life events in rational, grounded ways.
- Employ specific rhetorical and semiotic elements (such as freewriting, specificity, objectivity, word-choice, metaphor, imagery, humor, receptivity, audience-awareness, metalanguage, graphics and design, association, contiguity, transfer, music, and sound) to create messages that promote wellness.

Course Objectives

- Students read a wide range of print and nonprint texts to build an understanding of texts, of themselves, and of the cultures of the United State and the world; to acquire new information; to respond to the needs and demands of society and the workplace; and for personal fulfillment.
- Students apply a wide range of strategies to comprehend, interpret, evaluate, and appreciate texts.
- Students adjust their use of spoken, written, and visual language to communicate effectively with a variety of audiences and for different purposes.

- Students employ a wide range of strategies as they write and use different writing process elements appropriately to communicate with different audiences for a variety of purposes.
- Students conduct research on issues and interests by generating ideas and questions, and by posing problems.

(Standards for the English Language Arts. NCTE. 1996.)

TENTATIVE SCHEDULE

Note: Please be alert for any changes. When we don't have time to sufficiently discuss some readings in class, I may ask you to respond on the "Discussion Board" of the course web site. These entries should be posted no later than 5 pm on the Friday following their assignment in class on Tuesday night. *Also note that underlined parts of the following schedule denote writing due dates, responding to writing, etc.*

January 19

- Introductions; overview of course; review of syllabus.
- Why academic work should also enhance wellness (ppt.)Brainstorm (p. 117, DeSalvo) 30 potential ideas for narrative and turn in (anonymous) before you leave.

January 26

- Discuss "Introduction" to *Writing & Healing: Toward an Informed Practice* (Anderson and MacCurdy)
- Discuss "Suture, Stigma, and the Pages that Heal" in *Writing and Healing* (Anderson and MacCurdy)
- Discuss guidelines for small response groups.
- Begin Paper #1 In Class; Bring A Hand Mirror With You.
- Briefly review some proposed topics for narratives.
- Why process and fluency are basic to writing about trauma and academic writing; why Expressive Language is the matrix for all other forms of language/thinking

February 2

- Discuss Chapters 1–4 (pp. 3–69) in *Writing as a Way of Healing* (DeSalvo)
- Parallels between Academic Writing and writing as healing, including state and professional standards. Small Group Response to Paper # 1; bring copies.

February 9

- Discuss Chapters 5–8 (pp. 69–178) in *Writing as a Way of Healing* (DeSalvo).
- Begin Paper # 2 In Class! (GRAs rule; Fox in Minnesota.)

February 16

- Discuss Chapters 10-Epilogue (pp. 178–216) in *Writing as a Way of Healing* (DeSalvo) and "Dog Day Literacy" (Fox).
- Large group response to selected anonymous narrative.
- Small Group Response to Paper # 2, started in class, 2/9; bring copies.

February 23

- Discuss "Pain Management."
- Explore some Basic Principles of General Semantics: discuss excerpts from *Words and What They Do To You* (Minteer; on reserve) and excerpt from *Language in Thought and Action* (Hayakawa; on reserve).
- Small Group Response to Paper # 3; bring copies.

March 2

- Discuss "The Power of the Narrative: A Multiple Code Account" (Bucci)
- Continue response to selected anonymous papers.
- Small Group Response to Paper # 4; bring copies.

March 9

- Discuss "Burning Olivier: The Brief Private Burial of an Infant Son" (Foy).
- Small Group Response to Paper # 5; bring copies.

March 16

- Discuss "A Strange Unaccountable Something: Historicizing Sexual Abuse Essays" (Payne in Anderson & MacCurdy).
- Small Group Response to Paper # 6; bring copies.

March 23

- Discuss "A Personal View . . . : Four Cases of Student Depression." In *Student Depression: A Silent Crisis in Our Schools and Communities.* Lebrun, 2007.
- Catch Up on Small Group Responses to Papers 1–6 if needed!
- Meet with small groups and/or Instructor, GRAs re: Mini Case Study due 4–6. March 27—April 5: Spring Break

April 6

- Discuss Chapters 1–3 and Chapter 10 in *Finding a Voice*: ("What Is Changing Lives Through Literature?"; "Can We Change Lives?"; "Where Does Literacy Fit In, and What Does Gender Have to Do with It?" and "CLTL Teaching Strategies").
- *Optional:* Turn in Mini Case Study—as "finished" as possible—for instructor feedback.

April 13

- Discuss "The Place of Poetry Therapy in Psychology: Historical and Theoretical Foundations." In *Poetry Therapy: Theory and Practice.* Mazza, 2003.
- Discuss "Metaphor and Therapy." In *Healing with Stories: Your Casebook Collection for Using Therapeutic Metaphors.* Burns (ed.), 2007.
- Small Group Response to Paper # 7; bring copies.

April 20

- Discuss "All Writing is Autobiography" by Donald Murray.
- Discuss "Your Cheatin' Art:" by P. Elbow, to assist you with Collage Projects.
- Small Group Response to Paper # 8; bring copies.

April 27

- Complete course evaluations.
- Individual conferences with instructor.
- Small Group Response to Paper # 9; bring copies.

May 4

- Informal oral reports on case studies and/or Collage Projects.
- Small Group Response to Paper # 10; bring copies.

May 11

- Read aloud and discuss one assignment in large group—your "best" or favorite one, for whatever reason.
- Turn in polished draft of one writing-image(s) for Class Anthology, along with biographical paragraph and brief explanation of WHY you chose this piece. Bring copies for everyone in class. I will have cover page, Contents page, etc. We will assemble them before we leave!
- Turn in Collage Project and Final Mini Case Study.

COURSE ASSIGNMENTS AND GRADING PROCEDURE

Below are the main course requirements. Note that they assume consistent attendance and thoughtful participation in class activities.

1. *Final Collage Project.* Using Peter Elbow's chapter, "Your Cheatin' Art . . . as a guide, assemble *all of the weekly projects* into a "collage" project. This project will likely consist of two closely related parts: a visual-media component and a written component. Your collage project should be titled (thematically or in terms of your "conclusion" about

the total pieces). Your main goal should be to make as many connections as you can: a) between the verbal and visual messages—those that were created together, as well as those from different assignments and assigned readings; b) between your verbal and visual messages and the theories and research read in class; c) between your verbal and visual messages and professional teaching standards. An appendix should include all "process" materials, such as notes, prewritings, revisions, etc. Another appendix should consist of a writing explaining what you believe to be your 3–4 strongest pieces, with an explanation of how they fulfill the rubric for the weekly assignments.

Notes Re: Weekly Projects: 1) These 10 assignments will be given to you one group at a time, each group consisting of three assignments; 2) As these are composed over the semester, they will be collected and some pieces selected for sharing with the entire class, with author's names removed (optional). Nonetheless, please indicate on each piece if you would NOT like it shared with the class. 3) Please include the following brief information on the back of each paper or on a separate paper: A) What is the issue in this piece; B) What did you think/believe/feel before completing this piece? C) What did you think/believe/feel after finishing this piece? D) On a scale of 1–10, with ten representing "significant change," and one representing "absolutely no change," indicate the extent of this change overall. If no change, please explain or speculate why. *50%*

2. *Mini-Case Study.* This project should focus on 1–2 writers who employ writing (sometimes along with literature and media) as a way of healing. This person, preferably of student age, should complete any two of the brief assignments that you have completed in this course. For this report, complete these tasks: 1) Interview the writer about her or his experiences of completing the brief assignments, preferably after both are finished, and some time has elapsed. Ask the writer, which was most beneficial to her? Why? Which were least beneficial? Why? 2) Compare and contrast your writer's responses and written pieces to your own; and 3) Analyze and connect the most important information in #1 and #2 above to the course readings and other information from your instructor.

Note: You have the option of turning in a draft of this project well before its final due date (see schedule). Encourage your "subject" to dialogue with you on the course web site or through email, as well as through some face-to-face meetings, if at all possible. *Be sure to save all writings, drafts, prewritings, notes, email correspondence, tapes, transcripts, etc.;* these should be placed into an appendix. Suggested length: 5–7 double-spaced pages. *30%*

3. *Active Participation in Socratic Seminars focused on assigned readings.* These discussions will often begin with a brief, informal writing over the readings (e.g., your response to 2–4 questions re: the assigned readings). They will often be evaluated with a check-plus, check, or check-minus. Each team of 2 members will have a turn in leading discussion, responding to and evaluating the discussion and writings, and returning them the following week for my review, before I return them to their authors. See the web or Blackboard site for additional information on Socratic Seminars. *20%*

Academic Policies & Procedures

(My institution requires syllabi to contain "the small print" sections on the following policies and procedures: Professional Standards; Academic Honesty; Accessibility; and Intellectual Pluralism. I do not include the full statements here. While many faculty members [including me] often include these items automatically, they are especially important to include for such a course as this one.)

Syllabus Appendix A

Guidelines for the Final Project: Compose / Connect / Reflect

These guidelines *replace* the project guidelines on the course syllabus.

Assemble *all of your weekly paper assignments*—both verbal and visual components—into a single project or portfolio. This project will consist of ALL of your work for this course: the ten weekly papers (most with visuals) and the informal in-class writings.

Part I. General Directions
1. Please assemble your portfolio in any form you wish—a box, an accordion folder, a DVD or CD, using "Inspiration" or other software.

2. Your project should be titled (thematically or in terms of your overall "conclusion" about the total pieces). This title should appear on your cover, regardless of the type of "container" you use. Feel free to illustrate this cover/container in any way you wish, to reflect its contents.
3. Include a Table of Contents, clearly labeling every piece and where it can be found within your portfolio.
4. For *each paper,* include a cover sheet which provides the following information:

   A) What is the issue addressed in this piece?
   B) What did you think/believe/feel before completing this piece?
   C) What do you *currently* think/believe/feel about this piece?
   D) On a scale of 1–10, with ten representing "significant change," and one representing "absolutely no change," indicate the extent of this change overall. If no change, please explain or speculate why.

5. One or more appendices (they are lettered) should include all "process" materials, such as notes, pre-writings, notes taken in class, etc.
6. Revise—significantly—*any two* of your weekly assignments (verbal and visual parts). In a preface to each final revision (followed by the previous drafts), explain why you chose this piece to reformulate. Also, explain how each assignment addresses the rubric for the weekly assignments or does not fulfill the rubric, yet represents a strong example. Please explain your assertions. (Note: No single paper will demonstrate all of those criteria, so please select the most significant successes.)

Part 2. Directions for the Collage Project

Using your writing and images from this semester, "put them together" into some kind of whole piece. (For additional information, see Elbow's article on Collage). *A collage will suggest connections through arrangement, juxtapositions, etc., without stating them directly (this comes in IV, "Connections Paper" below).* While readers may not necessarily "know where you're going" while reading your project, by the end, they should have a clear idea of your main idea.

- Use at least five of your papers (or substantial excerpts).
- Use at least five images from papers—those already used or new ones.
- Use all or excerpts from at least two in-class freewritings and any written reflections.
- Use any format you like—printed pages, PowerPoint, PhotoStory, etc.

If you need to write new sentences or other parts for whatever reason, please do so.

Part 3. Directions for the Connections Paper

In a writing that introduces your portfolio of course work, please clearly explain the following types of connections that you believe appear in your work:

- Connections between the print and visual parts—those that were created together, as well as those between *different* assignments.
- Connections between your weekly assignments (both print and visual parts)—and the theories and research read in class.
- Connections between your assignments (both print and visual parts)—and professional teaching standards from NCTE/IRA that apply to the teaching and learning of thinking, writing, language, literature, or media. In one good paragraph, explain how any five of these standards are directly demonstrated in at least three of your weekly papers/projects.
- Connections made as a result of class discussion, small-group discussion of writings, or discussion with a colleague—in or out of class. You may also include connections made between your instructor's feedback and that received from others (including yourself).

Note: It may help you to paste your selected visuals (minimized) and excerpts (or "headlines" or notes that represent a single piece) on a large piece of butcher paper and then draw lines from text/visual to another text/visual. It may be easier, therefore, to write from this "map." If so, please include your map when you turn in the project.

Part IV. Directions for the Reflection Paper

- Look back over all your work and your connections writing, described above, and write a final reflective piece that explains the following points:
  - Identify the three assignments that were most significant, most important for you and briefly explain why. What were the kinds of thoughts and feelings you experienced that made them significant for you?
  - How will your work and this course affect your future teaching and writing?
  - Were any of your writings or other creative efforts a "Flow" experience, where you were challenged (but not overly so) and lost track of time and place as you delved deeply into the task?

Syllabus Appendix B

Recommended Readings

In addition to the categories below, please note the extensive lists of readings in the required books for this class!

Books & Articles

Pain and Possibility: Writing Your Way Through Personal Crisis. Gabrielle Rico, 1991.
Using Literature to Help Troubled Teenagers Cope with End-of-Life Issues Janet Allen
Emotion, Disclosure, and Health. Pennebaker (ed). 2002.
Bodily Discourses: When Students Write about Abuse and Eating Disorders. Payne, 2000.
The Courage to Heal: A Guide for Women Survivors of Child Sexual Abuse. Bass and Davis, 1994.
Presence of Mind: Writing and the Domain Beyond the Cognitive. Brand and Graves, 1994.
Emotional Intelligence. Goleman
Now and at the Hour. Cormier
UpDrafts: Case Studies in Teacher Renewal. Fox. 2001.
Stigma: Notes on the Management of Spoiled Identity. Goffmann.

Presence of Mind: Writing and the Domain Beyond the Cognitive. Brand and Graves (eds.).
Risky Writing: Self-Disclosure and Self-Transformation in the Classroom. Berman.
Notes from the Heart: Affective Issues in the Writing Classroom. McLeod.
Wrestling with the Angel: A Memoir of My Triumph over Illness. Max Lerner
Darkness Visible: A Memoir of Madness. William Styron
Writing Well: Creative Writing and Mental Health. Phillips and Penman
Writing as Therapy: Motivational Activities for the Developmentally Delayed. Stamatelos
"Crossing Lines." Delentiner. *College English,* 54.7 (1992)
The Psychology of Writing: The Affective Experience. Brand
Writing AIDS: Gay Literature, Language, and Analysis. Ed. by Murphy and Poirier.
It's Never About What It's About: What We Learned about Living while Waiting to Die. Kraus
Mind: An Essay on Human Feeling. Langer

Journals and Web Sites

Poetry as Therapy, http://www.spcsb.org/advoc/poetrytx.html
A Brief Overview of Poetry as Therapy, http://www.poetrytherapy.org/articles/pt.htm
Poetry Therapy, http://www.mickleigh.com/Poetry-Therapy.asp
Arts as a Force of Healing, Building, and Empowerment, http://www.artslynx.org/heal
JAMA, *Journal of the American Medical Association,* http://jama.ama.org/issues
Literature, Arts, and Medicine, http://www.endeavor.med.nyu.edu
Journal of Personality and Social Psychology
Native American Healing Methods, http://www.thebody.com/wa/spring98/native.html
Recovering Bodies: Illness, Disability and Life Writing by G. Thomas Cousser, http://brownalumnimagazine.com/story
Kathleen Adams Web Site, http://www.journaltherapy.com/kathleen_adams.htm
AIDS Community Research Initiative of America, http://www.criany.org/treatment_edu_summerupdate1999_resources.html

How Creativity Heals, http://www.kporterfield.com/healing/Healing_Index.html

This six-page document was compiled by the McGrath, Satterlee, et al., of the Louisville Writing Project of the National Writing Project. See http://writingproject.org. For additional sources, please see Resiliency in Schools: Making It Happen for Students and Educators, by Henderson, Milstein, and Parker. Full text is available at http://books.google.com/books.

Syllabus Appendix C

Basic Components or "Pre-Conditions" for Composing Therapeutic Language, Literature, & Media

Trust in audience (depends upon feedback processes)

- Fluency (eye, hand, brain coordination; increase wpm via consistent practice)
- Thinking / Feeling
- Objectivity & Toughness
- Positive (includes humor) / Negative
- Rationale (includes clarifying connections for students between therapeutic assignments and academic writing, work)
- Emphasis on writing process, especially invention, fluency, revision, and reformulation
- Flow experiences
- Imagery
- Voice / Tone
- Organization and Form
- Framing / Naming (via imagining, objectifying, & reformulating)
- Expressive Language / Thinking
- Eventually externalizing the products through publication, performance, and/or public recognition

Syllabus Appendix D

Possible Ways to Respond to Weekly Assignments

The following questions may assist you in responding to the therapeutic uses of written language by your colleagues, your students, and professional writers. *Of course, not every completed assignment can demonstrate all of these qualities.* The criteria come from DeSalvo, your instructor, and other sources. Feel free to use this when you discuss each other's writing in small groups, especially in your first few meetings.

Topic

1. Has the writer selected a topic that troubles, confuses, pains, or puzzles her? (See DeSalvo and Fox's key image/idea.)
2. Do you believe the writer may need professional counseling support for writing about this topic (see DeSalvo, p. 161, 176)?

Structure, Form

1. Overall, do major sections or chunks of the narrative proceed from 1) physical sensations, to 2) a narrative of the events/sensations, to 3) distanced reflection of the sensations and events?
2. Does the writer employ a clear form and sequence—one that reinforces a theme or meaning and not a mere chronology of events?
    a. Does the writer use subheadings?
    b. If so, which type of subheadings are most appropriate—those that refer to internal meaning (e.g., "The Rat Takes the Cheese") or those that employ external reference, such as "The Problem" and "The Solution"?
    c. Are the subheadings logical and parallel in form?
    d. Does the writer use transitions that refer to meaning?
    e. Does the writer use effective, brief subtitles and captions with images?
3. Are feelings in the piece clearly connected to *events?*
4. Does the writer often *connect* "then" with "now"?
5. Are there any gaps in the writer's story? i.e., will readers become distracted because they are wondering about something delayed for too long or omitted?

6. If the writer does not want to write about an event, does she instead write about her choice not to write about it—why she cannot or will not? (DeSalvo, p. 169).
7. What type of narrative would you label this one—the Chaos Narrative? The Restitution or Recovery Narrative? The Quest Narrative? Or some other type?

Tone, Voice

8. Does the piece avoid "moaning and groaning" or too much telling (vs. relying upon *showing*)?
9. Does the writer clearly *distinguish* between then and now, so that readers are not confused about what happened, when?
10. Does the writer use "the right words"—those that are precise, sharp, and economical? (This can include a brief explanation of why other words are rejected.)
11. Does the writer use visual, sound, and/or musical elements that are "right" for the message—that reinforce the message and not distract from it?
12. Does the writer inject some "balance" and "distance" into the piece by effectively using humor, verbally or visually?
13. Does the writer use dialogue to create a sense of immediacy for important scenes, to sharpen contrast between then and now?
14. Does the writer use imagery, including "originating" and key images, in different forms—visuals, figurative language, metaphors, similes, detailed description focused on all senses, etc. (e.g., p. 141 DeSalvo).
15. Does the writer use "negative emotion words, images, etc." and "positive emotion words, images, etc."?

Evidence, Connections, and Analysis:

16. Is the situation appropriately contextualized? Do readers know the larger picture (personal/local/regional/national/universal/natural)?
17. When appropriate, does the writer include some external or factual information (or secondary sources) to "ground" or augment the internal and subjective information? Does the writer analyze some of her own and others' language and imagery by using principles of General Semantics (e.g., the uses of generalities and abstractions, the uses of concrete language that is

"closer to reality," the either/or fallacy, the Is of Identity, and the map/territory analogy)?
18. When appropriate, does the writer explore issues by applying some principles from Csikszentmihalyi's *Flow: The Psychology of Optimal Experience?*
19. Are contradictions and tensions adequately resolved within the piece? By the end of the narrative, is seemingly unrelated material brought together to make a kind of new sense?
20. Does the writer communicate, in whatever form, what X looks like from the outside *and* what it feels like from the inside (p. 185, DeSalvo)?

Syllabus Appendix E

Possible Ideas for Reflecting on Writing about Trauma

Consider these criteria when responding to assignments that request you to "explain, analyze, and reflect" on your work (which you will also apply to your colleagues' work). You will be graded on the depth of your reflection to these questions.

1. What stage of the verbal/visual composing process are you now involved in? Are your actions appropriate for this stage?
2. What "healing benefits" do you think *might occur* when you finish this assignment?
3. Are you working on two or more pieces simultaneously? How does one affect the other?
4. Are you following your instincts or intuition during this work? If not, why not?
5. If you don't have a clear idea of what you want to do, are you constructing and composing anyway and trusting yourself? If not, why not?
6. What kind of overall tone or "atmosphere" do you want your product to convey?
7. Are you seeking and/or following any strong images associated with your topic, even if you have no idea what they "mean" now? Especially important are "originating images" (DeSalvo, p. 126–132 and Fox, "Mental Imagery and Writing"). If not, why not?

8. This type of "process writing" should include many of the qualities described on the handout, "Characteristics of Expressive Language," such as repetition, language that qualifies statements, expressions of doubt, hypothesizing, etc.

Syllabus Appendix F

Guidelines for Responding to Assignments in Small Groups

The following guidelines are adapted by your instructor from DeSalvo's *Writing as a Way of Healing: How Telling Our Stories Transforms Our Lives* (1999), pp. 210–212. Use these guidelines in addition to more generic ones often used in classrooms.

Whomever we share our work with while it's in process, we expect them to be empathic.

Vicious criticism reinforces the writer's deep-seated fear that the story shouldn't be told, that the story isn't important, that the story won't be believed. Vicious criticism can silence stories that must be told. We can suggest that our listeners not tell us whether they like our work or they don't, for whether they like it or not can't help us heal. It is impossible to "like" important survival narratives that nonetheless must be told. . . . We can say, "As you read, please tell me what you don't understand."

1. Act as a caring presence to enable the writer to really hear what he or she has composed. As we read our words aloud and/or view the assignment, we often immediately know what else we need to do and what we need to change. Jot these ideas down quickly.
2. Reflect back to the writer what she has composed—Peter Elbow calls this sharing "movies of your mind"—replaying exactly what happened as you heard the words and experience other symbols.
3. Tell the writer what you like *in the work* or what is effective *for you*—this is different from telling the writer that you do or don't like the work as a whole. When we learn—specifically—what makes our readers respond positively, we can make more accurate judgments about our work.

4. Work hard to help the writer achieve balance in all things—between positive and negative observations, between what happened and the current situation, between emotion and rationality, between subjectivity and objectivity.
5. Tell the writer when you perceive "holes" or gaps in the message—those places where the writer is so close to the story that he doesn't realize readers and viewers cannot possibly understand something. Example: After a student read a piece describing her brother's violence, a listener asked, "Where were your parents while this was happening?" In time, the writer discovered this was the most significant, unanswered question in her narrative and in her life.
6. Tell the writer where you would like to hear more. Writers whose voices have traditionally been silenced usually don't take much time in telling their story. What merits many pagers is often described in a paragraph or two. Barry Lane advises "exploding a moment."
7. Tell the writer about what you've observed about how she has survived—her victories, defeats, struggles. Focus on what you think the benefits of her reading and writing have been.
8. Help the writer to see the patterns in his narrative and in his life. Help him to see the images and metaphors he uses, the form he's chosen to construct reality, since he may not yet "see" the connections among ideas, people, and places that you do.

Appendix B: Research Questions

Note: At least two weeks before each participant's first interview, I sent them the following questions.

Introduction to Potential Research Questions
Please note the following items before we begin:
- For this study, "writing" should be interpreted very broadly, as any symbol system, genre, medium, etc.
- *Please don't be overwhelmed by the number of questions!* Just breeze through them and check those that most "resonate" with you, maybe jot a note or two for triggering your memory.
- In responding to questions, please try to think of one or two of your most successful, effective pieces of writing about trauma, as well as the processes of writing them.
- Most of your responses to questions will often elicit these typical follow-up questions: Why? What makes you think that? How? Can you give an example?
- Do you wish your real name to be used in any conference paper or publication? Please sign the release form. (You don't have to decide now.)
- You will have the opportunity to read and comment on early drafts of any material I produce about your discussions.
- I am willing co-author with you any type writing about trauma publication that may evolve from our discussions.

Session #1 will focus on your own writing about trauma: your perceptions of it, of the craft of such writing, etc. Session #2 will include any follow-up questions from Session 1 and focus on your analysis and response to others' writing about trauma given to you.

Can you please send me copies of a few examples of your own writing about trauma? These will be kept strictly confidential, of course. My plan is to read them and then email you a few questions about them.

If time allows, please read over these questions and make whatever notes you like. Of course, you may request NOT to respond to any of these questions.

I. OVERALL PERCEPTIONS OF WRITING AND TRAUMA

1. Describe your inner experience during your writing when it's going well.
2. Where do you locate the power of writing about trauma?
3. When and how did you first become convinced that writing about trauma was useful for you?
4. Do you view your writing about trauma as all rational or as all emotional? If a combination, what percentage of each? If this changes with each session, why and how?
5. To what degree does your writing about trauma focus (directly or indirectly) on how you are similar to other people? Explain.
6. To what degree does your writing about trauma focus (directly or indirectly) on how you are different from other people? Explain.
7. Are *both* similarities and differences reflected in your writing about trauma? Explain.
8. What metaphor or comparison best "crystallizes" your writing about trauma?
9. If we accept the notion that rhetoric, language, and learning are always related to issues of power, how and why might your own writing about trauma affect you in terms of power? How might it affect others?
10. Is your writing about trauma rooted in a need for stories, for narrative? ("Without stories, we are alienated from a deeper experience of self and world.")
11. Has your own writing about trauma evolved over time? Can you describe these changes? Have there been stages of development?
12. What does writing about trauma do for you? Why do you do it? (Does it help sort things out that are inside of you and that have not been verbalized well or not at all?)
13. Does your writing about trauma include both literal facts AND feelings about those facts? If both, what is the order; what needs to happen first?
14. When engaging in such writing, do words, images, feelings, facts, etc. "collide"? Do they do battle with each other?

15. Do you see specific, concrete changes in your life that might be a result of your writing about trauma? Changes in behavior, language, actions?
16. Do you consider your writing about trauma to be a means of "acceptance" or "forgiveness"? Explain.
17. What is the role of the "ordinary" in your writing about trauma? Are "ordinary" things, people, and events important? Does your perception of them change? How?
18. How does your writing about trauma affect your sense of individuality or "agency"?
19. Where is "spirituality" (not religion) or writing about trauma located for you in writing about trauma? (Text? Writer? Interaction? Other?)
20. Do you view your writing about trauma as a kind of "mediator" among your various "selves" or identities?
21. Do you view your writing about trauma as a kind of mediator between you and other people?
22. Does your writing about trauma help or hinder you in presenting yourself to the outside world?
23. Is your writing about trauma a kind of "rehearsal" for something? If so, what?
24. Can you describe your typical writing about trauma in terms of what is usually in the foreground and background?
25. How would you describe the movement or sequencing within your writing about trauma? From X to Y.
26. Does writing about trauma (or the intense focus on the self) ever become problematic for you?
27. Do you agree that writing about trauma is a form of "asking permission"? If so, of whom and why?
28. Does the writing about trauma you cannot (or do not) create ever "go underground," to later surface as something different (genre, action, behavior, etc.)?

II. Genre and Medium

1. Does humor play a role in your writing? Please explain.
2. Does your writing ever integrate other genres, such as poetry, drama, essay, or others?
3. Does your writing ever integrate other media, such as visuals, music, references, sound, etc.?
4. Do websites or email play a role in your writing? Why and how? Why not?
5. Are any of your writing topics or subjects manifested in other forms, such as objects, art, projects, photos, actions, behaviors, relationships, etc.? Please explain.

III. Global and Local Connections

1. To what degree do issues of global risk (e.g., climate change, economic failure, war, environmental degradation) affect your thinking and writing?
2. Do you ever "connect the dots" between the more impersonal global issues and your own topics? How and why?
3. Can you use a comparison or metaphor to describe how global risks relate to your writing topics?

IV. Craft of Writing

1. How does point-of-view work during your writing about trauma? Does it shift? Is it important?
2. Do you compose writing about trauma fast? Without worrying about grammar, punctuation, syntax, etc.?
3. How important is word choice in your writing about trauma?
4. How important is it to "name" things, actions, behaviors, etc. in your writing about trauma? Explain.
5. Can you describe, in general terms, your typical writing about trauma's beginning, middle, and end?
6. How important is information or secondary source material in your writing about trauma? If you have not used much secondary information, do you think it would be effective? Why?

7. How important is it to ask questions of yourself in your writing about trauma?
8. IF you ask questions of yourself, do you provide more than a single response or answer?
9. What "oppositions" or conflicts or tensions often appear in your writing about trauma?
10. Do you view any kind of tension as helpful in your writing about trauma?
11. Do you ever title your writing about trauma pieces? Is this important and why?
12. What are the roles of qualification in your writing about trauma?
13. What are the roles of detail and elaboration (i.e., becoming increasingly specific) in your writing about trauma?
14. How important is clarity, simplicity, S-V-O, and plain style in your writing about trauma?
15. Describe the syntax used in your writing about trauma: topics you want emphasized appear in main clause and less emphasis in subordinate clauses? Build up to most important points?
16. Do you often use cataloging or listing within your writing about trauma? Why and how?
17. What is the nature of your usual additions to writing about trauma? Your usual deletions?
18. If you ever revise your writing about trauma, why? Describe the nature of your changes.
19. Do you ever consciously shift POV in your writing about trauma? Why?
20. Are precise nouns or names important in your writing about trauma? i.e., are pronouns always clear or does a vague one suffice? Why?
21. Why should writers *revise* their writing about trauma? What are pros and cons?
22. How important is the conclusion of your writing about trauma pieces—of what you "return to" or where you "end up"?

23. How important is the use of "negatives" in your writing about trauma?

24. Is your writing about trauma overall concrete and specific—or abstract and general? What types of things are concrete and which are general? Why? Do these shift?

V. Voice/Persona in Writing

1. How would you describe your voice in your writing about trauma—the person behind the words?

2. Would you describe your writing about trauma as subjective? Objective? Or both? Or as something else?

3. Do you try to exercise objectivity in your writing about trauma? How and why? When does it not work to attempt objectivity?

4. Do you have more than one voice in your writing about trauma?

VI. Audience

1. How important is another person knowing about your writing about trauma? Do you ever summarize it or read it to another person(s)?

2. Do other readers or audiences affect what you write? Please explain.

3. What are the pros and cons of anonymity in your writing about trauma?

VII. Teaching, Learning, and Writing about Trauma

1. Should teachers employ writing about trauma in the classroom?

2. Should teachers have instruction in writing about trauma, regardless of how or when or if they use it?

3. Should teachers, themselves, engage in writing about trauma?

4. Do you have a specific text that you re-read, just for purposes of writing about trauma or easing off?

Appendix C: Assessing Thinking in Writing

Elements of Thinking in Student Writing

Dissonance. (A sense that things just don't add up, that our understanding is incomplete, that something is incongruous.)

- What sort of problems, ambiguities, ironies, questions, uncertainties, or conflicts do writers mention (or overlook)?
- Do writers point out things that surprise or puzzle them?
- Do they pose questions?
- Do they ever indicate that they are confused, uncertain, or ambivalent about something they have experienced?
- Do they comment on ways in which two strongly held beliefs (ideas, values) are inconsistent with each other?
- Do they notice ways in which people's actions seem inconsistent with their words?
- Do they mention ways in which something conflicts with what they had expected or would have preferred?

Selecting. (Being able to pay attention to some things, deemphasize others, and completely ignore others.)

- What kinds of information (observations, "facts," personal experiences, feelings, memories) do writers include in or exclude from their writing?
- When writers respond to literature or write personal narratives, do they focus solely on the events that happened, or do they include information about people's thoughts, feelings, and motivations?
- When they describe, do they look for details that will "show, not tell"?
- When they try to write persuasively or informatively, do they include the kind of information that is likely to be appropriate given the knowledge, needs or values of their intended readers?

Encoding/Representing. (Representing what we selected in a variety of ways—visual images, music, numbers, written and spoken language—some way to represent what we're thinking, feeling, observing, remembering, reading.)

- What sort of language do writers use to articulate their ideas (feelings, perceptions, memories)?
- When writers discuss personal events, do they use relatively abstract, generalized terms, or do they use language that reflects the personal significance of those events?
- When writers try to think through complicated issues, do they use highly emotional language that might limit their ability to see the complexity of a situation?
- Do they ever come up with metaphors that let them take a fresh look at the subject they are considering?
- Do they choose words whose connotations are appropriate for their subject matter, audience, and purpose?

Drawing on Prior Knowledge. (Trying to see how the present situation relates to what we already know)

- Do writers explicitly refer to things they already know in order to understand something new?
- When they read a complicated piece of literature, do writers comment on how this piece relates to other texts they have read or movies they have seen?
- When they encounter a difficult problem, do they use what they know from comparable problems or from prior schoolwork in order to solve it?
- When they are introduced to new concepts, do they consider ways in which those concepts apply to their personal experience or ways in which they are or are not compatible with what they've learned previously?

Seeing Relationships. (Asking how one thing causes another, how things are similar or different, how something interacts with its physical or social setting)

- What kinds of relationships (cause-effect, time, if . . . then, similarity, difference) do writers mention in their writing?
- Do writers note when and why things happen?
- Do they create hypothetical scenarios, speculating about how one thing might cause or lead up to another?
- Do they make distinctions, noticing ways in which something is different from something else?
- Do they classify or note similarities?
- Do they comment on how things change?
- Do they notice ways in which a person or object fits into his/her/its physical surroundings?

Considering Different Perspectives, (Trying to empathize with another person or asking how someone else's perceptions or interpretations might differ from our own)

- To what extent do writers try to consider ways in which other people might perceive, interpret, or respond to a given idea, fact, or experience?
- Do writers consider good news as well as bad, pro as well as con?
- Do they try to adopt another's perspective, trying to imagine how a character in a story might respond to a particular situation?
- Do they try to think of different conclusions that might be drawn from a particular set of data?
- Do they put themselves in their reader's place, trying to understand the knowledge, values, or needs with which that reader approaches their writing?
- When they disagree with someone, do they consider ways in which that person's views might possibly make sense?

Source: Adapted by Deborah Holland (course document) from Lee Odell's "Assessing Thinking: Glimpsing a Mind at Work." In *Evaluating Writing: The Role of Teachers' Knowledge About Text, Learning, and Culture,* 7–22. (Odell 1999)

About the Author

Roy F. Fox currently serves as Professor of English Education and former Chair of the Department of Learning, Teaching, & Curriculum at the University of Missouri. He previously served in the Department of English at Boise State University as that university's first Director of Campus Writing. In this capacity, he led the revision of the Freshman English writing program, developed campus-wide graduation requirements for writing ability, and established a Writing across the Disciplines Program with a grant from the National Endowment for the Humanities.

Fox's research focuses on the teaching and learning of language, writing, and media literacy—especially how people interact with television, film, and advertising messages. For the past decade these research interests have coalesced into his current focus on exploring how combinations of reading, writing, technology, and media can address physical and psychological trauma. In addition to numerous chapters and articles, Fox is the author of several books, including *Images in Language, Media, & Mind; Technical Communication: Problems and Solutions; Harvesting Minds: How TV Commercials Control Kids; UpDrafts: Case Studies in Teacher Renewal*; and *MediaSpeak: Three American Voices*. In 2010, Fox founded the journal, *Engaging Cultures & Voices: Learning through Media*. A former high school English teacher, *Fox* has received the *Maxine Christopher Shutz Award for Distinguished Teaching* and the *William T. Kemper Fellowship for Teaching Excellence*.

Photograph of the author by Beverly Fox.
Used by permission

INDEX

America 2000, 234
Anderson, Charles and Marian MacCurdy: *Writing & Healing; Towards an Informed Practice*, 8, 9, 15, 240
Angelou, Maya: *I Know Why the Caged Bird Sings*, 52, 217
anger, 15, 30, 81, 102, 134–35, 139, 149, 151, 174, 186, 227, 236, 241
assignments, 13, 50, 97, 127–28, 134, 139, 216; Conversation across Time, 55, 128, 158; Entrance into Another World, 53, 128; Fixing the Photo, 51, 52, 125; Getting Inside the Quote, 54; Monster and Angel, 34, 130–131, 152, 154; Snapshot Paper, 52; Synesthesia, 51, 128; The Mirror, 50; Therapeutic Meets Professional, 55; Your Objectivity Plus Their Objectivity, 52. *See also* projects

body image, 135, 139, 227
Britton, James: *Development of Writing Abilities, The*, 74, 235
broken homes, 227, 232
bullying, 101, 227
Burke, Kenneth: *Rhetoric of Motives, A*, 74, 221

cancer: and images, 9, 82–86, 152–157
Caring Bridge, 79–80, 83, 85, 89–93, 95–97, 99, 116, 220, 245, 249
case studies, 36, 208, 269
City of Hope Cancer Center, 15, 240
combustion, 46, 57
Common Core Standards, 232–233
commonplace book, 223
composing through trauma: 6–11, 47; as a basic human right, 226–237; defining, 7, 106, 112, 124, 208, 211, 214, 216, 223, 226–228, 231–232, 235; and fluency, 23–24, 28–29; and helping others, 224–225; meanings of, 6, 35, 37–38, 43, 132–133, 172, 175, 178, 206, 248; and narrative elements, 31; and physical and emotional health, 15–20; and prayer, 243–248; recommendations 226–248; research study, 68–76; and research, 237–243; and structure, 29, 31–34; symbols, 35–37. *See also* writing
connotations of, 38, 59, 289
contact zone, 41–42

293

critical lens, 73; and critical thinking, 10, 25, 28, 56, 74; and general semantics, 38, 48, 58, 74, 127, 265; and literature on trauma, 74; and narrative, 9, 13, 31–32, 40–41, 52, 61, 74, 77, 107; 120, 141, 218, 220, 266–267, 277–279, 281, 283; and semiotics, 59, 75

Csikszentmihalyi, Mihaly: *Flow: The Psychology of Optimal Experience*, 27, 114, 201–202, 246, 279. *See also* flow

cybertherapy, 239

death: 5–6, 242–243

Didion, Joan: *Year of Magical Thinking, The*; 16, 67, 171, 1994, 195, 203

Dierking, Rebecca: *Writing Down as a Way of Letting Go*, 31, 46, 69

Duke University, 15, 240

Eco, Umberto, 35, 75, 255

elaborate, 24, 86, 111

elaborating, 174, 178, 246

elaboration, 92

Elbow, Peter: *Writing Without Teachers*; 27, 40, 48, 60, 62, 75, 215, 246

Elbow, Peter and Belanoff, Pat: *A Community of Writers*, 62

empathy, 26, 38, 62, 67, 104, 238

English Education, 43, 46, 69, 70, 77, 113, 152

fabrications, 195

Fleckenstein, Kristie: *Embodied Literacies*, 46, 82, 125, 221, 255

flow: concept of Mihaly Csikszentmihalyi, 114–115, 201–202; and integrated self, 8, 9; and pleasure of, 196

Foy, George Michelson, 66, 218

Gardner, Howard: *Frames of Mind*, 75, 235

general semantics, 38, 48, 58–59, 74, 127

Hawkins, Robert, 239, 240

Hayakawa, S.I. and Hayakawa, A.: *Language in Thought and Action*, 58, 74, 81, 189, 220

helping the self through helping others, 191

HIV/AIDS education, 46

Holland, Deb, 47, 53

humor, 66, 89, 95, 100, 173, 184, 239

identities, 70, 75, 101. *See also* identity

identity, 8, 28, 58, 78, 101, 112, 122. *See also* identities

illiteracy, 227

imagery: 9; and metaphor 17–18; 35–37; and health, 36, 75; external and internal, 75, 84, 86, 127; roles of, 82–86. *See also* images

images: 36, 51–52, 82–85, 175–76; bleakness of, 51, 175, 203; and emotion, 81, 246; external, 69, 84, 86, 89, 116,

127, 134, 210, 218, 237, 242, 246, 247; framing through, 172, 175–179; and health, 124; manipulation of, 35, 51–52, 55, 59, 84, 85, 124–162, 216–217, 245; metaphoric, 17, 84, 178; mixed, 94, 166, 181; slowed down and speeded up, 84; stock, 156, 216; as symbols, 144–145, 155–156; *See also* imagery
inferences, 59
inner speech, 25, 114
Is of Identity, 58

James, William, 35, 112
Jefferson, Thomas, 16–20, 23, 35, 245, 246
John-Steiner, Vera: *Notebooks of the Mind*, 28, 36, 75, 82
Johnstone, Brick, 238
judgments, 38, 59, 167, 179

Kinneavy, James: *Theories of Discourse*, 74, 221
Kosslyn, Stephen: *Case for Mental Imagery, The*, 36, 74

ladder of abstraction, 59, 185, 187, 189
Lakoff, George: *Metaphors We Live By*, 75, 257
language: ambiguity in, 18, 172, 176, 177; association in, 59, 265; explicit, x, 104, 155, 167, 172; expressive, ix, 7, 14, 17, 19, 20, 25, 26, 28, 81, 211, 222, 235, 244; framing in, 170, 172, 176, 177, 178, 179; implicit, 172; meta-, 55, 69; naming in, 43, 88, 115, 172, 173, 175, 176, 178, 200, 204, 231; poetic, 17, 18, 19, 175; propaganda techniques in, 59; repetition of, 59, 84, 91, 171, 188, 194, 280; visible, 23, 27, 215; voice in, 9, 17, 29, 32, 62, 75, 77, 84, 106, 107, 121, 148, 155, 184, 195, 204, 205, 214, 246, 247, 249. *See also* therapeutic language, writing
Lapham, Lewis, 242
Lauer, Janice, 48
learning disorders, 227
letters of gratitude, 241
Lincoln, Abraham, 17–21, 23, 35, 52, 217
Lindemann, Erika: *Rhetoric for Writing Teachers, A*, 221, 236
longhand spasms, 18

MacCurdy, Marian, 36, 74
marijuana, 39, 58, 148, 150
McCarthy, Cormac: *The Road*, 175, 203, 223
McTavish, Fiyona, 239–240
meditation, 251
metaphor, and images, 17, 18, 103, 119, 176, 178, 240
Michelangelo, 247, 248
Miller, Richard E., 227
Miller, Richard L., 17
Moffett, James: *Coming on Center*, 74, 112, 234, 247. *See also* simultaneous differentiation and integration
molestation, 39–41

neural plasticity, 237

neuropsychology, 238
No Child Left Behind, 233
nonfiction: informational, 218; literary, 60, 61, 97, 214, 217
Nuland, Sherwin B.: *How We Die*, 243

objectivity, 57, 76, 103, 265, 281
Odell, Lee, 74, 208–209
online therapy, 239
order and control: illusion of, 90
orientation: extensional and intensional, 58

Paivio, Allan, 36, 74
palindrome, 34
paranoia, 45
pedagogy: 43–68; natural ability, 48
Pennebaker, James, 15, 74, 254
Piedmont Hospital, 15, 240
pilot study, 69
Postman, Neil: *Amusing Ourselves to Death*, 74, 227
post-secret.com, 239
Post-Traumatic Stress Disorder, 7, 15, 71, 240
poverty, 121, 190, 224, 227
professional standards, 48, 264, 267
projects, 50–55. *Also see* assignments
psychologists: Gestalt, 35, 75
qualification, 25, 103, 174

rape, 7, 26, 39, 71, 102, 126, 139, 141
reality TV, 39
reports, 19, 45, 59, 90, 210, 241

resilience, 225
rhetoric, 10, 28, 74, 209, 220, 221, 237, 283
rupture, 8, 41, 79, 88, 112, 113, 168, 193, 194
semiotics, 59, 75
Sheikh, Anees: 35, 36, 75, 124, 216
shock: initial, 194
simultaneous differentiation and integration, 109, 112, 192, 200, 203, 208, 219. *See also* James Moffett
sources: secondary, 33, 116, 218, 238
stream of consciousness: focusing of, 48, 53, 117, 128, 191, 220, 231, 236, 238; suspending of, 28, 114, 115, 193, 194, 200, 204–205, 213, 219; witnessing of, 28, 114–115, 176–177, 185, 193, 204–205, 219
Styron, William: *Darkness Visible*, 67, 275
substance abuse, 7, 101, 227, 229, 232, 238
suicide, 7, 17, 18, 71, 227, 229, 230
syllabus, 46, 47, 48, 49, 60, 61
symbolic identification: 84, 104

tangents, 95, 180
therapeutic language, 43, 46, 47
thinking: academic, 229, 231; logical 18; fluency in, 23–24; 27–29, 60, 109–111, 169, 182, 200–201, 215, 231, 246; higher order of, 25, 28; and writing production rate, 27; and mental imagery, 36; linear and propositional, 47; either/or, 70; visible,

63; magical, 67, 194–197; visual, 36, 75, 82, 124–125, 133; verbal, 82; process of, 112; and connecting, 41, 116, 121, 133, 170, 185, 189, 190–191, 208, 215, 220, 224, 231; relational, 127; and interplay of verbal and visual, 133–135; and reifying, repeating, and reminding, 170; and questioning, 179–185, 211; and connecting and interweaving, 185–190; and ladder of abstraction, 189–190; and solving problems, 193–194; enjoyment of, 201–202; and flow, 202; and "the other thing," 202–203; and simultaneous differentiation and integration, 109, 112, 192, 200, 203–204; faith in, 213–215; oppositions in, 73, 170, 215–216; and ignoring boundaries, 219; and rhetoric, 220–221; and speaking and listening, 246; comparing, 84, 103, 172, 231; defining, 7, 106, 112, 216, 231, 232; describing, 18, 43, 151, 204, 231, 239; dissonance in, 208; elaboration of, 92, 174; encoding, 208; enlarge context of, 38; evaluating, 25, 199, 231, 271; focusing of, 28, 48, 53, 114–117, 191, 193, 204–205, 219–220, 231; framing through names, 170; generalizing, 231; hypothesizing, 25, 231; inferences, 59; inquiring, 231; interweaving, 170, 215; judgments, 38, 59, 167, 179; meta-language of, 55, 69; metaphor, 17–18 25, 52, 62, 75, 84, 103, 109, 119, 124, 145, 166, 169, 170, 172, 176–179, 189, 224, 228, 231, 239–240; movement of mind, 148; nimbleness of mind, 180; observing, 74, 175, 193, 231; organizing, 23, 231, 234; qualification, 25, 103, 174; reports, 19, 45, 59, 90, 210, 241, 269; representing, 145, 208, 270, 272; researching, 38, 44, 46, 59, 211, 231; seeing relationships, 209; selecting, 116, 208, 231; solving problems, 69, 170, 215; specifying, 231; synthesizing, 60, 231; tensions in, 28, 81, 83, 88, 91, 123; transfer, 18, 25, 184; two-valued, 74, 155, 212; unsafe, 179; visualizing, 11, 231; wishful, 171, 196

transformation, 120, 129, 153, 247

Ulanov, Anna: *Primary Speech*, 244
Ulanov, Barry: *Primary Speech*, 244, 261

violence, 7, 15, 66, 224, 227, 229, 231, 241, 242, 281; physical, 6, 7, 14, 15, 25, 63, 71, 112, 113, 128, 157, 209, 227; psychological, 7, 15, 47, 71, 112, 113, 227, 237; virtual, 227

Vygotsky, Lev, 25, 74

ways of knowing, 47, 81

writing: agency in, 79, 86, 121–122, 148, 156; developmental, 44, 234; emotional/private, 79–90; empathy in, 26, 38, 62, 67, 104, 238; gaps in, 63–66, 227; grammar and mechanics of, 38; meditative, 168; private letters, 163–207; rational/public, 90–97; professional/public, 97–109; reformulation of, 276; revision of, 6, 64, 97, 104, 110–111, 127, 150, 172, 229; as basic human right, 226–237; as prayer, 243–248; as longhand spasms, 18–19; process of, 27, 43; and culture, 15–16; organization of, 29–32, 92–93; genres of, 93–100, 117–121; and reflecting on everyday life, 223–224; as dialogue, 16–17; apprehension about, 44, 249; blocking of, 211–213; journal, 163–165; and helping others, 224–226; faith in, 213–216; and rhetoric, 220–223; teachers of, 55–56; teaching of, 55, 100–109; and general semantics, 58–59; and reading, 60, 217–219; and chronological order, 61; responding to, 61–62; motivation for, 86–88, 167–170; comments on, 62; empathy with, 62; cycles of, 57; fluency, freedom, and flexibility in, 60–61; study of, 68–76; and *Caring Bridge*, 79; voice in, 9–11, 17, 72, 75, 77, 84, 101, 106–109, 121, 148, 155, 182, 184, 193, 195, 204–205, 214, 236, 239, 245–247, 249. *See also* composing.

YouTube, 34, 38

www.ingramcontent.com/pod-product-compliance
Lightning Source LLC
Chambersburg PA
CBHW030524230426
43665CB00010B/756